CAMBRIDGE TEXTS IN THE
HISTORY OF POLITICAL THOUGHT

———

L. T. HOBHOUSE
Liberalism and Other Writings

CAMBRIDGE TEXTS IN THE
HISTORY OF POLITICAL THOUGHT

Series editors
RAYMOND GEUSS
Reader in Philosophy, University of Cambridge

QUENTIN SKINNER
Regius Professor of Modern History, University of Cambridge

Cambridge Texts in the History of Political Thought is now firmly established as the major student textbook series in political theory. It aims to make available to students all the most important texts in the history of Western political thought, from ancient Greece to the early twentieth century. All the familiar classic texts will be included but the series seeks at the same time to enlarge the conventional canon by incorporating an extensive range of less well-known works, many of them never before available in a modern English edition. Wherever possible, texts are published in complete and unabridged form, and translations are specially commissioned for the series. Each volume contains a critical introduction together with chronologies, biographical sketches, a guide to further reading and any necessary glossaries and textual apparatus. When completed, the series will aim to offer an outline of the entire evolution of Western political thought.

For a list of titles published in the series, please see end of book.

L. T. HOBHOUSE

Liberalism and Other Writings

EDITED BY

JAMES MEADOWCROFT

Department of Politics
The University of Sheffield

CAMBRIDGE
UNIVERSITY PRESS

PUBLISHED BY THE PRESS SYNDICATE OF THE UNIVERSITY OF CAMBRIDGE
The Pitt Building, Trumpington Street, Cambridge, United Kingdom

CAMBRIDGE UNIVERSITY PRESS
The Edinburgh Building, Cambridge CB2 2RU, UK
40 West 20th Street, New York, NY 10011–4211, USA
477 Williamstown Road, Port Melbourne, VIC 3207, Australia
Ruiz de Alarcón 13, 28014 Madrid, Spain
Dock House, The Waterfront, Cape Town 8001, South Africa

http://www.cambridge.org

© Cambridge University Press 1994

This book is in copyright. Subject to statutory exception
and to the provisions of relevant collective licensing agreements,
no reproduction of any part may take place without
the written permission of Cambridge University Press.

First published 1994
Fourth printing 2006

Printed in the United Kingdom at the University Press, Cambridge

A catalogue record for this book is available from the British Library

Library of Congress Cataloguing in Publication data
Hobhouse, L. T. (Leonard Trelawney), 1864–1929.
Liberalism and other writings/L. T. Hobhouse; edited by James Meadowcroft.
p.   cm. – (Cambridge texts in the history of political thought)
Includes bibliographical references (p. xxxiii) and index.
ISBN 0 521 43112 3. – ISBN 0 521 43726 1 (pbk.)
1. Liberalism. 2. State, The.   I. Meadowcroft, James.
II. Title. III. Series.
JC571.H567   1994
320.5′1–dc20   93–19030 CIP

ISBN 0 521 43112 3 hardback
ISBN 0 521 43726 1 paperback

wv

Contents

Contents

Acknowledgements

I would like to thank Michael Freeden and Geraint Williams for their assistance and encouragement.

Introduction

Leonard Trelawny Hobhouse was the most sophisticated intellectual exponent of the 'New Liberalism' which emerged in Britain in the closing years of the nineteenth century. A determined advocate of political and social reform, who worked for years as a journalist on the progressive liberal press, Hobhouse also had a distinguished academic career, occupying the first professorial chair in sociology to be established at a British university. As a political theorist, Hobhouse is most significant for his attempt to reformulate liberalism to recognize more adequately the claims of community, establish the centrality of basic welfare rights, and legitimate an activist democratic state.

Leonard Hobhouse was born in the Cornish village of St Ive in 1864. The son of Caroline Trelawny and an Anglican clergyman, Reginald Hobhouse, he was brought up in comfortable circumstances. Schooled at Marlborough, he went on to Corpus Christi College, Oxford, earning a first-class degree in Greats in 1887. After graduation, Hobhouse stayed on in Oxford, first as a Prize Fellow at Merton College, and later as a full Fellow of Corpus Christi. By the mid-1890s Hobhouse began to feel cramped by the confines of academia; and, eager to play some more definite part in the crusade for social reform, he abandoned his Oxford career to take up a position with the liberal *Manchester Guardian* in 1897. He remained with the paper as a full-time leader writer until 1902. Between 1903 and 1905 he worked as Secretary to the anti-protectionist Free Trade Union. Next followed another stint of full-time journalism – this time as political editor for the London-based, left-liberal daily, *The Tribune*. Then, in the autumn of 1907, Hobhouse re-oriented his

ix

energies back towards teaching and research by accepting the newly created chair of sociology at the University of London – a post he retained until his death in 1929. Hobhouse never abandoned his interest in the practical politics of reform, however, and for many years he continued to make a substantial contribution to the editorial pages of the *Manchester Guardian*.

Hobhouse was a prolific writer – a fact that occasioned snide comments from some academic quarters – and a collection of his journalistic pieces would fill several volumes. His substantive works spanned an impressive range of disciplines, dealing particularly with philosophy, politics, and sociology, but touching also on issues that might today be regarded as the preserve of physiology, psychology, and anthropology. Issues in political theory were addressed most directly in *The Labour Movement* (1893), *Democracy and Reaction* (1904), *Liberalism* (1911), *Social Evolution and Political Theory* (1911), *The Metaphysical Theory of the State* (1918), and *The Elements of Social Justice* (1922).

The period spanned by the publication of these volumes was one of the more turbulent phases of the modern British polity, during which many of the parameters of twentieth-century political life were established. Welfare and taxation policy, the regulation of trade union activity, the definition of the franchise, the constitutional position of the Lords and the Commons, the status of Ireland, and the conduct of Imperial policy were the focus of acute political struggles. Hobhouse lived through two major wars, the Boer War (1899–1902) and the First World War (1914–18). He experienced the high-tide of Edwardian Liberalism – with its innovative social legislation, the 'People's Budget' of 1909–10, and the clipping of the Lords' wings by the Parliament Act of 1911 – and he witnessed the rapid falling away of Liberal support as Labour came into its own in the early 1920s.

For Hobhouse, as for many of the educated young men who came of age in the late 1880s and 1890s, the liberalism which looked back towards principles elaborated earlier in the century held little attraction. There seemed to be insufficient recognition of the psychic and moral interdependence of the individuals who made up society. The ritual injunctions to self-help could be perverted too readily into an encouragement of indifference or selfishness. Above all, the idea that all social ills would vanish once the interference of government had been eliminated appeared frankly naive.

During the first phase of his development as a political thinker, Hobhouse was largely concerned with the critique of 'individualism' – both as a philosophical doctrine which ignored the intimate moral bond between individual and society, and as a political dogma which set narrow limits on permissible forms of state action. While still an undergraduate, Hobhouse had staked out a position towards the left of Liberalism, expressing sympathy for Irish Home Rule, the extension of the suffrage, and *The Radical Programme* – a volume of essays which served as something of a manifesto for Radical Liberals in the mid-1880s (Preface by Joseph Chamberlain, 1885). As his sojourn at Oxford continued Hobhouse became increasingly receptive to the claims of labour, entered into contact with a number of prominent Fabians, and began to class himself as a 'collectivist'. His first book, *The Labour Movement*, was a product of this period; ranging over a wider set of themes than the title might suggest, the volume not only discussed trade union and co-operative organization, but also advocated a significant extension of collective control of economic activity through state and municipal action. Of course, to be a 'collectivist' in the late 1880s and 1890s was not necessarily to repudiate liberalism – but it did imply rejection of the 'individualist' bias of traditional liberalism, and scepticism towards the cautious orientation of the Liberal leadership.

By the early years of the new century there had been a discernible shift in mood and emphasis in Hobhouse's work: his youthful enthusiasm for collectivism had been somewhat tempered, and he displayed a renewed appreciation for the virtues of earlier liberal thinkers. In the late 1890s Hobhouse became preoccupied with the relation between the Imperial reflex and domestic reform, and convinced that lust for Empire had served to drive urgent social questions from the political agenda. He opposed British intervention during the Boer War in South Africa, and was dismayed that leading Fabians and prominent Liberals sympathetic to a more activist state had been seduced by the Imperial dream. In *Democracy and Reaction*, Hobhouse discussed the obsession with Empire and examined the intellectual props of what he considered to be a revolt against sound humanistic values. He particularly targeted the pseudo-scientific application of the idea of the biological 'struggle for existence' to human social life (to justify the old claim that 'Might is Right'), and Idealism – which, by considering 'every institution and every belief' to be a 'manifestation of a spiritual principle', threw 'a gloss over stupidity, and prejudice, and caste, and tradition' (pp. 78–9). Hobhouse praised the doctrines of earlier Liberal reformers like Cobden, insisting that although their hostility to the domestic responsibilities of government would now be misplaced, their resistance to Imperial aggrandizement remained pertinent, and he complained that 'the socialistic development of Liberalism' had to some extent 'paved the way for Imperialism by diminishing the credit of the school which had stood most stoutly for the doctrines of liberty, fair dealing, and forbearance in international affairs' (p. 12).

From this point on, Hobhouse generally identified himself as a liberal, a new liberal, or a liberal socialist, rather than simply a 'collectivist'. To some extent this reflected a gradual change in the accepted usage of 'collectivism' – the term was increasingly deployed to denote support for the mechanism of generalized state ownership, and associated with the nascent Labour Party – but it was also evidence of a shift in Hobhouse's concerns. Certainly he came to regard the struggle between 'Democracy and Reaction', rather than the contradiction between 'Individualism and Collectivism', as the fundamental political divide facing his generation.

In this context, a recurrent theme of Hobhouse's writing became the need to reconcile what he described as 'the two branches' of the democratic and humanitarian movement – liberalism and socialism. On the one hand Hobhouse argued that only a practical alliance of progressive currents could block the forces of reaction, and on the other he emphasized the essential affinity between liberal and socialist goals: an entirely consistent liberalism would, he suggested, imply a considerable dose of the social provision, social regulation, and social ownership usually associated with socialism; while a reasonable and workable socialism would attach permanent value to the liberal ideals of individual freedom and political democracy. And yet, if Hobhouse freely admitted that his own approach accepted 'many of the ideas that go to make up the framework of Socialist teaching (*Liberalism*, p. 101)', he made it clear that his primary intellectual attachment was to liberalism; in a sense, he believed that liberalism was the stronger, more fundamental movement – that it had deeper historical roots and that its accomplishments were more solid.

Two earlier liberal theorists with whom Hobhouse shared an obvious affinity were John Stuart Mill and Thomas Hill Green. Although critical of Mill's 'individualism', Hobhouse always had a warm regard for his determination to 'apply standards of rational justice to human affairs', and he praised Mill's insistence upon both 'liberation for the individual, and mutual aid as between individuals' (*The Nation* 7 (1910), p. 246). From Green, Hobhouse absorbed the ideas of a common good, of society as a more intimate moral union, and of liberty as a power to achieve self-expansion. Both Herbert Spencer and Auguste Comte influenced Hobhouse's idea of sociology as a positive science, with an emphasis on evolution passing down from the English theorist, and the image of a self-directing humanity being accepted from the French thinker.

Hobhouse was a well known critic of Idealism; indeed, his first major philosophical work, *The Theory of Knowledge* (1896), was intended as a Realist critique of the essential Idealist 'fallacy' – 'that consciousness must in some way sustain in its existence the reality that it knows, that what exists for knowledge exists only by our knowledge' (p. 539). And, in *The Metaphysical Theory of the State*, written twenty years later, he delivered a biting attack on Idealist political theory as represented in the works of Hegel and the English philosopher, Bernard Bosanquet. Yet despite his antipathy towards Idealism, Hobhouse drew upon Hegel, and this influence is evident in Hobhouse's conception of a universal developmental process in which a spiritual principle inherent in reality grows and achieves self-consciousness. Indeed, Hobhouse described

> the whole course of . . . physical, biological, and social evolution [as] . . . a process wherein mind grows from the humblest of beginnings to an adult vigour, in which it can – as in the creed of humanity it does – conceive the idea of directing its own course . . .
>
> (*Morals in Evolution*, 1906, p. 596)

Hobhouse's idea of upward development, of a movement of mind from lower to higher, was the product of a creative synthesis of strands drawn from Idealism and from the Darwinist evolutionary theory which so profoundly influenced late-nineteenth-century social thought. It is the essential theme which unites his contributions to various intellectual domains: in *Mind in Evolution* (1901) Hobhouse examined the emergence of higher mental powers in the course of animal evolution; in *Morals in Evolution* he presented a history of the expansion of human ethical consciousness; in *Development and Purpose* (1913) he offered an evolutionary ontology; and his sociological works, such as *Social Development: Its Nature and Conditions* (1924), were largely concerned with documenting the advance of human social institutions.

While acknowledging that history displayed no smooth pattern of advance, Hobhouse insisted that over the long haul progress was a reality – developed social forms, in which ethical principles were more soundly established, emerged and proliferated. With time, the rational elements of social life grew more substantial, and human beings acquired the ability to self-consciously orient society in the direction of further improvement. According to Hobhouse, belief in progress lay at the very foundation of the movement for social reform; indeed, he insisted that ultimately 'every constructive social doctrine rests on the conception of human progress' (*Liberalism*, p. 65).

In the years after the First World War Hobhouse lost something of his earlier optimism and experienced a degree of alienation from the ongoing process of party politics. The scale of the carnage in Europe severely tested his faith in social advance, while the electoral collapse of the Liberals and their turn away from social reform made prospects for revitalizing the Party remote. Like many a pre-war reform liberal, Hobhouse was drawn towards Labour – and yet he could never entirely accept the organization's close association with the trade unions, or feel comfortable with the more doctrinaire socialists in its ranks. To some extent, Hobhouse found himself a theorist without a natural home: a reform liberal in a time when Liberal fortunes were waning.

Hobhouse's *Liberalism*

Not the most elaborate or scholarly of Hobhouse's writings, *Liberalism* is nevertheless his most enduring work. The book was one of three commissioned by the editors of the Home University Library of Modern Knowledge to introduce their readers to contemporary political argument. Ramsay MacDonald's *The Socialist Movement* (1911) and Hugh Cecil's *Conservatism* (1912) were its companion volumes. *Liberalism* appeared while the controversy over the 1909–10 budget (which increased death duties, imposed a super-tax on high incomes, and introduced a tax on profits in land transactions) was still fresh in the public memory, but before the Parliament Act of 1911 was finally accepted by the House of Lords. Although written in a popular style, it is a theoretical work of some subtlety.

The fundamental challenge Hobhouse had to confront in writing the book was to explain how the activist state he championed could be justified according to the essential principles of a creed which had for so long been associated with the struggle for freedom of the individual from state interference. To make good his case, Hobhouse invoked two basic stratagems: first, he presented a distinctive interpretation of liberal history – one which sought to establish the liberal interventionist state as the logical, indeed the inevitable, outgrowth of earlier liberal endeavour; and second, he provided his own positive theoretic reconstruction of liberal political doctrine.

To some extent these two arguments were developed sequentially: the early sections of *Liberalism* are largely concerned with history, while the later chapters of the book explicitly present Hobhouse's version of liberal theory. Yet the division is not so clear cut. Theoretical elements central to Hobhouse's reconstructive effort – such as the principle of citizenship and the idea of harmony – are introduced right from the outset, while only in the final chapter is the historical account completed.

Hobhouse made his argument about history by appealing to the ideas of continuity, change, and progress. In the first place, he suggested that the differences between the old and the new liberalism were less extensive than most critics imagined. The list of fundamental liberties introduced in the second chapter of *Liberalism* was one whose significance could be appreciated in the main by all liberals. Moreover, despite changes in the political conjuncture or in the theoretical articulation of liberalism, the rational and emancipatory character of the creed could be seen as a constant. According to Hobhouse, 'liberalism' was 'a movement fairly denoted' by its 'name – a movement of liberation, a clearance of obstructions, an opening of channels for the flow of free spontaneous vital activity' (p. 22). It was true that earlier liberals had mistrusted the state; but careful consideration of the principles on which the older liberals had based their activity revealed that these principles could legitimate a more comprehensive range of regulatory intervention than their originators had believed necessary.

Hobhouse's second tack was to insist upon the great change in economic, social, and political circumstances which separated his generation from earlier liberals. Half a century of practical experience had taught liberals that free trade and freedom of contract were not, as originally had been hoped, sufficient to secure steady progress and universal prosperity. Above all, Hobhouse pointed to the altered character of the state itself. In the days of Bentham, or even Cobden, government had resembled a closed corporation, administration was inefficient, and power had been concentrated in the hands of the aristocracy. It was not surprising that liberals had mistrusted the state. By the outset of the twentieth century, however, British government had been transformed – through the growth of an efficient and relatively impartial professional civil service on one hand, and the progressive extension of the franchise on the other. Hobhouse spoke of a shift between two eras of liberal endeavour: during the first, more negative, phase the movement had been concerned with breaking the mould of traditional society; during the subsequent, positive phase of social reconstruction the liberal model of the social order would be fully worked out. A more active and 'positive' understanding of the state was appropriate to this later stage of democratic reconstruction.

Hobhouse's final point was to emphasize the advance of social philosophy, and to postulate a progressive deepening of liberal self-consciousness. It was not just that the state-shy liberals of the older generation had faced different circumstances, but also that they had accepted a somewhat one-sided view of social life, and that they had but partially grasped what was implied by the full development of the liberal ideal. The third, fourth, and fifth chapters of *Liberalism* trace the progress of liberal theory as a movement which passed from the 'theory of the Natural Order' formulated by thinkers such as Locke, Rousseau, and Paine to the utilitarianism of Bentham and James Mill, and then moved on through the hey-day of 'laissez-faire', to arrive at the more balanced views of Gladstone and John Stuart Mill. At each stage, Hobhouse suggests that 'partial solutions gave occasion for deeper probings' (p. 23): the strengths and weaknesses of each liberal variant prepared the way for the subsequent re-formulation of core beliefs.

Weaving together these three broad strands, Hobhouse arrives at a version of liberal history in which the new, state-reliant, social reform-oriented liberalism appears simultaneously as the authentic continuator, the appropriate contemporary expression, and the more profound outgrowth of earlier liberal thought.

This brings us to Hobhouse's own substantive reconstruction of liberal theory – formally presented in outline in the sixth chapter of *Liberalism*, and elaborated in the remainder of the book. The central unifying concepts which Hobhouse invoked to articulate his vision of liberal theory were those of 'the organic' view of society, and the 'harmonic' understanding of the good or the desirable.

Organic imagery was something of a staple in late-nineteenth-century British political argument. As Hobhouse deployed organicism, it was intended to counter the claims both of 'individualism' and of 'extreme collectivism' by establishing the subtle mutualism of the individual/social bond. Against those who endorsed an abstract notion of the individual and an atomistic conception of social constitution, Hobhouse argued that as a 'mental and moral being' the modern individual was largely a social product (p. 60). Furthermore, society could not adequately be conceived as an assemblage of pre-formed individuals – rather it comprised a more intimate union. Against those who would exaggerate the claims of society, Hobhouse insisted that the social whole was not some mysterious or transcendent power, but simply the members taken in their inter-connections.

With respect to ethical principle, Hobhouse argued that the 'organic' conception of the relation between individual and society could reconcile potentially conflicting appeals to individual right on the one hand, and to the requirements of social welfare on the other. He insisted that rights could not spring from the individual as an abstract entity; rather, they were socially grounded – with each right finding its justification as a condition of social well-being. According to Hobhouse the 'organic' perspective avoided undue subordination of the individual to society because it recognized that society itself was composed 'wholly of persons'. Thus, while the rights of the individual were relative to the requirements of social welfare, 'the common good to which each man's rights' was subordinate was 'a good in which each man' had 'a share' (p. 61). Hobhouse explained, 'this share consists in realizing his capacities of feeling, of loving, of mental and physical energy, and in realizing these he plays his part in the social life'.

Thus according to Hobhouse there was no fundamental or necessary contradiction between the rights of individuals and the requirements of social welfare. An individual 'right' which conflicted with the permanent interests of society – which weakened the capacity of society's members to make the most of themselves – was not a genuine moral right. Not every form of individual self-expansion was desirable; freedom for some must not be predicated on stunted life chances for others. Society upheld those rights for individuals which, in balance, enhanced opportunities for self-development along lines compatible with the development of others. The challenge for social ethics was to discover that configuration of individual and collective rights and duties which would minimize friction and maximize generalized self-realization.

Hobhouse believed that each human being had a unique identity, the ability to accomplish a distinctive set of achievements, and the capacity to make a specific contribution to communal existence. Indeed, he claimed that

> Liberalism is the belief that society can safely be founded on this self-directing power of personality, that it is only on this foundation that a true community can be built, and that so established its foundations are so deep and so wide that there is no limit that we can place to the extent of the building.
>
> (p. 59)

For the individual, the good consisted in the realization of his or her potential in a balanced expansion of personality. For society, it lay in the simultaneous and mutually reinforcing fulfilment of each of its members. This was the essential bearing of Hobhouse's 'harmonic principle': on the one hand, the various dimensions of an individual life should be harmonized in a well-rounded personality; on the other, the trajectories to self-realization adopted by the different members of the community should harmonize in a general flourishing. Note that for Hobhouse it was not sufficient that collisions among individuals be avoided; 'true harmony' implied positive support – that for each person there be 'possibilities of development' so as 'actively to further the development of others' (p. 62).

Now Hobhouse was quite prepared to admit that, in this complete form, harmony represented 'an ideal . . . perhaps beyond the power of man to realize' (p. 65). Nevertheless, he insisted that the impulse to advance towards a more perfect harmony was an imperative for the rational subject. Above all, Hobhouse emphasized that to approximate true harmony it was necessary to deploy conscious effort. Earlier generations of liberals had been mistaken to assume that if each man acted according to the principles of enlightened self-interest, the outcome would necessarily be the best for the community as a whole. The 'harmonic' vision did not postulate that there was

> an actually existing harmony requiring nothing but prudence and coolness of judgement for its effective operation, but only that there is a possible ethical harmony, to which, partly by discipline, partly by the improvement of the conditions of life, men might attain, and that in such attainment lies the social ideal.
>
> (p. 62)

There were many possible lines of social development – but most led to suffering and conflict. The harmonic way was a narrow path, and to keep to it required conscious adjustment to reconcile the diverse moments of social life.

This deliberate displacement of liberty – and the positing of harmony at the core of liberalism – was the most striking formal innovation Hobhouse introduced in the course of articulating a liberal variant more sympathetic to the activist democratic state. But this was just one of a series of conceptual redefinitions and theoretical arguments which served to break any necessary connection between liberalism and minimal government.

When discussing liberty, Hobhouse emphasized that it was important relative to a specific end – the realization of personality; that a set of liberties that could assure opportunities for self-fulfilment to all depended upon a complex system of social restraints; and, that substantive freedom could be eroded by widespread economic inequality. In *Liberalism*, the state appears not as an external force ordering the lives of its subjects, but as an association of citizens collectively and consciously regulating the terms of their mutual interactions. State coercion is deemed legitimate not only to uphold rights – to prevent groups or individuals from injuring others – but also to make effective the will of the community in cases where necessary collective action would otherwise be frustrated by recalcitrant individuals. Moreover, making much of a point raised earlier by John Stuart Mill, Hobhouse argued that a great deal of state action is essentially non-coercive, representing the mobilization of social resources for collective ends.

Responsibility was not to be viewed solely in terms of the individual, but also in terms of society. If the individual had a duty to be self-supporting, then the community had an obligation to assure employment opportunities for every citizen. Although it was not for the state to 'feed, house, or clothe' its citizens, it was its duty to assure that 'economic conditions are such that the normal man who is not defective in mind or body or will can by useful labour feed, house, and clothe himself and his family' (p. 76).

Property rights were to be subordinate to the requirements of the common good: if individual property was essential to the growth of personality, then all citizens must have access to such property. Furthermore, Hobhouse argued that property had a 'social' dimension, and that wealth was in part a collective creation. Taxation of income could therefore be presented as the social re-absorption of a common product, rather than state confiscation of the fruits of individual labour.

Considering the nature of economic justice, Hobhouse argued that it depended upon an 'equation between function and sustenance' – each economic element should receive a reward sufficient to 'stimulate and maintain' its activity throughout its life (p. 92). However, market-mediated pay rates did not necessarily assure this equitable reward for labour, because in bargaining with owners, property-less workers suffered structural disadvantage. Once again the ground was prepared for remedial government action. Hobhouse insisted:

> the 'right to work' and the right to a 'living wage' are just as valid as the rights of person or property. That is to say, they are integral conditions of a good social order.
>
> (p. 76)

In Chapter VIII of *Liberalism* Hobhouse applied these and other principles to support a greatly increased regulatory role for the state. Many of the specific measures he advocated – such as the introduction of old-age pensions and health insurance, taxation of land values, and maintaining a distinction between earned and unearned income – closely followed the Liberal legislative agenda. However, the comprehensive scope of Hobhouse's vision of an activist, redistributive, egalitarian state went considerably beyond the pragmatic adjustments favoured by the mainstream Party leadership.

Even as he advocated reform, Hobhouse made it clear that he

did not favour an integral socialism which centralized all economic decision-making in the hands of the state. He argued that 'in production the personal factor is vital', and he defended those 'elements of individual right and personal independence, of which Socialism at times appears oblivious' (pp. 95–6, 101). Both 'Mechanical Socialism' (a term Hobhouse used to denote revolutionary or Marxist-inspired socialist variants) and 'Official Socialism' (an expression he applied to the Fabians) were explicitly rejected (pp. 81–2).

The final chapter of *Liberalism* reviews British political developments over the preceding half-century. Considering the prospects for popular government, Hobhouse argues that democracy is 'the necessary basis of the Liberal idea' (p. 109). Not that liberals regard this as the only legitimate form of government – for in some circumstances democracy may be inappropriate; rather it is that in the absence of democracy society suffers a permanent loss: for the people do not jointly assume responsibility for ordering the conditions of their common life. In other words, the process of collective self-government is itself part of the good life. With respect to its essence, Hobhouse understood democracy to imply the formation of a common will, something that is possible only when citizens take an intelligent interest in public affairs. As to its form, there was still much to be done to perfect the machinery of British democracy; among the measures Hobhouse considered were: proportional representation; reform of the powers and composition of the upper house; decision by popular referendum; and the substantial decentralization of powers to regional government.

Other writings

The other texts included in this collection originally appeared during a four-year period (1910 to 1913) which brackets the publication of *Liberalism*. They have been selected to round out the presentation of Hobhouse's political thought and provide further clarification of his views on a number of points raised by the longer work.

The first piece, *Government by the People*, was issued as a pamphlet by the People's Suffrage Federation in 1910. Written at the height of the constitutional wrangle over the Lords' veto, it is a straightforward plea for the speedy introduction of universal suffrage. Hobhouse makes his argument from social utility, insisting that democracy is less open to abuse than alternative forms of government; that it is the 'natural guardian of popular rights'; and that it favours 'government by public discussion', secures the responsibility of public officials, and permits the expression of 'larger social forces' (p. 131). The work is particularly interesting in that it highlights how the concerns about democracy had shifted in the interval since the publication of John Stuart Mill's *Considerations on Representative Government* (1861). It is not the danger of mob rule, or 'tyranny of the majority', that Hobhouse considers, but the risk that electoral politics will be dominated by an 'oligarchy of wealth', and the cynic's argument that for the average citizen the vote confers such a minute share of political responsibility that it is virtually meaningless. On both counts, Hobhouse's answer is to invoke the idea of democracy as facilitating the expression of groups and organized interests.

The next two selections – 'The Growth of the State' and 'The Individual and the State' – were published originally as Chapters VI and IX of *Social Evolution and Political Theory*. A re-write of eight lectures which Hobhouse had delivered at Columbia University in New York, this volume was centrally concerned with the nature of progress.

'The Growth of the State' is the pivotal chapter of this work in which Hobhouse attempts to prove that progress has been a real feature of human social evolution, by tracing the emergence of the state and the increasingly consistent application of the citizenship principle on which it is founded. This text provides a more detailed discussion of the three-stage classificatory schema of social types which makes a brief appearance in the first chapter of *Liberalism*, and clarifies Hobhouse's view of the ethical foundations of the modern state. It brings out the teleological character of Hobhouse's theory: for on his account, the modern democratic state – with its universal citizenship, elaborate individual freedoms, and complex system of rights and duties – is in some sense immanent within the citizenship principle as first tried out in the Greek city-state of antiquity. Taken in conjunction with the other texts included here, it also suggests that Hobhouse believed that the contemporary British state fell short of consistently embodying the citizenship principle in at least four ways: the Edwardian constitution was not fully democratic; the absence of welfare rights and the existence of exaggerated concentrations of wealth constantly threatened 'to reduce political and civic equality to a meaningless form of words' (p. 147); the state continued to exercise despotic dominion over subject peoples in the Empire; and, self-government was denied to minority nationalities (like the Irish) within the metropole.

'The Individual and the State' is the concluding chapter of *Social Evolution and Political Theory*, in which Hobhouse considers how individual liberty and social control can be successfully reconciled in the modern polity. The discussion covers much the same ground as the sixth and seventh chapters of *Liberalism*, but the exposition is more concise and straightforward. Hobhouse defines the 'sphere of the state' to be 'securing those common ends in which uniformity or, more generally, concerted action, is necessary' (p. 159); and, invoking a phrase which would have pleased T. H. Green, he suggested that 'the further development of the state lies in such an extension of public control as makes for the fuller liberty of the life of the mind' (p. 164). This piece also features a clear presentation of Hobhouse's perspective on the relationship between the right and the good, as well as further commentary on progress.

'Irish Nationalism and Liberal Principle' was first published in 1912 in *The New Irish Constitution*, an impressive collection of essays – on Irish history, Irish nationalism, and the constitutional arrangements to be introduced under Home Rule – commissioned by the liberal Committee of the Eighty Club, and edited by J. H. Morgan, Professor of Constitutional Law at University College, London. Hobhouse's essay was written in the months leading up to the introduction of the third Home Rule Bill, before the Irish crisis had assumed its most acute form, with threats of Army mutiny, and civil war. The piece reveals a rather subtle appreciation of the reality of national sentiment, and of the futility of applying force to maintain irreconciled nationalities within a unitary state. According to Hobhouse, the 'test of nationality lies in history', and when history has established that a national group has a persistent desire for autonomy, liberals must recognize that only by satisfying this demand can the liberty of all concerned parties be enhanced.

The final selection, 'The Historical Evolution of Property, in Fact and in Idea', originally appeared in 1913 in *Property: Its Duties and Rights Historically, Philosophically and Religiously Regarded*, a volume of essays edited by Charles Gore, Bishop of Oxford. In this article Hobhouse presents a brief description of the development of property as a social institution, and a survey of some of the leading political–theoretic approaches to property rights. The most important distinction Hobhouse introduces is one between 'property for use' and 'property for power': on the one hand, property serves individuals as the material foundation for an ordered, autonomous life; and on the other, property is 'a form of social organization, whereby the labour of those who have it not is directed by and for the enjoyment of those that have' (p. 181). In the modern world, ownership is concentrated in the hands of a few, while most lack minimal access to productive resources. For Hobhouse, the solution lay not in the abolition of private property, which was valuable for the fulfilment of personality, but in restoring

> to society a direct ownership of some things, but an eminent ownership of all things material to the production of wealth, securing 'property for use' to the individual, and retaining 'property for power' for the democratic state.
>
> (p. 198)

To the modern reader many aspects of Hobhouse's discussion may appear unsatisfactory. His belief in progress as a palpable reality, as advance down a single line, jars with more cautious late-twentieth-century assessments. Universalist assumptions, agent-centred explanation, and the almost exclusively rationalist account of human behaviour typical of Hobhouse have been subject to much modern criticism. We may wonder whether Hobhouse did not underestimate the significance of endemic conflict in determining patterns of social life, and whether the economic and political reforms he advocated could have been expected to secure the free development of each along mutually beneficial paths. Certainly, Hobhouse's belief that 'no essential element of social value has to be purchased at the expense of ... any other element of essential value' would be thought by many to have been overly sanguine (p. 165).

Most contemporary liberals would be repelled by the teleological dimension of Hobhouse's theory. Many would object to his easy slippage from the language of individual liberty into the idiom of collective freedom, and to his readiness to restrict the individual in order that 'majoritarian' freedoms may prevail. Some might query the degree to which Hobhouse makes individual welfare rights dependent upon the willingness to perform social duties – in particular the duty to strive to be 'self-supporting'. Others would question his brushing aside of the worry that state action might foster a culture of dependence. More fundamentally, it might be objected that Hobhouse exaggerates the unity of belief and purpose prevailing among the citizens of a modern democratic state, and that a liberal theory which is to give adequate recognition to the plurality of individual and group ends must abandon the politics of the common good for a right-prioritizing ethos.

Notwithstanding such objections, there is much to be gleaned from Hobhouse's political writings. In the first place, they provide valuable insight into the character of turn-of-the-century liberalism. They reveal the kinds of arguments invoked by the more thoughtful proponents of reform, as well as telling us something about the political beliefs of those with whom the New Liberals did battle. To read Hobhouse is to gain access to an important phase in the history of British liberal theory, and to encounter the intellectual controversy surrounding institutional changes which did much to shape the subsequent character of twentieth-century political life.

Liberalism and related writings also provide an illustration of how a political thinker, working within the framework of an established tradition, adapts inherited ideas to confront new circumstances. Existing conceptual categories are redefined; the relationships among concepts are adjusted; emphasis is switched from one element to another; and the result is a theory which in a sense is at one with tradition, but in another breaks new ground.

This suggests a further element to be gained from Hobhouse's writings: an appreciation of the essential complexity of the liberal political tradition. Today it is so often assumed that liberals can be easily categorized – as individualists, for instance; or as defenders of free markets, the existing property system, and quiescent government; or perhaps as advocates of a state which maintains strict neutrality with respect to competing conceptions of the good life. Hobhouse does not correspond to such stereotypes; and yet the general character of his thinking is recognizably liberal. Thus, his theory can encourage us to consider the particularities of modern liberal variants, and to reflect upon long-term continuities in the pattern of liberal belief.

Finally, Hobhouse's theorizing is sufficiently sophisticated that it can provoke us to reflect anew upon political problems of our own time. Hobhouse's discussions of the relationships between freedom and social control, and between individual self-reliance and collective responsibility; of the extent to which economic inequality and democratic citizenship are compatible; and of the possible reconciliation of liberalism and moderate socialism, touch issues which still preoccupy us today. And, while we may find Hobhouse's vision of progress no longer compelling, we may wonder whether there is not something to his suggestion that some theory of progress is an essential foundation for any sustained movement for social reform.

Principal events in the life of L. T. Hobhouse

1864	Born, St Ive, Cornwall.
1877	Attends Marlborough College.
1883	Wins scholarship to Corpus Christi College, Oxford.
1885	Gladstone introduces Irish Home Rule Bill and Liberal Party splits.
1886	Conservatives win election and Lord Salisbury becomes Prime Minister with massive Unionist support.
1887	Hobhouse graduates from university with a First in Greats, and wins election as a Prize Fellow at Merton College.
1891	Hobhouse marries Nora Hadwen.
1892	Liberals form government.
1893	*The Labour Movement* published. Second Irish Home Rule Bill defeated in the House of Lords.
1894	Hobhouse elected Tutorial Fellow of Corpus Christi College, Oxford.
1895	Unionists return to power under Lord Salisbury.
1896	*The Theory of Knowledge* published.
1897	Hobhouse leaves Oxford for Manchester, to take up position as writer on the *Manchester Guardian*.
1899	Outbreak of Boer War in southern Africa.
1901	*Mind in Evolution* published. Death of Queen Victoria.
1902	Hobhouse leaves Manchester for London. For the next quarter-century he remains an active contributor to the *Manchester Guardian*.

1903	Hobhouse becomes Secretary of the anti-protectionist Free Trade Union. Contributes to founding of the Sociological Society.
1904	*Democracy and Reaction* published.
1905	Hobhouse accepts post as Political Editor of the liberal daily *The Tribune*.
1906	Liberal Party wins landslide election victory under Campbell-Bannerman. *Morals in Evolution* published.
1907	Hobhouse takes up the Martin White Chair of Sociology at the University of London. Edits first issues of the *Sociological Review*.
1908	Asquith replaces Campbell-Bannerman as Liberal Prime Minister. Old Age Pensions enacted.
1909	Introduction of the Lloyd George Budget.
1910	Two general elections (January and December) return the Liberals to power and signal popular support for the Budget, and for the ascendancy of the Commons over the Lords. Death of Edward VII; George V becomes King.
1911	*Liberalism,* and *Social Evolution and Political Theory* published. Hobhouse becomes a Director of the *Manchester Guardian*. National Insurance Act introduces sickness and disability insurance. Parliament Act adopted.
1912	Third Home Rule Bill introduced by Liberal government.
1913	*Development and Purpose* published.
1914	Outbreak of Great War in Europe.
1915	*The World in Conflict* published. Coalition government established to provide war leadership.
1916	*Questions of War and Peace* published. Lloyd George replaces Asquith as Prime Minister.
1918	*The Metaphysical Theory of the State* published. Armistice concludes fighting in Europe. Hobhouse begins to assume responsibilities chairing Trades Boards.
1921	*The Rational Good* published.
1922	*The Elements of Social Justice* published. Coalition government falls; election returns Conservatives under Bonar Law; Labour becomes largest opposition party.
1923	Stanley Baldwin replaces Bonar Law as Conservative Prime Minister. General election reduces Conservative strength.

1924   *Social Development: Its Nature and Conditions* published. Minority Labour government lasts nine months. General election returns Conservatives to power and reduces Liberals to forty seats.

1925   Hobhouse elected Fellow of the British Academy. Death of Nora Hobhouse.

1929   Death of Leonard Hobhouse.

Further reading

Works by Hobhouse

Readers wishing to extend their encounter with Hobhouse's political thought should turn first to *Democracy and Reaction* (2nd edition, London, 1909), next to the more complex and sharply polemical *The Metaphysical Theory of the State* (London, 1918), and then to Hobhouse's most comprehensive work of political theory, *The Elements of Social Justice* (London, 1922). Those interested in Hobhouse's perspective on sociology should consult *Social Development: Its Nature and Conditions* (London, 1924). *The Rational Good: A Study in the Logic of Practice* (London, 1921) provides an exposition of Hobhouse's ethical theory, while the more difficult *Development and Purpose: An Essay Towards a Philosophy of Evolution* (2nd edition, London, 1927) elaborates the teleological evolutionist framework of his philosophical system.

Hobhouse produced many essays and short articles. Among the more significant pieces which deal directly with politics are: 'The Ethical Basis of Collectivism', *International Journal of Ethics* 8 (1898), 137–56; 'The Foreign Policy of Collectivism', *Economic Review* 9 (1899), 197–220; 'The Constitutional Issue', *Contemporary Review* 91 (1907), 312–18; 'The Prospects of Liberalism', *Contemporary Review* 93 (1908), 349–58; 'The Lords and the Constitution', *Contemporary Review* 96 (1909), 641–51; 'The Contending Forces', *English Review* 4 (1910), 359–71; 'The New Spirit in America', *Contemporary Review* 100 (1911), 1–11; and 'The Prospects for Anglo-Saxon Democracy', *Atlantic Monthly* 109 (1912), 345–52. Many of Hobhouse's more important pieces on sociology have been collected in *Sociology and Philosophy: A Centenary Collection of Essays and Articles* (ed. Morris

Ginsberg, London, 1966), including: 'The Roots of Modern Sociology' (Hobhouse's 1907 Inaugural Lecture at the London School of Economics); 'The Law of the Three Stages' (first published in the *Sociological Review* 1 (1908), 262–79); and 'Sociology' (first published in *Hastings' Encyclopedia of Religion and Ethics*, 1920, vol. 11, 654–65). Also included in this volume are interesting pieces on 'Comparative Ethics' and 'Comparative Psychology' (which originally appeared in *Encyclopedia Britannica*, 14th edition, 1929, vol. 6, 156–64 and 167–70) and an important article outlining the general lines of Hobhouse's philosophical perspective – 'The Philosophy of Development' (first published in *Contemporary British Philosophy*, 1st series, ed. J. Muirhead, London, 1924).

Political, social, and intellectual context

A short introduction to pre-war British political ideas can be found in Ernest Barker's *Political Thought in England: 1848–1914* (London, 1915). A more recent and substantial survey of British political thinking since the mid-nineteenth century can be found in *The Ideological Heritage* (London, 1983), the second volume of W. H. Greenleaf's *The British Political Tradition*. Other works which help set Hobhouse's writings in context are: Richard Bellamy, ed., *Victorian Liberalism: Nineteenth Century Political Thought and Practice* (London, 1990); Michael Bentley, *The Climax of Liberal Politics: British Liberalism in Theory and Practice 1868–1918* (London, 1987); George L. Bernstein, *Liberalism and Liberal Politics in Edwardian England* (Winchester, Mass., 1986); Peter Clarke, 'The Progressive Movement in England', *Transactions of the Royal Historical Society*, 5th series 24 (1974), 159–81; H. V. Emy, *Liberals, Radicals and Social Politics* (Cambridge, 1973); Michael Freeden, 'Biological and Evolutionary Roots of the New Liberalism in England', *Political Theory* 4 (1976), 471–90, and *Liberalism Divided: A Study in British Political Thought 1914–1939* (Oxford, 1986); R. Pearson and G. Williams, *Political Thought and Public Policy in the Nineteenth Century* (London, 1984); and Andrew Vincent and Raymond Plant, *Philosophy, Politics and Citizenship: the Life and Thought of the British Idealists* (Oxford, 1984).

Recent studies of British political thinkers with whom Hobhouse interacted can be found in: A. M. McBriar, *An Edwardian Mixed Doubles: the Bosanquets and the Webbs* (Oxford, 1987); Peter Nicholson, *The Political Philosophy of the British Idealists: Selected Studies* (Cambridge, 1990); and M. W. Taylor, *Men Versus the State: Herbert Spencer and Late Victorian Individualism* (Oxford, 1992).

Discussion of Hobhouse

A brief introduction to Hobhouse's political ideas is provided by Peter Weiler's 'The New Liberalism of L. T. Hobhouse', *Victorian Studies* 16 (1972), 141–61. Other useful short studies include: Ernest Barker's 'Leonard Trelawney Hobhouse: 1864–1929', *Proceedings of the British Academy* 15 (1929), 536–54; Peter Clarke's 'Introduction' to Hobhouse's *Democracy and Reaction* (Brighton, 1972); and Morris Ginsberg's 'Introduction' to *Sociology and Philosophy*.

The most sophisticated modern study of Hobhouse is Stefan Collini's *Liberalism and Sociology: L. T. Hobhouse and Political Argument in England 1880–1914* (Cambridge, 1979). Useful earlier works include Hugh Carter, *The Social Theories of L. T. Hobhouse* (Durham, N.C. 1927), and John E. Owen, *L. T. Hobhouse, Sociologist* (London, 1974). Although not exclusively devoted to Hobhouse, M. S. Freeden's *The New Liberalism: An Ideology of Social Reform* (Oxford, 1978) includes valuable discussion of Hobhouse's political thought. Also of considerable interest are: Peter Clarke, *Liberals and Social Democrats* (Cambridge, 1978); and Peter Weiler, *The New Liberalism: Liberal Social Theory in Great Britain 1889–1914* (New York, 1982).

Biographical material, together with a longer evaluative essay by Ginsberg, and short pieces by Hobhouse, can be found in *L. T. Hobhouse: His Life and Work*, ed. J. A. Hobson and Morris Ginsberg (London, 1931). Recent articles on Hobhouse include: Stefan Collini, 'Hobhouse, Bosanquet and the State: Philosophical Idealism and Political Argument in England: 1880–1918', *Past and Present* 72 (1976), 86–111; C. M. Griffin, 'L. T. Hobhouse and the Idea of Harmony', *Journal of the History of Ideas* 35 (1974), 647–61; and John W. Seaman, 'L. T. Hobhouse and the Theory of Social Liberalism', *Canadian Journal of Political Science* 11 (1978), 777–801.

Biographical notes

ARISTOTLE (384–322 BC). Greek philosopher who studied at Plato's Academy in Athens, tutored Alexander the Great, and taught on many issues including natural science, logic, metaphysics, and ethics. The *Politics*, which starts with an analysis of the essential nature of political association, is often regarded as the first systematic and empirically grounded investigation of political phenomena.

BACON, Francis (1561–1626). English philosopher and statesman. At various times Bacon served as Solicitor-General, Attorney-General, and Lord Chancellor, and his writings include *The Advancement of Learning* (1605).

BENTHAM, Jeremy (1748–1832). English philosopher, jurist, and advocate of reform. Bentham championed Utilitarianism, arguing that all social institutions should be judged according to the extent that they promoted the greatest happiness of the greatest number.

BISMARCK, Otto Eduard Leopold von (1815–98). Prussian Prime Minister who strove to unite the German principalities under a conservative monarchical constitution, and became first Imperial Chancellor of the new German Reich under Emperor William I in 1871. Bismarck was known for his ruthless suppression of opposition and calculated use of war to achieve political ends.

BOOTH, Charles (1840–1916). A shipowner, statistician, and social investigator, Booth served as president of the Royal Statistical Society between 1892 and 1894. He is best remembered for his influential *Life and Labour of the People in London* (1891–1903), a seventeen-volume study which did much to document the scale of poverty in the British capital.

BRIGHT, John (1811–89). British politician who held a Parliamentary seat for over forty years, and served under Gladstone as President of the Board of Trade (1868–70). A close associate of Cobden, Bright assumed a prominent role in the campaign to repeal the Corn Laws, and supported the Reform Act of 1867. A determined advocate of 'laissez-faire', he resisted the introduction of factory and health acts and opposed Gladstone's policy of Home Rule for Ireland.

CAMPBELL-BANNERMAN, Henry (1836–1908). A Liberal politician who held various ministerial posts under Gladstone, assumed leadership of the Party in the Commons in 1899, and served as Prime Minister from December 1905 until ill-health compelled him to resign in 1908. A moderate Liberal, wary of foreign entanglements, who took up the struggle to curtail the powers of the House of Lords after his landslide victory in 1906, Campbell-Bannerman was popular with the progressive wing of his Party.

CARLYLE, Thomas (1795–1881). One of the most influential literary figures of his day, Carlyle was an acerbic critic of the materialism, vulgarity, and corruption of modern society. He opposed 'laissez-faire' while it was in the ascendant, denounced the follies of democracy, and upheld diligence, duty, and authority. Among his influential works were *The French Revolution* (1837), *Past and Present* (1843), and *History of Frederick the Great* (1858–65).

COBDEN, Richard (1804–65). Free Trade and the promotion of international concord are the causes with which Cobden's name is most closely associated. A Manchester manufacturer who made a fortune in the calico trade, Cobden was a founder of the Anti-Corn Law League, and was later elected to Parliament. Cobden opposed the Crimean War, organized conferences to promote international arbitration and peace, and negotiated a tariff reduction agreement with France in 1860.

FAGUET, Auguste Emile (1847–1916). French literary figure and Professor at the Sorbonne, whose enormous output included works of literary and cultural criticism, philosophy, and politics.

GAMALIEL ('the elder') (died *c.* AD 50). Jewish religious leader, reported to be the grandson of Hillel. Teacher of the apostle Paul, Gamaliel was noted for his liberal interpretation of law and tradition.

GEORGE, Henry (1839–97). An American writer on economic affairs, George attacked the landholders' monopoly and advocated the introduction of a 'single tax' on the (pre-improvement) value of land. His book *Progress and Poverty* (1879), which related poverty to the landlords' absorption as rent of the wealth generated by increases in labour productivity, caused a considerable stir in Britain and the United States.

GLADSTONE, William Ewart (1809–98). The pre-eminent states-man of his day, Gladstone was Prime Minister on four occasions: 1868–74, 1880–5, 1886, and 1892–4. He helped secure the disestab-lishment of the Irish church (1869), protection for Irish tenants (1870 and 1881), and the extension of the vote to agricultural labourers (the 'County franchise') in 1885. His attempt to introduce Home Rule for Ireland split the Liberal Party and brought about the down-fall of his administration in 1886. A second attempt to obtain Home Rule was rejected by the Lords in 1893.

GREEN, Thomas Hill (1836–82). An Idealist philosopher, Fellow of Balliol College, and later Whyte's Professor of Moral Philosophy at Oxford, Green exerted an important influence on the succeeding generation of political philosophers. His most important works, which were both published posthumously, are *Prolegomena to Ethics* (1883), and *Lectures on the Principles of Political Obligation* (1895).

HOBHOUSE, J. Cam (1786–1869). A Radical politician who served as Secretary of War (1832–3) and President of the Board of Control (1835–41 and 1846–52). A close friend of Byron, J. Cam Hobhouse supported a range of progressive causes in his youth, although he became more cautious in later life.

LOCKE, John (1632–1704). English philosopher and political theor-ist, whose defence of toleration, and argument that government exists to preserve the life and liberties of the people, and that should it fail to do so it may be legitimately resisted, has an important place in the liberal canon. Locke's most influential works are *An Essay Concerning Human Understanding*, *A Letter Concerning Toleration*, and *Two Treatises of Government*.

MACHIAVELLI, Niccolò (1469–1527). Secretary and diplomat to the Florentine government, and author of two major political treatises – *The Prince* and *The Discourse on the First Ten Books of Titus Livy*. A republican and an Italian patriot, Machiavelli is associated with the idea that statecraft cannot be bound by conventional moral norms.

MAZZINI, Giuseppe (1805–72). An Italian patriot and revolutionary who fought to unite Italy under a republican government. In 1832 Mazzini established a secret society – 'Young Italy' – to work towards these ends; he also served as a member of the republican government in Rome during the abortive revolution of 1848.

METTERNICH, Prince Klemens Winzel Nepomuk Lohar von (1773–1859). Austrian statesman who helped reassert his country's status as a European power during the first half of the nineteenth century. A bitter opponent of liberal ideas and movements, Metternich was associated with repressive domestic policies. He was finally forced from office by the revolutionary upsurge of 1848.

MILL, James (1773–1836). A close friend and disciple of Jeremy Bentham, James Mill worked to popularize the teachings of his mentor. Mill campaigned for legal and administrative reform, and supported a vast extension of the franchise to end the landed aristocracy's domination of Parliament. Among his important works are *The History of British India* (1817), *An Essay on Government* (1820), and *Elements of Political Economy* (1821).

MILL, John Stuart (1806–73). English philosopher, economist, and liberal political theorist. The son of James Mill, he was raised an orthodox utilitarian; but contact with Continental thinking and the Romantic movement led him to reject the original formulation of the creed. A champion of individual liberty, Mill in later life described himself as a 'socialist'. His writings, many of which became almost instant classics, include: *Logic* (1843), *Principles of Political Economy* (1848), *On Liberty* (1869), *Utilitarianism* (1861), and *The Subjection of Women* (1869).

MORRIS, William (1834–98). English Romantic poet, artist, craftsman, and designer, who rebelled against the materialistic norms of industrial civilization. An early socialist and anti-capitalist campaigner, Morris had a fond regard for what he took to be the simple, wholesome, and organic life of the medieval village community. Among his many works are the epic poem, *Sigurd the Volsung* (1875), and a novel describing a British socialist utopia, *News from Nowhere* (1883).

NICHOLAS I (1796–1855). Czar of Russia from 1825 until 1855; conservative autocrat noted for crushing revolutionary nationalist movements in Europe – as in Poland (1830–1) and Hungary (1849) – and attempting to expand Russian influence south, by wresting territory from the Ottoman Empire.

PAINE, Thomas (1737–1809). Radical and republican publicist, who was born in England and participated in the revolutionary upheavals in America and France. In *Common Sense* (1776) he called for the American colonies to issue an immediate declaration of independence, while in *The Rights of Man* he defended the French revolution against the attacks of Edmund Burke.

PARNELL, Charles Stuart (1846–91). Irish nationalist politician who led Irish MPs committed to Home Rule in the British Parliament from 1877. Elected President of the Land League, Parnell prosecuted a militant campaign to stop the eviction of Irish tenant farmers. His career was ruined when it was revealed through divorce proceedings that he had had a protracted liaison with the wife of a prominent supporter.

PEEL, Robert (1788–1850). British Tory statesman who as a young man opposed Catholic emancipation. As Prime Minister he introduced many administrative reforms and was responsible for repealing the Corn Laws in 1846.

PLACE, Francis (1771–1854). English reformer, and friend of Jeremy Bentham and the two Mills. Place led the campaign for the repeal of statutes prohibiting trade unions in the early 1820s, supported the great Reform Bill of 1832, and helped draft the petition which set out the Chartists' demands in 1838.

PLATO (427–347 BC). Greek philosopher who studied under Socrates until the latter's death in 399 BC. Plato founded the Academy in Athens. In the *Republic* he considers the meaning of justice both in the human soul, and in an ideal polity.

PYM, John (1584–1643). English statesman who played a leading role in defending the rights of Parliament in the political struggle with Charles I.

ROUSSEAU, Jean-Jacques (1712–78). French philosopher, writer, and social thinker. A radical contract theorist, and an admirer of the citizenship communities of classic antiquity, Rousseau denounced the systematic dependence fostered by modern commercial society. His most famous political writings are the *Discourse on the Origin of Inequality* (1755) and *The Social Contract* (1762).

ROWNTREE, Benjamin Seebohm (1871–1954). A manufacturer and social researcher who served as an adviser to the Liberal Chancellor of the Exchequer, David Lloyd George. Rowntree's *Poverty: A Study of Town Life* (1901), an investigation of conditions in his home town of York, was a pioneering application of statistical methods to the study of poverty, and firmly established the prevalence of large-scale deprivation outside the capital.

SALISBURY, Marquess of (Robert Arthur Talbot Gascoyne Cecil) (1830–1903). Conservative politician who assumed leadership of the opposition in the Lords from 1881, and served as Prime Minister 1885–6, 1886–92, and 1895–1902. An opponent of democracy, social reform, and Irish Home Rule, Salisbury was a cautious but consistent Imperialist who prosecuted the Boer War.

SELKIRK, Alexander (1676–1721). A Scots sailor who spent four and a half years stranded on an island after having been set down by a passing ship. His case inspired the protagonist for Daniel Defoe's famous novel *Robinson Crusoe*.

SHAFTESBURY, Lord (Anthony Ashley Cooper) (1801–85). English philanthropist who entered Parliament in 1826 as Lord Ashley, and became seventh Earl of Shaftesbury in 1851. An evangelical reformer, Shaftesbury campaigned for a broad range of factory legislation, securing among other measures the passage of an Act in 1842 which forbade the employment in underground mines of children under ten and women.

SPENCER, Herbert (1820–1903). British philosopher and sociologist who attempted to provide a comprehensive evolutionary philosophy in his multi-volume *Synthetic Philosophy*. A self-professed 'individualist',

Spencer was a determined opponent of governmental interference. Considered a major thinker by his contemporaries, he has been judged harshly by posterity. Today his best known work is the anti-state polemic, *The Man Versus the State* (1884), but a more sophisticated version of his political theory can be found in *The Principles of Ethics* (1892, 1893).

STERLING, John (1806–44). British essayist and poet who founded a London literary club and became a friend of Thomas Carlyle. Despite differences, the two men formed a strong attachment and in 1851 Carlyle published *Life of Sterling*, an affectionate portrait of his companion.

TACITUS, Publius Cornelius (AD c.55–c.117). Roman political leader, orator, and historian. In the *Histories* and the *Annals* (which are only partially preserved) he dealt with the history of the Empire from the end of the reign of Augustus until Domitian (AD 14–96).

TIBERIUS (Tiberius Claudius Nero Caesar) (42 BC to AD 37). A successful military commander, who succeeded Augustus as Emperor of Rome (AD 14–37).

TOLSTOY, Count Leo Nikalaevich (1828–1910). Russian novelist and moral philosopher, who came to advocate a doctrine of non-resistance. His works include *War and Peace* (1866) and *Anna Karenina* (1875–7).

TORQUEMADA, Tomás de (c. 1420–98). Dominican monk appointed Grand Inquisitor by Pope Innocent VIII. He directed the conduct of the Inquisition in Spain.

TOYNBEE, Arnold (1852–83). A student of T. H. Green, who pioneered the university settlement movement, and advocated an evangelical socialism and self-sacrificing service to the community. He died young and left no substantial body of written work, but for a time inspired idealistic reformers from the educated classes. In his memory, Toynbee Hall was founded in the Whitechapel district of London's East End in 1884.

WEBB, Sydney and Beatrice (1859–1947 and 1858–1943). Most famous of the English Fabian socialists. Sidney Webb was one of the original Fabian essayists; became a Labour MP in 1920; served as

President of the Board of Trade in the first Labour government; and eventually sat as a Labour Peer. Beatrice was a member of the famous Royal Commission on the Poor Laws (1905–9). Their many works include a massive history of English local government, published between 1903 and 1929.

LIBERALISM

CHAPTER I

Before Liberalism

The modern State is the distinctive product of a unique civilization. But it is a product which is still in the making, and a part of the process is a struggle between new and old principles of social order. To understand the new, which is our main purpose, we must first cast a glance at the old. We must understand what the social structure was, which – mainly, as I shall show, under the inspiration of Liberal ideas – is slowly but surely giving place to the new fabric of the civic State. The older structure itself was by no means primitive. What is truly primitive is very hard to say. But one thing is pretty clear. At all times men have lived in societies, and ties of kinship and of simple neighbourhood underlie every form of social organization. In the simplest societies it seems probable that these ties – reinforced and extended, perhaps, by religious or other beliefs – are the only ones that seriously count. It is certain that of the warp of descent and the woof of intermarriage there is woven a tissue out of which small and rude but close and compact communities are formed. But the ties of kinship and neighbourhood are effective only within narrow limits. While the local group, the clan, or the village community are often the centres of vigorous life, the larger aggregate of the Tribe seldom attains true social and political unity unless it rests upon a military organization. But military organization may serve not only to hold one tribe together but also to hold other tribes in subjection, and thereby, at the cost of much that is most valuable in primitive life, to establish a larger and at the same time a more orderly society. Such an order once established does not, indeed, rest on naked force. The rulers become invested with a sacrosanct authority. It may be that

3

they are gods or descendants of gods. It may be that they are blessed and upheld by an independent priesthood. In either case the powers that be extend their sway not merely over the bodies but over the minds of men. They are ordained of God because they arrange the ordination. Such a government is not necessarily abhorrent to the people nor indifferent to them. But it is essentially government from above. So far as it affects the life of the people at all, it does so by imposing on them duties, as of military service, tribute, ordinances, and even new laws, in such wise and on such principles as seem good to itself. It is not true, as a certain school of jurisprudence held, that law is, as such, a command imposed by a superior upon an inferior, and backed by the sanctions of punishment.[1] But though this is not true of law in general it is a roughly true description of law in that particular stage of society which we may conveniently describe as the Authoritarian.

Now, in the greater part of the world and throughout the greater part of history the two forms of social organization that have been distinguished are the only forms to be found. Of course, they themselves admit of every possible variation of detail, but looking below these variations we find the two recurrent types. On the one hand, there are the small kinship groups, often vigorous enough in themselves, but feeble for purposes of united action. On the other hand, there are larger societies varying in extent and in degree of civilization from a petty negro kingdom to the Chinese Empire, resting on a certain union of military force and religious or quasi-religious belief which, to select a neutral name, we have called the principle of Authority. In the lower stages of civilization there appears, as a rule, to be only one method of suppressing the strife of hostile clans, maintaining the frontier against a common enemy, or establishing the elements of outward order. The alternative to authoritarian rule is relapse into the comparative anarchy of savage life.

But another method made its appearance in classical antiquity. The city state of ancient Greece and Italy was a new type of social organization. It differed from the clan and the commune in several

---

[1] Following Jeremy Bentham, John Austin (1790–1859) – in his influential *Lectures on Jurisprudence* (London, 1863) – defined positive law as a command of a political superior backed by threat of coercive sanction. [Numbered footnotes are by the editor; lettered footnotes are by Hobhouse himself. Editorial additions to Hobhouse's footnotes are enclosed in square brackets.]

ways. In the first place it contained many clans and villages, and perhaps owed its origin to the coming together of separate clans on the basis not of conquest but of comparatively equal alliance. Though very small as compared with an ancient empire or a modern state it was much larger than a primitive kindred. Its life was more varied and complex. It allowed more free play to the individual, and, indeed, as it developed, it suppressed the old clan organization and substituted new divisions, geographical or other. It was based, in fact, not on kinship as such, but on civic right, and this it was which distinguished it not only from the commune, but from the Oriental monarchy. The law which it recognized and by which it lived was not a command imposed by a superior government on a subject mass. On the contrary, government was itself subject to law, and law was the life of the state, willingly supported by the entire body of free citizens. In this sense the city state was a community of free men. Considered collectively its citizens owned no master. They governed themselves, subject only to principles and rules of life descending from antiquity and owing their force to the spontaneous allegiance of successive generations. In such a community some of the problems that vex us most presented themselves in a very simple form. In particular the relation of the individual to the community was close, direct, and natural. Their interests were obviously bound up together. Unless each man did his duty the State might easily be destroyed and the population enslaved. Unless the State took thought for its citizens it might easily decay. What was still more important, there was no opposition of church and state, no fissure between political and religious life, between the claims of the secular and the spiritual, to distract the allegiance of the citizens, and to set the authority of conscience against the duties of patriotism. It was no feat of the philosophical imagination, but a quite simple and natural expression of the facts to describe such a community as an association of men for the purpose of living well. Ideals to which we win our way back with difficulty and doubt arose naturally out of the conditions of life in ancient Greece.

On the other hand, this simple harmony had very serious limitations, which in the end involved the downfall of the city system. The responsibilities and privileges of the associated life were based not on the rights of human personality but on the rights of citizenship, and citizenship was never co-extensive with the community. The population included slaves or serfs, and in many cities there were large classes descended from the original conquered population, personally free but excluded from the governing circle. Notwithstanding the relative simplicity of social conditions the city was constantly torn by the disputes of faction – in part probably a legacy from the old clan organization, in part a consequence of the growth of wealth and the newer distinction of classes. The evil of faction was aggravated by the ill-success of the city organization in dealing with the problem of inter-state relations. The Greek city clung to its autonomy, and though the principle of federalism which might have solved the problem was ultimately brought into play, it came too late in Greek history to save the nation.

The constructive genius of Rome devised a different method of dealing with the political problems involved in expanding relations. Roman citizenship was extended till it included all Italy and, later on, till it comprised the whole free population of the Mediterranean basin. But this extension was even more fatal to the free self-government of a city state. The population of Italy could not meet in the Forum of Rome or the Plain of Mars to elect consuls and pass laws, and the more widely it was extended the less valuable for any political purpose did citizenship become. The history of Rome, in fact, might be taken as a vast illustration of the difficulty of building up an extended empire on any basis but that of personal despotism resting on military force and maintaining peace and order through the efficiency of the bureaucratic machine. In this vast mechanism it was the army that was the seat of power, or rather it was each army at its post on some distant frontier that was a potential seat of power. The 'secret of the empire' that was early divulged was that an emperor could be made elsewhere than at Rome, and though a certain sanctity remained to the person of the emperor, and legists cherished a dim remembrance of the theory that he embodied the popular will, the fact was that he was the choice of a powerful army, ratified by the God of Battles, and maintaining his power as long as he could suppress any rival pretender. The break-up of the Empire through the continual repetition of military strife was accelerated, not caused, by the presence of barbarism both within and without the frontiers. To restore the elements of order a compromise between central and local jurisdictions was necessary, and the vassal became a local prince owning an allegiance, more or less real as the case might be, to a distant sovereign. Meanwhile, with the prevailing disorder the mass of the population in Western Europe lost its freedom, partly through conquest, partly through the necessity of finding a protector in troublous times. The social structure of the Middle Ages accordingly assumed the hierarchical form which we speak of as the Feudal system. In this thoroughgoing application of the principle of authority every man, in theory, had his master. The serf held of his lord, who held of a great seigneur, who held of the king. The king in the completer theory held of the emperor, who was crowned by the Pope, who held of St Peter. The chain of descent was complete from the Ruler of the universe to the humblest of the serfs." But within this order the growth of industry and commerce raised up new centres of freedom. The towns in which men were learning anew the lessons of association for united defence and the regulation of common interests, obtained charters of rights from seigneur or king, and on the Continent even succeeded in establishing complete independence. Even in England, where from the Conquest the central power was at its strongest, the corporate towns became for many purposes self-governing communities. The city state was born again, and with it came an outburst of activity, the revival of literature and the arts, the rediscovery of ancient learning, the rebirth of philosophy and science.

The mediaeval city state was superior to the ancient in that slavery was no essential element in its existence. On the contrary, by welcoming the fugitive serf and vindicating his freedom it contributed powerfully to the decline of the milder form of servitude. But like the ancient state it was seriously and permanently weakened by internal faction, and like the ancient state it rested the privileges of its members not on the rights of human personality, but on the responsibilities of citizenship. It knew not so much liberty as 'liberties', rights of corporations secured by charter, its own rights as a whole secured against king or feudatory and the rest of the world, rights of gilds and crafts within it, and to men or women only as they were members of such bodies. But the real weakness of the city state was once more

---

" This is, of course, only one side of mediaeval theory, but it is the side which lay nearest to the facts. The reverse view, which derives the authority of government from the governed, made its appearance in the Middle Ages partly under the influence of classical tradition. But its main interest and importance is that it served as a starting-point for the thought of a later time. On the whole subject the reader may consult Gierke, *Political Theories of the Middle Age*, translated by Maitland (Cambridge University Press [, 1900]).

its isolation. It was but an islet of relative freedom on, or actually within, the borders of a feudal society which grew more powerful with the generations. With the improvement of communications and of the arts of life, the central power, particularly in France and England, began to gain upon its vassals. Feudal disobedience and disorder were suppressed, and by the end of the fifteenth century great unified states, the foundation of modern nations, were already in being. Their emergence involved the widening and in some respects the improvement of the social order; and in its earlier stages it favoured civic autonomy by suppressing local anarchy and feudal privilege. But the growth of centralization was in the end incompatible with the genius of civic independence, and perilous to such elements of political right as had been gained for the population in general as the result of earlier conflicts between the crown and its vassals.

We enter on the modern period, accordingly, with society constituted on a thoroughly authoritarian basis, the kingly power supreme and tending towards arbitrary despotism, and below the king the social hierarchy extending from the great territorial lord to the day-labourer. There is one point gained as compared to earlier forms of society. The base of the pyramid is a class which at least enjoys personal freedom. Serfdom has virtually disappeared in England, and in the greater part of France has either vanished or become attenuated to certain obnoxious incidents of the tenure of land. On the other hand, the divorce of the English peasant from the soil has begun, and has laid the foundation of the future social problem as it is to appear in this country.

The modern State accordingly starts from the basis of an authoritarian order, and the protest against that order, a protest religious, political, economic, social, and ethical, is the historic beginning of Liberalism. Thus Liberalism appears at first as a criticism, sometimes even as a destructive and revolutionary criticism. Its negative aspect is for centuries foremost. Its business seems to be not so much to build up as to pull down, to remove obstacles which block human progress, rather than to point the positive goal of endeavour or fashion the fabric of civilization. It finds humanity oppressed, and would set it free. It finds a people groaning under arbitrary rule, a nation in bondage to a conquering race, industrial enterprise obstructed by social privileges or crippled by taxation, and it offers relief. Everywhere it is removing superincumbent weights, knocking off fetters, clearing away obstructions. Is it doing as much for the reconstruction that will be necessary when the demolition is complete? Is Liberalism at bottom a constructive or only a destructive principle? Is it of permanent significance? Does it express some vital truth of social life as such, or is it a temporary phenomenon called forth by the special circumstances of Western Europe, and is its work already so far complete that it can be content to hand on the torch to a newer and more constructive principle, retiring for its own part from the race, or perchance seeking more backward lands for missionary work? These are among the questions that we shall have to answer. We note, for the moment, that the circumstances of its origin suffice to explain the predominance of critical and destructive work without therefrom inferring the lack of ultimate reconstructive power. In point of fact, whether by the aid of Liberalism or through the conservative instincts of the race, the work of reconstruction has gone on side by side with that of demolition, and becomes more important generation by generation. The modern State, as I shall show, goes far towards incorporating the elements of Liberal principle, and when we have seen what these are, and to what extent they are actually realized, we shall be in a better position to understand the essentials of Liberalism, and to determine the question of its permanent value.

CHAPTER II

The Elements of Liberalism

I cannot here attempt so much as a sketch of the historical progress of the Liberalizing movement. I would call attention only to the main points at which it assailed the old order, and to the fundamental ideas directing its advance.

1 Civil Liberty

Both logically and historically the first point of attack is arbitrary government, and the first liberty to be secured is the right to be dealt with in accordance with law. A man who has no legal rights against another, but stands entirely at his disposal, to be treated according to his caprice, is a slave to that other. He is 'rightless', devoid of rights. Now, in some barbaric monarchies the system of rightlessness has at times been consistently carried through in the relations of subjects to the king. Here men and women, though enjoying customary rights of person and property as against one another, have no rights at all as against the king's pleasure. No European monarch or seignior has ever admittedly enjoyed power of this kind, but European governments have at various times and in various directions exercised or claimed powers no less arbitrary in principle. Thus, by the side of the regular courts of law which prescribe specific penalties for defined offences proved against a man by a regular form of trial, arbitrary governments resort to various extrajudicial forms of arrest, detention, and punishment, depending on their own will and pleasure. Of such a character is punishment by 'administrative' process in Russia at the present day; imprisonment by *lettre de cachet* in France under the *ancien régime*; all executions by so-called martial law in times of rebellion, and the suspension of various ordinary guarantees of immediate and fair trial in Ireland. Arbitrary government in this form was one of the first objects of attack by the English Parliament in the seventeenth century, and this first liberty of the subject was vindicated by the Petition of Right, and again by the Habeas Corpus Act. It is significant of much that this first step in liberty should be in reality nothing more nor less than a demand for law. 'Freedom of men under government', says Locke, summing up one whole chapter of seventeenth-century controversy, 'is to have a standing rule to live by, common to every one of that society and made by the legislative power erected in it'.[2]

The first condition of universal freedom, that is to say, is a measure of universal restraint. Without such restraint some men may be free but others will be unfree. One man may be able to do all his will, but the rest will have no will except that which he sees fit to allow them. To put the same point from another side, the first condition of free government is government not by the arbitrary determination of the ruler, but by fixed rules of law, to which the ruler himself is subject. We draw the important inference that there is no essential antithesis between liberty and law. On the contrary, law is essential to liberty. Law, of course, restrains the individual; it is therefore opposed to his liberty at a given moment and in a given direction. But, equally, law restrains others from doing with him as they will. It liberates him from the fear of arbitrary aggression or coercion, and this is the only way, indeed, the only sense, in which liberty *for an entire community* is attainable.

There is one point tacitly postulated in this argument which should not be overlooked. In assuming that the reign of law guarantees liberty to the whole community, we are assuming that it is impartial. If there is one law for the Government and another for its subjects, one for noble and another for commoner, one for rich and another for poor, the law does not guarantee liberty for all. Liberty in this respect implies equality. Hence the demand of Liberalism for such a procedure as will ensure the impartial application of law. Hence the demand for the independence of the judiciary to secure equality as between the Government and its subjects. Hence the demand

[2] John Locke, *Two Treatises of Government* (1689/90), Book II, chap. iv.

for cheap procedure and accessible courts. Hence the abolition of privileges of class.* Hence will come in time the demand for the abolition of the power of money to purchase skilled advocacy.

2 Fiscal Liberty

Closely connected with juristic liberty, and more widely felt in everyday life, is the question of fiscal liberty. The Stuarts brought things to a head in this country by arbitrary taxation. George III brought things to a head in America by the same infallible method. The immediate cause of the French Revolution was the refusal of the nobles and the clergy to bear their share of the financial burden. But fiscal liberty raises more searching questions than juristic liberty. It is not enough that taxes should be fixed by a law applying universally and impartially, for taxes vary from year to year in accordance with public needs, and while other laws may remain stable and unchanged for an indefinite period, taxation must, in the nature of the case, be adjustable. It is a matter, properly considered, for the Executive rather than the Legislature. Hence the liberty of the subject in fiscal matters means the restraint of the Executive, not merely by established and written laws, but by a more direct and constant supervision. It means, in a word, responsible government, and that is why we have more often heard the cry, 'No taxation without representation', than the cry, 'No legislation without representation.' Hence, from the seventeenth century onwards, fiscal liberty was seen to involve what is called political liberty.

3 Personal Liberty

Of political liberty it will be more convenient to speak later. But let us here observe that there is another avenue by which it can be, and, in fact, was, approached. We have seen that the reign of law is the first step to liberty. A man is not free when he is controlled by other

* In England 'benefit of clergy' was still a good plea for remission of sentence for a number of crimes in the seventeenth century. At that time all who could read could claim benefit, which was therefore of the nature of a privilege for the educated class. The requirement of reading, which had become a form, was abolished in 1705, but peers and clerks in holy orders could still plead their clergy in the eighteenth century, and the last relics of the privilege were not finally abolished till the nineteenth century.

men, but only when he is controlled by principles and rules which all society must obey, for the community is the true master of the free man. But here we are only at the beginning of the matter. There may be law, and there may be no attempt, such as the Stuarts made, to set law aside, yet (1) the making and maintenance of law may depend on the will of the sovereign or of an oligarchy, and (2) the content of the law may be unjust and oppressive to some, to many, or to all except those who make it. The first point brings us back to the problem of political liberty, which we defer. The second opens questions which have occupied a great part of the history of Liberalism, and to deal with them we have to ask what types of law have been felt as peculiarly oppressive, and in what respects it has been necessary to claim liberty not merely through law, but by the abolition of bad law and tyrannical administration.

In the first place, there is the sphere of what is called personal liberty – a sphere most difficult to define, but the arena of the fiercest strife of passion and the deepest feelings of mankind. At the basis lies liberty of thought – freedom from inquisition into opinions that a man forms in his own mind' – the inner citadel where, if anywhere, the individual must rule. But liberty of thought is of very little avail without liberty to exchange thoughts – since thought is mainly a social product; and so with liberty of thought goes liberty of speech and liberty of writing, printing, and peaceable discussion. These rights are not free from difficulty and dubiety. There is a point at which speech becomes indistinguishable from action, and free speech may mean the right to create disorder. The limits of just liberty here are easy to draw neither in theory nor in practice. They lead us immediately to one of the points at which liberty and order may be in conflict, and it is with conflicts of this kind that we shall have to deal. The possibilities of conflict are not less in relation to the connected right of liberty in religion. That this liberty is absolute cannot be contended. No modern state would tolerate a form of religious worship which should include cannibalism, human sacrifice, or the burning of witches. In point of fact, practices of this kind – which follow quite naturally from various forms of primitive belief that are most sincerely

---

' See an interesting chapter in Faguet's *Libéralisme* [(Paris, 1903)], which points out that the common saying that thought is free is negated by any inquisition which compels a man to disclose opinions, and penalizes him if they are not such as to suit the inquisitor.

held – are habitually put down by civilized peoples that are responsible for the government of less developed races. The British law recognizes polygamy in India, but I imagine it would not be open either to a Mahommedan or a Hindu to contract two marriages in England. Nor is it for liberty of this kind that the battle has been fought.

What, then, is the primary meaning of religious liberty? Externally, I take it to include the liberties of thought and expression, and to add to these the right of worship in any form which does not inflict injury on others or involve a breach of public order. This limitation appears to carry with it a certain decency and restraint in expression which avoids unnecessary insult to the feelings of others; and I think this implication must be allowed, though it makes some room for strained and unfair applications. Externally, again, we must note that the demand for religious liberty soon goes beyond mere toleration. Religious liberty is incomplete as long as any belief is penalized, as, for example, by carrying with it exclusion from office or from educational advantages. On this side, again, full liberty implies full equality. Turning to the internal side, the spirit of religious liberty rests on the conception that a man's religion ranks with his own innermost thought and feelings. It is the most concrete expression of his personal attitude to life, to his kind, to the world, to his own origin and destiny. There is no real religion that is not thus drenched in personality; and the more religion is recognized for spiritual the starker the contradiction is felt to be that any one should seek to impose a religion on another. Properly regarded, the attempt is not wicked, but impossible. Yet those sin most against true religion who try to convert men from the outside by mechanical means. They have the lie in the soul, being most ignorant of the nature of that for which they feel most deeply.

Yet here again we stumble on difficulties. Religion is personal. Yet is not religion also eminently social? What is more vital to the social order than its beliefs? If we send a man to gaol for stealing trash, what shall we do to him whom, in our conscience and on our honour, we believe to be corrupting the hearts of mankind, and perhaps leading them to eternal perdition? Again, what in the name of liberty are we to do to men whose preaching, if followed out in act, would bring back the rack and the stake? Once more there is a difficulty of delimitation which will have to be fully sifted. I will only remark here that our practice has arrived at a solution which, upon the whole, appears to have worked well hitherto, and which has its roots in principle. It is open to a man to preach the principles of Torquemada or the religion of Mahomet. It is not open to men to practise such of their precepts as would violate the rights of others or cause a breach of the peace. Expression is free, and worship is free as far as it is the expression of personal devotion. So far as they infringe the freedom, or, more generally, the rights of others, the practices inculcated by a religion cannot enjoy unqualified freedom.

4 Social Liberty

From the spiritual we turn to the practical side of life. On this side we may observe, first, that Liberalism has had to deal with those restraints on the individual which flow from the hierarchic organization of society, and reserve certain offices, certain forms of occupation, and perhaps the right or at least the opportunity of education generally, to people of a certain rank or class. In its more extreme form this is a caste system, and its restrictions are religious or legal as well as social. In Europe it has taken more than one form. There is the monopoly of certain occupations by corporations, prominent in the minds of eighteenth-century French reformers. There is the reservation of public appointments and ecclesiastical patronage for those who are 'born', and there is a more subtly pervading spirit of class which produces a hostile attitude to those who could and would rise; and this spirit finds a more material ally in the educational difficulties that beset brains unendowed with wealth. I need not labour points which will be apparent to all, but have again to remark two things. (1) Once more the struggle for liberty is also, when pushed through, a struggle for equality. Freedom to choose and follow an occupation, if it is to become fully effective, means equality with others in the opportunities for following such occupation. This is, in fact, one among the various considerations which lead Liberalism to support a national system of free education, and will lead it further yet on the same lines. (2) Once again, though we may insist on the rights of the individual, the social value of the corporation or quasi-corporation, like the Trade Union, cannot be ignored. Experience shows the necessity of some measure of collective regulation in industrial matters, and in the adjustment of such regulation to individual liberty serious difficulties of principle emerge. We shall have to refer to these in the next section. But one point is relevant at this stage. It is clearly a matter of Liberal principle that membership of a corporation should not depend on any hereditary qualification, nor be set about with any artificial difficulty of entry, where by the term artificial is meant any difficulty not involved in the nature of the occupation concerned, but designed for purposes of exclusiveness. As against all such methods of restriction, the Liberal case is clear.

It has only to be added here that restrictions of sex are in every respect parallel to restrictions of class. There are, doubtless, occupations for which women are unfit. But, if so, the test of fitness is sufficient to exclude them. The 'open road for women' is one application, and a very big one, of the 'open road for talent', and to secure them both is of the essence of Liberalism.

5   Economic Liberty

Apart from monopolies, industry was shackled in the earlier part of the modern period by restrictive legislation in various forms, by navigation laws, and by tariffs. In particular, the tariff was not merely an obstruction to free enterprise, but a source of inequality as between trade and trade. Its fundamental effect is to transfer capital and labour from the objects on which they can be most profitably employed in a given locality, to objects on which they are less profitably employed, by endowing certain industries to the disadvantage of the general consumer. Here, again, the Liberal movement is at once an attack on an obstruction and on an inequality. In most countries the attack has succeeded in breaking down local tariffs and establishing relatively large Free Trade units. It is only in England, and only owing to our early manufacturing supremacy, that it has fully succeeded in overcoming the Protective principle, and even in England the Protectionist reaction would undoubtedly have gained at least a temporary victory but for our dependence on foreign countries for food and the materials of industry. The most striking victory of Liberal ideas is one of the most precarious. At the same time, the battle is one which Liberalism is always prepared to fight over again. It has led to no back stroke, no counter-movement within the Liberal ranks themselves.

It is otherwise with organized restrictions upon industry. The old regulations, which were quite unsuited to the conditions of the time, either fell into desuetude during the eighteenth century, or were formally abolished during the earlier years of the industrial revolution. For a while it seemed as though wholly unrestricted industrial enterprise was to be the progressive watchword, and the echoes of that time still linger. But the old restrictions had not been formally withdrawn before a new process of regulation began. The conditions produced by the new factory system shocked the public conscience; and as early as 1802[3] we find the first of a long series of laws, out of which has grown an industrial code that year by year follows the life of the operative, in his relations with his employer, into more minute detail. The first stages of this movement were contemplated with doubt and distrust by many men of Liberal sympathies. The intention was, doubtless, to protect the weaker party, but the method was that of interference with freedom of contract. Now the freedom of the sane adult individual – even such strong individualists as Cobden recognized that the case of children stood apart – carried with it the right of concluding such agreements as seemed best to suit his own interests, and involved both the right and the duty of determining the lines of his life for himself. Free contract and personal responsibility lay close to the heart of the whole Liberal movement. Hence the doubts felt by so many Liberals as to the regulation of industry by law. None the less, as time has gone on, men of the keenest Liberal sympathies have come not merely to accept but eagerly to advance the extension of public control in the industrial sphere, and of collective responsibility in the matter of the education and even the feeding of children, the housing of the industrial population, the care of the sick and aged, the provision of the means of regular employment. On this side Liberalism seems definitely to have retraced its steps, and we shall have to inquire closely into the question whether the reversal is a change of principle or of application.

Closely connected with freedom of contract is freedom of association. If men may make any agreement with one another in their mutual interest so long as they do not injure a third party, they may apparently agree to act together permanently for any purposes of common interest on the same conditions. That is, they may form

[3] In 1802 an Act was passed to regulate the hours and working conditions of parish apprentices.

associations. Yet at bottom the powers of an association are something very different from the powers of the individuals composing it; and it is only by legal pedantry that the attempt can be made to regulate the behaviour of an association on principles derived from and suitable to the relations of individuals. An association might become so powerful as to form a state within the state, and to contend with government on no unequal terms. The history of some revolutionary societies, of some ecclesiastical organizations, even of some American trusts might be quoted to show that the danger is not imaginary. Short of this, an association may act oppressively towards others and even towards its own members, and the function of Liberalism may be rather to protect the individual against the power of the association than to protect the right of association against the restriction of the law. In fact, in this regard, the principle of liberty cuts both ways, and this double application is reflected in history. The emancipation of trade unions, however, extending over the period from 1824 to 1906, and perhaps not yet complete, was in the main a liberating movement, because combination was necessary to place the workman on something approaching terms of equality with the employer, and because tacit combinations of employers could never, in fact, be prevented by law. It was, again, a movement to liberty through equality. On the other hand, the oppressive capacities of a trade union could never be left out of account, while combinations of capital, which might be infinitely more powerful, have justly been regarded with distrust. In this there is no inconsistency of principle, but a just appreciation of a real difference of circumstance. Upon the whole it may be said that the function of Liberalism is not so much to maintain a general right of free association as to define the right in each case in such terms as make for the maximum of real liberty and equality.

6   Domestic Liberty

Of all associations within the State, the miniature community of the Family is the most universal and of the strongest independent vitality. The authoritarian state was reflected in the authoritarian family, in which the husband was within wide limits absolute lord of the person and property of wife and children. The movement of liberation consists (1) in rendering the wife a fully responsible individual, capable of holding property, suing and being sued, conducting business on her own account, and enjoying full personal protection against her husband; (2) in establishing marriage as far as the law is concerned on a purely contractual basis, and leaving the sacramental aspect of marriage to the ordinances of the religion professed by the parties; (3) in securing the physical, mental, and moral care of the children, partly by imposing definite responsibilities on the parents and punishing them for neglect, partly by elaborating a public system of education and of hygiene. The first two movements are sufficiently typical cases of the interdependence of liberty and equality. The third is more often conceived as a Socialistic than a Liberal tendency, and, in point of fact, the State control of education gives rise to some searching questions of principle, which have not yet been fully solved. If, in general, education is a duty which the State has a right to enforce, there is a countervailing right of choice as to the lines of education which it would be ill to ignore, and the mode of adjustment has not yet been adequately determined either in theory or in practice. I would, however, strongly maintain that the general conception of the State as Over-parent is quite as truly Liberal as Socialistic. It is the basis of the rights of the child, of his protection against parental neglect, of the equality of opportunity which he may claim as a future citizen, of his training to fill his place as a grown-up person in the social system. Liberty once more involves control and restraint.

7 Local, Racial, and National Liberty

From the smallest social unit we pass to the largest. A great part of the liberating movement is occupied with the struggle of entire nations against alien rule, with the revolt of Europe against Napoleon, with the struggle of Italy for freedom, with the fate of the Christian subjects of Turkey, with the emancipation of the negro, with the national movement in Ireland and in India. Many of these struggles present the problem of liberty in its simplest form. It has been and is too often a question of securing the most elementary rights for the weaker party; and those who are not touched by the appeal are deficient rather in imagination than in logic or ethics. But at the back of national movements very difficult questions do arise. What is a nation as distinct from a state? What sort of unity does it constitute, and what are its rights? If Ireland is a nation, is Ulster one? and if Ulster is a British and Protestant nation, what of the Catholic half of Ulster? History has in some cases given us a practical answer. Thus, it has shown that, enjoying the gift of responsible government, French and British, despite all historical quarrels and all differences of religious belief, language, and social structure, have fused into the nation of Canada. History has justified the conviction that Germany was a nation, and thrown ridicule on the contemptuous saying of Metternich that Italy was a geographical expression. But how to anticipate history, what rights to concede to a people that claims to be a self-determining unit, is less easy to decide. There is no doubt that the general tendency of Liberalism is to favour autonomy, but, faced as it is with the problems of subdivision and the complexity of group with group, it has to rely on the concrete teaching of history and the practical insight of statesmanship to determine how the lines of autonomy are to be drawn. There is, however, one empirical test which seems generally applicable. Where a weaker nation incorporated with a larger or stronger one can be governed by ordinary law applicable to both parties to the union, and fulfilling all the ordinary principles of liberty, the arrangement may be the best for both parties. But where this system fails, where the government is constantly forced to resort to exceptional legislation or perhaps to de-liberalize its own institutions, the case becomes urgent. Under such conditions the most liberally-minded democracy is maintaining a system which must undermine its own principles. The Assyrian conqueror, Mr Herbert Spencer remarks, who is depicted in the bas-reliefs leading his captive by a cord, is bound with that cord himself. He forfeits his liberty as long as he retains his power.

Somewhat similar questions arise about race, which many people wrongly confuse with nationality. So far as elementary rights are concerned there can be no question as to the attitude of Liberalism. When the political power which should guarantee such rights is brought into view, questions of fact arise. Is the Negro or the Kaffir mentally and morally capable of self-government or of taking part in a self-governing State? The experience of Cape Colony tends to the affirmative view. American experience of the negro gives, I take it, a more doubtful answer. A specious extension of the white man's rights to the black may be the best way of ruining the black. To destroy tribal custom by introducing conceptions of individual property, the free disposal of land, and the free purchase of gin may be the handiest method for the expropriator. In all relations with weaker peoples we move in an atmosphere vitiated by the insincere use of high-sounding words. If men say equality, they mean oppression by forms of justice. If they say tutelage, they appear to mean the kind of tutelage extended to the fattened goose. In such an atmosphere, perhaps, our safest course, so far as principles and deductions avail at all, is to fix our eyes on the elements of the matter, and in any part of the world to support whatever method succeeds in securing the 'coloured' man from personal violence, from the lash, from expropriation, and from gin; above all, so far as it may yet be, from the white man himself. Until the white man has fully learnt to rule his own life, the best of all things that he can do with the dark man is to do nothing with him. In this relation, the day of a more constructive Liberalism is yet to come.

8   International Liberty

If non-interference is the best thing for the barbarian many Liberals have thought it to be the supreme wisdom in international affairs generally. I shall examine this view later. Here I merely remark: (1) It is of the essence of Liberalism to oppose the use of force, the basis of all tyranny. (2) It is one of its practical necessities to withstand the tyranny of armaments. Not only may the military force be directly turned against liberty, as in Russia, but there are more subtle ways, as in Western Europe, in which the military spirit eats into free institutions and absorbs the public resources which might go to the advancement of civilization. (3) In proportion as the world becomes free, the use of force becomes meaningless. There is no purpose in aggression if it is not to issue in one form or another of national subjection.

9   Political Liberty and Popular Sovereignty

Underlying all these questions of right is the question how they are to be secured and maintained. By enforcing the responsibility of the executive and legislature to the community as a whole? Such is the general answer, and it indicates one of the lines of connection between the general theory of liberty and the doctrine of universal suffrage and the sovereignty of the people. The answer, however, does not meet all the possibilities of the case. The people as a whole might be careless of their rights and incapable of managing them. They might be set on the conquest of others, the expropriation of the rich, or on any form of collective tyranny or folly. It is perfectly possible that from the point of view of general liberty and social progress a limited franchise might give better results than one that is more extended. Even in this country it is a tenable view that the extension of the suffrage in 1884 tended for some years to arrest the development of liberty in various directions. On what theory does the principle of popular sovereignty rest, and within what limits does it hold good? Is it a part of the general principles of liberty and equality, or are other ideas involved? These are among the questions which we shall have to examine.

We have now passed the main phases of the Liberal movement in very summary review, and we have noted, first, that it is coextensive with life. It is concerned with the individual, the family, the State. It touches industry, law, religion, ethics. It would not be difficult, if space allowed, to illustrate its influence in literature and art, to describe the war with convention, insincerity, and patronage, and the struggle for free self-expression, for reality, for the artist's soul. Liberalism is an all-penetrating element of the life-structure of the modern world. Secondly, it is an effective historical force. If its work is nowhere complete, it is almost everywhere in progress. The modern State as we see it in Europe outside Russia, in the British colonies, in North and South America, as we begin to see it in the Russian empire and throughout the vast continent of Asia, is the old authoritarian society modified in greater or less degree by the absorption of Liberal principles. Turning, thirdly, to those principles themselves, we have recognized Liberalism in every department as a movement fairly denoted by the name – a movement of liberation, a clearance of obstructions, an opening of channels for the flow of free spontaneous vital activity. Fourthly, we have seen that in a large number of cases what is under one aspect a movement for liberty is on another side a movement towards equality, and the habitual association of these principles is so far confirmed. On the other hand, lastly, we have seen numerous cases in which the exacter definition of liberty and the precise meaning of equality remain obscure, and to discuss these will be our task. We have, moreover, admittedly regarded Liberalism mainly in its earlier and more negative aspect. We have seen it as a force working within an old society and modifying it by the loosening of the bonds which its structure imposed on human activity. We have yet to ask what constructive social scheme, if any, could be formed on Liberal principles; and it is here, if at all, that the fuller meaning of the principles of Liberty and Equality should appear, and the methods of applying them be made out. The problem of popular sovereignty pointed to the same need. Thus the lines of the remainder of our task are clearly laid down. We have to get at the fundamentals of Liberalism, and to consider what kind of structure can be raised upon the basis which they offer. We will approach the question by tracing the historic movement of Liberal thought through certain well-marked phases. We shall see how the problems which have been indicated were attacked by successive thinkers, and how partial solutions gave occasion for deeper probings. Following the guidance of the actual movement of ideas, we shall reach the centre and heart of Liberalism, and we shall try to form a conception of the essentials of the Liberal creed as a constructive theory of society. This conception we shall then apply to the greater questions, political and economic, of our own day; and this will enable us finally to estimate the present position of Liberalism as a living force in the modern world and the prospect of transforming its ideals into actualities.

CHAPTER III

The Movement of Theory

Great changes are not caused by ideas alone; but they are not effected without ideas. The passions of men must be aroused if the frost of custom is to be broken or the chains of authority burst; but passion of itself is blind and its world is chaotic. To be effective men must act together, and to act together they must have a common understanding and a common object. When it comes to be a question of any far-reaching change, they must not merely conceive their own immediate end with clearness. They must convert others, they must communicate sympathy and win over the unconvinced. Upon the whole, they must show that their object is possible, that it is compatible with existing institutions, or at any rate with some workable form of social life. They are, in fact, driven on by the requirements of their position to the elaboration of ideas, and in the end to some sort of social philosophy; and the philosophies that have driving force behind them are those which arise after this fashion out of the practical demands of human feeling. The philosophies that remain ineffectual and academic are those that are formed by abstract reflection without relation to the thirsty souls of human kind.

In England, it is true, where men are apt to be shy and unhandy in the region of theory, the Liberal movement has often sought to dispense with general principles. In its early days and in its more moderate forms, it sought its ends under the guise of constitutionalism. As against the claims of the Stuart monarchy, there was a historic case as well as a philosophic argument, and the earlier leaders of the Parliament relied more on precedent than on principle. This method was embodied in the Whig tradition, and runs on to our own time, as one of the elements that go to make up the working constitution of the Liberal mind. It is, so to say, the Conservative element in Liberalism, valuable in resistance to encroachments, valuable in securing continuity of development, for purposes of re-construction insufficient. To maintain the old order under changed circumstances may be, in fact, to initiate a revolution. It was so in the seventeenth century. Pym and his followers could find justification for their contentions in our constitutional history, but to do so they had to go behind both the Stuarts and the Tudors; and to apply the principles of the fourteenth and fifteenth centuries in 1640 was, in effect, to institute a revolution. In our own time, to maintain the right of the Commons against the Lords is, on the face of it, to adhere to old constitutional right, but to do so under the new circumstances which have made the Commons representative of the nation as a whole is, in reality, to establish democracy for the first time on a firm footing, and this, again, is to accomplish a revolution.

Now, those who effect a revolution ought to know whither they are leading the world. They have need of a social theory – and in point of fact the more thorough-going apostles of movement always have such a theory; and though, as we have remarked, the theory emerges from the practical needs which they feel, and is therefore apt to invest ideas of merely temporary value with the character of eternal truths, it is not on this account to be dismissed as of secondary importance. Once formed, it reacts upon the minds of its adherents, and gives direction and unity to their efforts. It becomes, in its turn, a real historic force, and the degree of its coherence and adequacy is matter, not merely of academic interest, but of practical moment. Moreover, the onward course of a movement is more clearly understood by appreciating the successive points of view which its thinkers and statesmen have occupied than by following the devious turnings of political events and the tangle of party controversy. The point of view naturally affects the whole method of handling problems, whether speculative or practical, and to the historian it serves as a centre around which ideas and policies that perhaps differ, and even conflict with one another, may be so grouped as to show their underlying affinities. Let us then seek to determine the principal points of view which the Liberal movement has occupied, and distinguish the main types of theory in which the passion for freedom has sought to express itself.

The first of these types I will call the theory of the Natural Order. The earlier Liberalism had to deal with authoritarian government in church and state. It had to vindicate the elements of personal, civil, and economic freedom; and in so doing it took its stand on the rights of man, and, in proportion as it was forced to be constructive, on the supposed harmony of the natural order. Government claimed supernatural sanction and divine ordinance. Liberal theory replied in effect that the rights of man rested on the law of Nature, and those of government on human institution. The oldest 'institution' in this view was the individual, and the primordial society the natural grouping of human beings under the influence of family affection, and for the sake of mutual aid. Political society was a more artificial arrangement, a convention arrived at for the specific purpose of securing a better order and maintaining the common safety. It was, perhaps, as Locke held, founded on a contract between king and people, a contract which was brought to an end if either party violated its terms. Or, as in Rousseau's view, it was essentially a contract of the people with one another, an arrangement by means of which, out of many conflicting individual wills, a common or general will could be formed. A government might be instituted as the organ of this will, but it would, from the nature of the case, be subordinate to the people from whom it derived authority. The people were sovereign. The government was their delegate.

Whatever the differences of outlook that divide these theories, those who from Locke to Rousseau and Paine worked with this order of ideas agreed in conceiving political society as a restraint to which men voluntarily submitted themselves for specific purposes. Political institutions were the source of subjection and inequality. Before and behind them stood the assemblage of free and equal individuals. But the isolated individual was powerless. He had rights which were limited only by the corresponding rights of others, but he could not, unless chance gave him the upper hand, enforce them. Accordingly, he found it best to enter into an arrangement with others for the mutual respect of rights; and for this purpose he instituted a government to maintain his rights within the community and to guard the community from assault from without. It followed that the function of government was limited and definable. It was to maintain the natural rights of man as accurately as the conditions of society allowed, and to do naught beside. Any further action employing the compulsory power of the State was of the nature of an infringement of the understanding on which government rested. In entering into the compact, the individual gave up so much of his rights as was necessitated by the condition of submitting to a common rule – so much, and no more. He gave up his natural rights and received in return civil rights, something less complete, perhaps, but more effective as resting on the guarantee of the collective power. If you would discover, then, what the civil rights of man in society should be, you must inquire what are the natural rights of man,[4] and how far they are unavoidably modified in accommodating the conflicting claims of men with one another. Any interference that goes beyond this necessary accommodation is oppression. Civil rights should agree as nearly as possible with natural rights, or, as Paine says, a civil right is a natural right exchanged.[4]

This conception of the relations of the State and the individual long outlived the theory on which it rested. It underlies the entire teaching of the Manchester school. Its spirit was absorbed, as we shall see, by many of the Utilitarians. It operated, though in diminishing force, throughout the nineteenth century; and it is strongly held by contemporary Liberals like M. Faguet, who frankly abrogate its speculative foundations and rest their case on social utility. Its strength is, in effect, not in its logical principles, but in the compactness and consistency which it gives to a view of the functions of the State which responds to certain needs of modern society. As long as those needs were uppermost, the theory was of living value. In proportion as they have been satisfied and other needs have emerged, the requirement has arisen for a fuller and sounder principle.

But there was another side to the theory of nature which we must not ignore. If in this theory government is the marplot[5] and authority the source of oppression and stagnation, where are the springs of progress and civilization? Clearly, in the action of individuals. The

---

[4] *Cf.* the preamble to the Declaration of the Rights of Man by the French National Assembly in 1789. The Assembly lays down 'the natural, inalienable, and sacred rights of man', in order, among other things, 'that the acts of the legislative power and those of the executive power, being capable of being at every instant compared with the end of every political institution, may be more respected accordingly'.

[4] Paine wrote: 'every civil right grows out of a natural right; or, in other words, is a natural right exchanged' (*Rights of Man* (1791/2), Part I).

[5] 'marplot': 'one who mars or defeats a plot or design by officious interference, or hinders the success of any undertaking' (*OED*).

more the individual receives free scope for the play of his faculties, the more rapidly will society as a whole advance. There are here the elements of an important truth, but what is the implication? If the individual is free, any two individuals, each pursuing his own ends, may find themselves in conflict. It was, in fact, the possibility of such conflict which was recognized by our theory as the origin and foundation of society. Men had to agree to some measure of mutual restraint in order that their liberty might be effective. But in the course of the eighteenth century, and particularly in the economic sphere, there arose a view that the conflict of wills is based on misunderstanding and ignorance, and that its mischiefs are accentuated by governmental repression. At bottom there is a natural harmony of interests. Maintain external order, suppress violence, assure men in the possession of their property, and enforce the fulfilment of contracts, and the rest will go of itself. Each man will be guided by self-interest, but interest will lead him along the lines of greatest productivity. If all artificial barriers are removed, he will find the occupation which best suits his capacities, and this will be the occupation in which he will be most productive, and therefore, socially, most valuable. He will have to sell his goods to a willing purchaser, therefore he must devote himself to the production of things which others need, things, therefore, of social value. He will, by preference, make that for which he can obtain the highest price, and this will be that for which, at the particular time and place and in relation to his particular capacities, there is the greatest need. He will, again, find the employer who will pay him best, and that will be the employer to whom he can do the best service. Self-interest, if enlightened and unfettered, will, in short, lead him to conduct coincident with public interest. There is, in this sense, a natural harmony between the individual and society. True, this harmony might require a certain amount of education and enlightenment to make it effective. What it did not require was governmental 'interference', which would always hamper the causes making for its smooth and effectual operation. Government must keep the ring, and leave it for individuals to play out the game. The theory of the natural rights of the individual is thus supplemented by a theory of the mutual harmony of individual and social needs, and, so completed, forms a conception of human society which is *prima facie* workable, which, in fact, contains important elements of truth, and which was responsive to the needs of a great class, and to many of the requirements of society as a whole, during a considerable period.

On both sides, however, the theory exhibits, under criticism, fundamental weaknesses which have both a historical and a speculative significance. Let us first consider the conception of natural rights. What were these rights, and on what did they rest? On the first point men sought to be explicit. By way of illustration we cannot do better than quote the leading clauses of the Declaration of 1789.[c, 6]

> *Article I.* – Men are born and remain free and equal in rights. Social distinctions can only be founded on common utility.
>
> *Article II.* – The end of every political association is the conservation of the natural and imprescriptible rights of man.[f] These rights are liberty, property, security (*la sûreté*), and resistance to oppression.
>
> *Article III.* – The principle of all sovereignty resides essentially in the nation. . .
>
> *Article IV.* – Liberty consists in the power to do anything that does not injure others; thus, the exercise of the natural rights of every man has only such limits as assure to other members of society the enjoyment of the same rights. These limits can only be determined by law.
>
> *Article VI.* – The law is the expression of the general will. All citizens have a right to take part (*concourir*), personally or by their representatives, in its formation.

The remainder of this article insists on the impartiality of law and the equal admission of all citizens to office. The Declaration of 1793 is more emphatic about equality, and more rhetorical. Article III reads, 'All men are equal by nature and before the law.'

It is easy to subject these articles to a niggling form of criticism in which their spirit is altogether missed. I would ask attention only to one or two points of principle.

---

[c] The comparison of the Declaration of the Assembly in 1789 with that of the Convention in 1793 is full of interest, both for the points of agreement and difference, but would require a lengthy examination. I note one or two points in passing.

[f] Contrast 1793, Art. I: 'The end of society is the common happiness. Government is instituted to guarantee to man the enjoyment of his natural and imprescriptible rights.'

[6] The Declaration of the Rights of Man was adopted by the French National Assembly on 26 August 1789. The Declaration of the Rights of Man and the Citizen was adopted by the more radical Convention in June 1793. Both statements served as preambles to draft post-revolutionary constitutions.

(*a*) What are the rights actually claimed? 'Security' and 'resistance to oppression' are not in principle distinct, and, moreover, may be taken as covered by the definition of liberty. The meaning at bottom is 'Security for liberty in respect of his person and property is the right of every man.' So expressed, it will be seen that this right postulates the existence of an ordered society, and lays down that it is the duty of such a society to secure the liberty of its members. The right of the individual, then, is not something independent of society, but one of the principles which a good social order must recognize.

(*b*) Observe that equality is limited by the 'common utility', and that the sphere of liberty is ultimately to be defined by 'law'. In both cases we are referred back from the individual either to the needs or to the decision of society as a whole. There are, moreover, two definitions of liberty. (1) It is the power to do what does not injure others. (2) It is a right limited by the consideration that others must enjoy the same rights. It is important to bear in mind that these two definitions are highly discrepant. If my right to knock a man down is only limited by his equal right to knock me down, the law has no business to interfere when we take to our fists. If, on the other hand, I have no right to injure another, the law should interfere. Very little reflection suffices to show that this is the sounder principle, and that respect for the equal liberty of another is not an adequate definition of liberty. My right to keep my neighbour awake by playing the piano all night is not satisfactorily counterbalanced by his right to keep a dog which howls all the time the piano is being played. The right of a 'sweater' to pay starvation wages is not satisfactorily limited by the corresponding right which his employee would enjoy if he were in a position to impose the same terms on some one else. Generally, the right to injure or take advantage of another is not sufficiently limited by the right of that other if he should have the power to retaliate in kind. There is no right to injure another; and if we ask what is injury we are again thrown back on some general principle which will override the individual claim to do what one will.

(*c*) The doctrine of popular sovereignty rests on two principles. (1) It is said to reside in the nation. Law is the expression of the general will. Here the 'nation' is conceived as a collective whole, as a unit. (2) Every citizen has the right to take part in making the law. Here the question is one of individual right. Which is the real ground of democratic representation – the unity of the national life, or the inherent right of the individual to be consulted about that which concerns himself?

Further, and this is a very serious question, which is the ultimate authority – the will of the nation, or the rights of the individual? Suppose the nation deliberately decides on laws which deny the rights of the individual, ought such laws to be obeyed in the name of popular sovereignty, or to be disobeyed in the name of natural rights? It is a real issue, and on these lines it is unfortunately quite insoluble.

These difficulties were among the considerations which led to the formation of the second type of Liberal theory, and what has to be said about the harmony of the natural order may be taken in conjunction with this second theory to which we may now pass, and which is famous as The Greatest Happiness Principle.

Bentham, who spent the greater part of his life in elaborating the greatest happiness principle as a basis of social reconstruction, was fully alive to the difficulties which we have found in the theory of natural rights. The alleged rights of man were for him so many anarchical fallacies. They were founded on no clearly assignable principle, and admitted of no demonstration. 'I say I have a right.' 'I say you have no such right.' Between the disputants who or what is to decide? What was the supposed law of nature? When was it written, and by whose authority? On what ground do we maintain that men are free or equal? On what principle and within what limits do we or can we maintain the right of property? There were points on which, by universal admission, all these rights have to give way. What is the right of property worth in times of war or of any overwhelming general need? The Declaration itself recognized the need of appeal to common utility or to the law to define the limits of individual right. Bentham would frankly make all rights dependent on common utility, and therewith he would make it possible to examine all conflicting claims in the light of a general principle. He would measure them all by a common standard. Has a man the right to express his opinion freely? To determine the question on Bentham's lines we must ask whether it is, on the whole, useful to society that the free expression of opinion should be allowed, and this, he would say, is a question which may be decided by general reasoning and by experience of results. Of course, we must take the rough with the smooth. If the free expression of opinion is allowed, false opinion will find utterance and will mislead many. The question would be, does the loss involved in the promulgation of error counterbalance the gain to be derived from unfettered discussion? and Bentham would hold himself free to judge by results. Should the State maintain the rights of private property? Yes, if the admission of those rights is useful to the community as a whole. No, if it is not useful. Some rights of property, again, may be advantageous, others disadvantageous. The community is free to make a selection. If it finds that certain forms of property are working to the exclusive benefit of individuals and the prejudice of the common weal, it has good ground for the suppression of those forms of property, while it may, with equal justice, maintain other forms of property which it holds sound as judged by the effect on the common welfare. It is limited by no 'imprescriptible' right of the individual. It may do with the individual what it pleases provided that it has the good of the whole in view. So far as the question of right is concerned the Benthamite principle might be regarded as decidedly socialistic or even authoritarian. It contemplates, at least as a possibility, the complete subordination of individual to social claims.

There is, however, another side to the Benthamite principle, to understand which we must state the heads of the theory itself as a positive doctrine. What is this social utility of which we have spoken? In what does it consist? What is useful to society, and what harmful? The answer has the merit of great clearness and simplicity. An action is good which tends to promote the greatest possible happiness of the greatest possible number of those affected by it. As with an action, so, of course, with an institution or a social system. That is useful which conforms to this principle. That is harmful which conflicts with it. That is right which conforms to it, that is wrong which conflicts with it. The greatest happiness principle is the one and supreme principle of conduct. Observe that it imposes on us two considerations. One is the *greatest* happiness. Now happiness is defined as consisting positively in the presence of pleasure, negatively in the absence of pain. A greater pleasure is then preferable to a lesser, a pleasure unaccompanied by pain to one involving pain. Conceiving pain as a minus quantity of pleasure, we may say that the principle requires us always to take quantity and pleasure into account, and nothing else. But, secondly, the *number* of individuals affected is material. An act might cause pleasure to one and pain to two. Then it is wrong, unless, indeed, the pleasure were very great and the pain in each case small. We must balance the consequences, taking all individuals affected into account, and 'everybody must count for one and nobody for more than one'. This comment is an integral part of the original formula. As between the happiness of his father, his child, or himself, and the happiness of a stranger, a man must be impartial. He must only consider the quantity of pleasure secured or pain inflicted.

Now, in this conception of measurable quantities of pleasure and pain there is, as many critics have insisted, something unreal and academic. We shall have to return to the point, but let us first endeavour to understand the bearing of Bentham's teaching on the problems of his own time and on the subsequent development of Liberal thought. For this purpose we will keep to what is real in his doctrine, even if it is not always defined with academic precision. The salient points that we note, then, are (1) the subordination of all considerations of right to the considerations of happiness, (2) the importance of number, and (3) as the other side of the same doctrine, the insistence on equality or impartiality between man and man. The common utility which Bentham considers is the happiness experienced by a number of individuals, all of whom are reckoned for this purpose as of equal value. This is the radical individualism of the Benthamite creed, to be set against that socialistic tendency which struck us in our preliminary account.

In this individualism, equality is fundamental. Everybody is to count for one, nobody for more than one, for every one can feel pain and pleasure. Liberty, on the other hand, is not fundamental, it is a means to an end. Popular sovereignty is not fundamental, for all government is a means to an end. Nevertheless, the school of Bentham, upon the whole, stood by both liberty and democracy. Let us consider their attitude.

As to popular government, Bentham and James Mill reasoned after this fashion. Men, if left to themselves, that is to say, if neither trained by an educational discipline nor checked by responsibility, do not consider the good of the greatest number. They consider their own good. A king, if his power is unchecked, will rule in his own interest. A class, if its power is unchecked, will rule in its own interest. The only way to secure fair consideration for the happiness of all is to allow to all an equal share of power. True, if there is a conflict the majority will prevail, but they will be moved each by consideration of

33

his own happiness, and the majority as a whole, therefore, by the happiness of the greater number. There is no inherent right in the individual to take a part in government. There is a claim to be considered in the distribution of the means of happiness, and to share in the work of government as a means to this end. It would follow, among other things, that if one man or one class could be shown to be so much wiser and better than others that his or their rule would, in fact, conduce more to the happiness of the greater number than a popular system, then the business of government ought to be entrusted to that man or that class and no one else ought to interfere with it.

The whole argument, however, implies a crude view of the problem of government. It is, of course, theoretically possible that a question should present itself, detached from other questions, in which a definite measurable interest of each of the seven millions or more of voters is at stake. For example, the great majority of English people drink tea. Comparatively few drink wine. Should a particular sum be raised by a duty on tea or on wine? Here the majority of tea-drinkers have a measurable interest, the same in kind and roughly the same in degree for each; and the vote of the majority, if it could be taken on this question alone and based on self-interest alone, might be conceived without absurdity as representing a sum of individual interests. Even here, however, observe that, though the greatest number is considered, the greatest happiness does not fare so well. For to raise the same sum the tax on wine will, as less is drunk, have to be much larger than the tax on tea, so that a little gain to many tea-drinkers might inflict a heavy loss on the few wine-drinkers, and on the Benthamite principle it is not clear that this would be just. In point of fact it is possible for a majority to act tyrannically, by insisting on a slight convenience to itself at the expense, perhaps, of real suffering to a minority. Now the Utilitarian principle by no means justifies such tyranny, but it does seem to contemplate the weighing of one man's loss against another's gain, and such a method of balancing does not at bottom commend itself to our sense of justice. We may lay down that if there is a rational social order at all it must be one which never rests the essential indispensable condition of the happiness of one man on the unavoidable misery of another, nor the happiness of forty millions of men on the misery of one. It may be temporarily expedient, but it is eternally unjust, that one man should die for the people.

We may go further. The case of the contemplated tax is, as applied to the politics of a modern State, an unreal one. Political questions cannot be thus isolated. Even if we could vote by referendum on a special tax, the question which voters would have to consider would never be the revenue from and the incidence of that tax alone. All the indirect social and economic bearings of the tax would come up for consideration, and in the illustration chosen people would be swayed, and rightly swayed, by their opinion, for example, of the comparative effects of tea-drinking and wine-drinking. No one element of the social life stands separate from the rest, any more than any one element of the animal body stands separate from the rest. In this sense the life of society is rightly held to be organic, and all considered public policy must be conceived in its bearing on the life of society as a whole. But the moment that we apply this view to politics, the Benthamite mode of stating the case for democracy is seen to be insufficient. The interests of every man are no doubt in the end bound up with the welfare of the whole community, but the relation is infinitely subtle and indirect. Moreover, it takes time to work itself out, and the evil that is done in the present day may only bear fruit when the generation that has done it has passed away. Thus, the direct and calculable benefit of the majority may by no means coincide with the ultimate good of society as a whole; and to suppose that the majority must, on grounds of self-interest, govern in the interests of the community as a whole is in reality to attribute to the mass of men full insight into problems which tax the highest efforts of science and of statesmanship. Lastly, to suppose that men are governed entirely by a sense of their interests is a many-sided fallacy. Men are neither so intelligent nor so selfish. They are swayed by emotion and by impulse, and both for good and for evil they will lend enthusiastic support to courses of public policy from which, as individuals, they have nothing to gain. To understand the real value of democratic government, we shall have to probe far deeper into the relations of the individual and society.

I turn lastly to the question of liberty. On Benthamite principles there could be no question here of indefeasible individual right. There were even, as we saw, possibilities of a thorough-going Socialism or of an authoritarian paternalism in the Benthamite principle. But two great considerations told in the opposite direction. One arose from the circumstances of the day. Bentham, originally a man of somewhat conservative temper, was driven into Radicalism comparatively late in life by the indifference or hostility of the governing classes to his schemes of reform. Government, as he saw it, was of the nature of a close corporation with a vested interest hostile to the public weal, and his work is penetrated by distrust of power as such. There was much in the history of the time to justify his attitude. It was difficult at that time to believe in an honest officialdom putting the commonwealth above every personal or corporate interest, and reformers naturally looked to individual initiative as the source of progress. Secondly, and this was a more philosophic argument, the individual was supposed to understand his own interest best, and as the common good was the sum of individual interests, it followed that so far as every man was free to seek his own good, the good of the greatest number would be most effectually realized by general freedom of choice. That there were difficulties in reconciling self-interest with the general good was not denied. But men like James Mill, who especially worked at this side of the problem, held that they could be overcome by moral education. Trained from childhood to associate the good of others with his own, a man would come, he thought, to care for the happiness of others as for the happiness of self. For, in the long run, the two things were coincident. Particularly in a free economic system, as remarked above, each individual, moving along the line of greatest personal profit, would be found to fulfil the function of greatest profit to society. Let this be understood, and we should have true social harmony based on the spontaneous operation of personal interest enlightened by intelligence and chastened by the discipline of unruly instinct.

Thus, though their starting-point was different, the Benthamites arrived at practical results not notably divergent from those of the doctrine of natural liberty; and, on the whole, the two influences worked together in the formation of that school who in the reform period exercised so notable an influence on English Liberalism, and to whose work we must now turn.

CHAPTER IV

'Laissez-faire'

The school of Cobden is affiliated in general outlook both to the doctrine of natural liberty and to the discipline of Bentham. It shared with the Benthamites the thoroughly practical attitude dear to the English mind. It has much less to say of natural rights than the French theorists. On the other hand, it is saturated with the conviction that the unfettered action of the individual is the mainspring of all progress.[f] Its starting-point is economic. Trade is still in fetters. The worst of the archaic internal restrictions have, indeed, been thrown off. But even here Cobden is active in the work of finally emancipating Manchester from manorial rights that have no place in the nineteenth century. The main work, however, is the liberation of foreign trade. The Corn Laws,[7] as even the tariff reformers of our own day admit, were conceived in the interest of the governing classes. They frankly imposed a tax on the food of the masses for the benefit of the landlords, and as the result of the agricultural and industrial revolutions which had been in progress since 1760, the

---

[f] 'If I were asked to sum up in a sentence the difference and the connection (between the two schools) I would say that the Manchester men were the disciples of Adam Smith and Bentham, while the Philosophical Radicals followed Bentham and Adam Smith' (F. W. Hirst, [Free Trade and Other Fundamental Doctrines of] the Manchester School [(London, 1903)], Introduction, p. xi). Lord [John] Morley, in the concluding chapter of his [The] Life of [Richard] Cobden [(London, 1881), vol. 2, p. 483], points out that it was the view of 'policy as a whole' in connection with the economic movement of society which distinguished the school of Cobden from that of the Benthamites.

[7] Enacted at the end of the Napoleonic wars, the Corn Laws were intended to support domestic agricultural prices through a tariff on the sale of imported grain.

masses had been brought to the lowest point of economic misery. Give to every man the right to buy in the cheapest and sell in the dearest market, urged the Cobdenite, and trade would automatically expand. The business career would be open to the talents. The good workman would command the full money's worth of his work, and his money would buy him food and clothing at the lowest rate in the world's market. Only so would he get the full value of his work, paying toll to none. Taxes there must be to carry on government, but if we looked into the cost of government we found that it depended mostly on armaments. Why did we need armaments? First, because of the national antagonisms aroused and maintained by a protective system. Free commercial intercourse between nations would engender mutual knowledge, and knit the severed peoples by countless ties of business interests. Free Trade meant peace, and once taught by the example of Great Britain's prosperity, other nations would follow suit, and Free Trade would be universal. The other root of national danger was the principle of intervention. We took it on ourselves to set other nations right. How could we judge for other nations? Force was no remedy. Let every people be free to work out its own salvation. Things were not so perfect with us that we need go about setting the houses of other people in order. To complete personal freedom, there must be national freedom. There must also be colonial freedom. The colonies could no longer be governed in the interests of the mother country, nor ought they to require standing garrisons maintained by the mother country. They were distant lands, each, if we gave it freedom, with a great future of its own, capable of protecting itself, and developing with freedom into true nationhood. Personal freedom, colonial freedom, international freedom, were parts of one whole. Non-intervention, peace, restriction of armaments, retrenchment of expenditure, reduction of taxation, were the connected series of practical consequences. The money retrenched from wasteful military expenditure need not all be remitted to the taxpayer. A fraction of it devoted to education – free, secular, and universal – would do as much good as when spent on guns and ships it did harm. For education was necessary to raise the standard of intelligence, and provide the substantial equality of opportunity at the start without which the mass of men could not make use of the freedom given by the removal of legislative restrictions. There were here elements of a more constructive view for which Cobden and his friends have not always received sufficient credit.

In the main, however, the teaching of the Manchester school tended both in external and in internal affairs to a restricted view of the function of government. Government had to maintain order, to restrain men from violence and fraud, to hold them secure in person and property against foreign and domestic enemies, to give them redress against injury, that so they may rely on reaping where they have sown, may enjoy the fruits of their industry, may enter unimpeded into what arrangements they will with one another for their mutual benefit. Let us see what criticism was passed on this view by the contemporaries of Cobden and by the loud voice of the facts themselves. The old economic régime had been in decay throughout the eighteenth century. The divorce of the labourer from the land was complete at the time when the Anti-Corn Law League[8] was formed. The mass of the English peasantry were landless labourers working for a weekly wage of about ten or twelve shillings, and often for a good deal less. The rise of machine industry since 1760 had destroyed the old domestic system and reduced the operative in the towns to the position of a factory hand under an employer, who found the road to wealth easy in the monopoly of manufacture enjoyed by this country for two generations after the Napoleonic war. The factory system early brought matters to a head at one point by the systematic employment of women and young children under conditions which outraged the public conscience when they became known. In the case of children it was admitted from an early date, it was urged by Cobden himself, that the principle of free contract could not apply. Admitting, for the sake of argument, that the adult could make a better bargain for himself or herself than any one could do for him or her, no one could contend that the pauper child apprenticed by Poor Law guardians to a manufacturer had any say or could have any judgement as to the work which it was set to do. It had to be protected, and experience showed that it had to be protected by law. Free contract did not solve the question of the helpless child. It left it to be 'exploited' by the employer in his own interest, and whatever

---

[*] Founded in 1839, the Anti-Corn Law League led a vigorous campaign for the repeal of the Corn Laws and for Free Trade.

regard might be shown for its health and well-being by individuals was a matter of individual benevolence, not a right secured by the necessary operation of the system of liberty.

But these arguments admitted of great extension. If the child was helpless, was the grown-up person, man or woman, in a much better position? Here was the owner of a mill employing five hundred hands. Here was an operative possessed of no alternative means of subsistence seeking employment. Suppose them to bargain as to terms. If the bargain failed, the employer lost one man and had four hundred and ninety-nine to keep his mill going. At worst he might for a day or two, until another operative appeared, have a little difficulty in working a single machine. During the same days the operative might have nothing to eat, and might see his children going hungry. Where was the effective liberty in such an arrangement? The operatives themselves speedily found that there was none, and had from an early period in the rise of the machine industry sought to redress the balance by combination. Now, combination was naturally disliked by employers, and it was strongly suspect to believers in liberty because it put constraint upon individuals. Yet trade unions gained the first step in emancipation through the action of Place and the Radicals in 1824,[9] more perhaps because these men conceived trade unions as the response of labour to oppressive laws which true freedom of competition would render superfluous than because they founded any serious hopes of permanent social progress upon Trade Unionism itself. In point of fact, the critical attitude was not without its justification. Trade Unionism can be protective in spirit and oppressive in action. Nevertheless, it was essential to the maintenance of their industrial standard by the artisan classes, because it alone, in the absence of drastic legislative protection, could do something to redress the inequality between employer and employed. It gave, upon the whole, far more freedom to the workman than it took away, and in this we learn an important lesson which has far wider application. In the matter of contract true freedom postulates substantial equality between the parties. In proportion as one party is in a position of vantage, he is able to dictate his terms. In proportion as the other party is in a weak position, he must accept unfavourable terms. Hence

---

[9] Francis Place and the Radical parliamentarian Joseph Hume were instrumental in securing the repeal, in 1824, of the Combination Acts prohibiting trade union organization.

the truth of Walker's dictum[10] that economic injuries tend to perpetuate themselves. The more a class is brought low, the greater its difficulty in rising again without assistance. For purposes of legislation the State has been exceedingly slow to accept this view. It began, as we saw, with the child, where the case was overwhelming. It went on to include the 'young person' and the woman – not without criticism from those who held by woman's rights, and saw in this extension of tutelage an enlargement of male domination. Be that as it may, public opinion was brought to this point by the belief that it was intervening in an exceptional manner to protect a definite class not strong enough to bargain for itself. It drew the line at the adult male; and it is only within our own time, and as the result of a controversy waged for many years within the trade union world itself, that legislation has avowedly undertaken the task of controlling the conditions of industry, the hours, and at length, through the institution of Wages Boards in 'sweated industries', the actual remuneration of working people without limitation of age or sex. To this it has been driven by the manifest teaching of experience that liberty without equality is a name of noble sound and squalid result.

In place of the system of unfettered agreements between individual and individual which the school of Cobden contemplated, the industrial system which has actually grown up and is in process of further development rests on conditions prescribed by the State, and within the limits of those conditions is very largely governed by collective arrangements between associations of employers and employed. The law provides for the safety of the worker and the sanitary conditions of employment. It prescribes the length of the working day for women and children in factories and workshops, and for men in mines and on railways.* In the future it will probably deal freely with the hours of men. It enables wages boards to establish a legal minimum wage in scheduled industries which will undoubtedly grow in number. It makes employers liable for all injuries suffered by operatives in the

---

* Indirectly it has for long limited the hours of men in factories owing to the interdependence of the adult male with the female and child operative.

[10] Francis Walker, then President of the Massachusetts Institute of Technology, argued in his highly regarded treatise on *Political Economy* (London, 1887) that under the conditions of 'impaired competition' which prevail in the real world 'the tendency of purely economic forces . . . is continually to aggravate the disadvantages from which any person or class may suffer in the beginning' (p. 265).

course of their employment, and forbids any one to 'contract out' of this obligation. Within these limits, it allows freedom of contract. But at this point, in the more highly developed trades, the work is taken up by voluntary associations. Combinations of men have been met by combinations of employers, and wages, hours, and all the details of the industrial bargain are settled by collective agreement through the agency of a joint board with an impartial chairman or referee in case of necessity for an entire locality and even an entire trade. So far have we gone from the free competition of isolated individuals.

This development is sometimes held to have involved the decay and death of the older Liberalism. It is true that in the beginning factory legislation enjoyed a large measure of Conservative support. It was at that stage in accordance with the best traditions of paternal rule, and it commended itself to the religious convictions of men of whom Lord Shaftesbury was the typical example. It is true, also, that it was bitterly opposed by Cobden and Bright. On the other hand, Radicals like J. Cam Hobhouse took a leading part in the earlier legislation, and Whig Governments passed the very important Acts of 1833 and 1847.[11] The cleavage of opinion, in fact, cut across the ordinary divisions of party. What is more to the purpose is that, as experience ripened, the implications of the new legislation became clearer, and men came to see that by industrial control they were not destroying liberty but confirming it. A new and more concrete conception of liberty arose and many old presuppositions were challenged.

Let us look for a moment at these presuppositions. We have seen that the theory of *laissez-faire* assumed that the State would hold the ring. That is to say, it would suppress force and fraud, keep property safe, and aid men in enforcing contracts. On these conditions, it was maintained, men should be absolutely free to compete with one another, so that their best energies should be called forth, so that each should feel himself responsible for the guidance of his own life, and exert his manhood to the utmost. But why, it might be asked, on these conditions, just these and no others? Why should the State ensure protection of person and property? The time was when the

---

[11] The Act of 1833 covered most textile mills, prohibiting work by children under nine, and regulating the hours and making compulsory the provision of some schooling for older children; the Act of 1847 limited the employment of young people in certain industries to ten hours a day.

strong man armed kept his goods, and incidentally his neighbour's goods too if he could get hold of them. Why should the State intervene to do for a man that which his ancestor did for himself? Why should a man who has been soundly beaten in physical fight go to a public authority for redress? How much more manly to fight his own battle! Was it not a kind of pauperization to make men secure in person and property through no efforts of their own, by the agency of a state machinery operating over their heads? Would not a really consistent individualism abolish this machinery? 'But', the advocate of *laissez-faire* may reply, 'the use of force is criminal, and the State must suppress crime'. So men held in the nineteenth century. But there was an earlier time when they did not take this view, but left it to individuals and their kinsfolk to revenge their own injuries by their own might. Was not this a time of more unrestricted individual liberty? Yet the nineteenth century regarded it, and justly, as an age of barbarism. What, we may ask in our turn, is the essence of crime? May we not say that any intentional injury to another may be legitimately punished by a public authority, and may we not say that to impose twelve hours' daily labour on a child was to inflict a greater injury than the theft of a purse for which a century ago a man might be hanged? On what principle, then, is the line drawn, so as to specify certain injuries which the State may prohibit and to mark off others which it must leave untouched? Well, it may be said, *volenti non fit injuria*. No wrong is done to a man by a bargain to which he is a willing party. That may be, though there are doubtful cases. But in the field that has been in question the contention is that one party is not willing. The bargain is a forced bargain. The weaker man consents as one slipping over a precipice might consent to give all his fortune to one who will throw him a rope on no other terms. This is not true consent. True consent is free consent, and full freedom of consent implies equality on the part of both parties to the bargain. Just as government first secured the elements of freedom for all when it prevented the physically stronger man from slaying, beating, despoiling his neighbours, so it secures a larger measure of freedom for all by every restriction which it imposes with a view to preventing one man from making use of any of his advantages to the disadvantage of others.

There emerges a distinction between unsocial and social freedom. Unsocial freedom is the right of a man to use his powers without regard to the wishes or interests of any one but himself. Such freedom is theoretically possible for an individual. It is antithetic to all public control. It is theoretically impossible for a plurality of individuals living in mutual contact. Socially it is a contradiction, unless the desires of all men were automatically attuned to social ends. Social freedom, then, for any epoch short of the millennium rests on restraint. It is a freedom that can be enjoyed by all the members of a community, and it is the freedom to choose among those lines of activity which do not involve injury to others. As experience of the social effects of action ripens, and as the social conscience is awakened, the conception of injury is widened and insight into its causes is deepened. The area of restraint is therefore increased. But, inasmuch as injury inflicted is itself crippling to the sufferer, as it lowers his health, confines his life, cramps his powers, so the prevention of such injury sets him free. The restraint of the aggressor is the freedom of the sufferer, and only by restraint on the actions by which men injure one another do they as a whole community gain freedom in all courses of conduct that can be pursued without ultimate social disharmony.

It is, therefore, a very shallow wit that taunts contemporary Liberalism with inconsistency in opposing economic protection while it supports protective legislation for the manual labourer. The two things have nothing in common but that they are restraints intended to operate in the interests of somebody. The one is a restraint which, in the Liberal view, would operate in favour of certain industries and interests to the prejudice of others, and, on the whole, in favour of those who are already more fortunately placed and against the poorer classes. The other is a restraint conceived in the interest primarily of the poorer classes with the object of securing to them a more effective freedom and a nearer approach to equality of conditions in industrial relations. There is point in the argument only for those who conceive liberty as opposed to restraint as such. For those who understand that all social liberty rests upon restraint, that restraint of one man in one respect is the condition of the freedom of other men in that respect, the taunt has no meaning whatever. The liberty which is good is not the liberty of one gained at the expense of others, but the liberty which can be enjoyed by all who dwell together, and this liberty depends on and is measured by the completeness with which by law, custom, or their own feelings they are restrained from mutual injury.

Individualism, as ordinarily understood, not only takes the policeman and the law court for granted. It also takes the rights of property for granted. But what is meant by the rights of property? In ordinary use the phrase means just that system to which long usage has accustomed us. This is a system under which a man is free to acquire by any method of production or exchange within the limits of the law whatever he can of land, consumable goods, or capital; to dispose of it at his own will and pleasure for his own purposes, to destroy it if he likes, to give it away or sell it as it suits him, and at death to bequeath it to whomsoever he will. The State, it is admitted, can take a part of a man's property by taxation. For the State is a necessity, and men must pay a price for security; but in all taxation the State on this view is taking something from a man which is 'his', and in so doing is justified only by necessity. It has no 'right' to deprive the individual of anything that is his in order to promote objects of its own which are not necessary to the common order. To do so is to infringe individual rights and make a man contribute by force to objects which he may view with indifference or even with dislike. 'Socialistic' taxation is an infringement of individual freedom, the freedom to hold one's own and do as one will with one's own. Such seems to be the ordinary view.

But a consistent theory of liberty could not rest wholly satisfied with the actual system under which property is held. The first point of attack, already pressed by the disciples of Cobden, was the barrier to free exchange in the matter of land. It was not and still is not easy for the landless to acquire land, and in the name of free contract Cobden and his disciples pressed for cheap and unimpeded transfer. But a more searching criticism was possible. Land is limited in amount, certain kinds of land very narrowly limited. Where there is limitation of supply monopoly is always possible, and against monopoly the principles of free competition declared war. To Cobden himself, free trade in land was the pendant to free trade in goods. But the attack on the land monopoly could be carried much further, and might lead the individualist who was in earnest about his principles to march a certain distance on parallel lines with the Socialist enemy. This has, in fact, occurred in the school of Henry George.

This school holds by competition, but by competition only on the basis of a genuine freedom and equality for all individuals. To secure this basis, it would purge the social system of all elements of monopoly, of which the private ownership of land is in its view the most important. This object, it maintains, can be secured only through the absorption by the State of all elements of monopoly value. Now, monopoly value accrues whenever anything of worth to men of which the supply is limited falls into private hands. In this case competition fails. There is no check upon the owner except the limitations of demand. He can exact a price which bears no necessary relation to the cost of any effort of his own. In addition to normal wages and profits, he can extract from the necessities of others a surplus, to which the name of economic rent is given. He can also hold up his property and refuse to allow others to make use of it until the time when its full value has accrued, thereby increasing the rent which he will ultimately receive at the cost of much loss in the interim to society.

Monopolies in our country fall into three classes. There is, first, the monopoly of land. Urban rents, for example, represent not merely the cost of building, nor the cost of building plus the site, as it would be if sites of the kind required were unlimited in amount. They represent the cost of a site where the supply falls short of the demand, that is to say, where there is an element of monopoly. And site value – the element in the actual cost of a house or factory that depends on its position – varies directly with the degree of this monopoly. This value the land nationalizer contends is not created by the owner. It is created by society. In part it is due to the general growth of the country to which the increase of population and the rise of town life is to be attributed. In part it depends on the growth of the particular locality, and in part on the direct expenditure of the ratepayers' money in sanitation and other improvements which make the place one where people can live and industry can thrive. Directly and indirectly, the community creates the site value. The landlord receives it, and, receiving it, can charge any one who wants to live or carry on industry upon the site with rent to the full amount. The land-nationalizer, looking at rights of property purely from the point of view of the individual, denies the justice of this arrangement, and he sees no solution except this – that the monopoly value should pass back to the community which creates it. Accordingly, he favours the taxation of site value to its full amount. Another element of monopoly arises from industries in which competition is inapplicable – the supply of gas and water, for example, a tramway service, and in some conditions a railway service. Here competition may be wasteful if not altogether impossible; and here again, on the lines of a strictly consistent individualism, if the industry is allowed to fall into private hands the owners will be able to secure something more than the normal profits of competitive industry. They will profit by monopoly at the expense of the general consumer, and the remedy is public control or public ownership. The latter is the more complete and efficacious remedy, and it is also the remedy of municipal socialism. Lastly, there may be forms of monopoly created by the State, such as the sale of liquor as restricted by the licensing system. In accordance with competitive ideas the value so created ought not to pass into private hands, and if on social grounds the monopoly is maintained, the taxation of licensed premises ought to be so arranged that the monopoly value returns to the community.

Up to this point a thoroughly consistent individualism can work in harmony with socialism, and it is this partial alliance which has, in fact, laid down the lines of later Liberal finance. The great Budget of 1909 had behind it the united forces of Socialist and individualist opinion. It may be added that there is a fourth form of monopoly which would be open to the same double attack, but it is one of which less has been heard in Great Britain than in the United States. It is possible under a competitive system for rivals to come to an agreement. The more powerful may coerce the weaker, or a number of equals may agree to work together. Thus competition may defeat itself, and industry may be marshalled into trusts or other combinations for the private advantage against the public interest. Such combinations, predicted by Karl Marx as the appointed means of dissolving the competitive system, have been kept at bay in this country by Free Trade. Under Protection they constitute the most urgent problem of the day. Even here the railways, to take one example, are rapidly moving to a system of combination, the economies of which are obvious, while its immediate result is monopoly, and its assured end is nationalization.

Thus individualism, when it grapples with the facts, is driven no small distance along Socialist lines. Once again we have found that to maintain individual freedom and equality we have to extend the sphere of social control. But to carry through the real principles of Liberalism, to achieve social liberty and living equality of rights, we shall have to probe still deeper. We must not assume any of the rights of property as axiomatic. We must look at their actual working and consider how they affect the life of society. We shall have to ask whether, if we could abolish all monopoly on articles of limited supply, we should yet have dealt with all the causes that contribute to social injustice and industrial disorder, whether we should have rescued the sweated worker, afforded to every man adequate security for a fair return for an honest day's toil, and prevented the use of economic advantage to procure gain for one man at the expense of another. We should have to ask whether we had the basis of a just delimitation between the rights of the community and those of the individual, and therewith a due appreciation of the appropriate ends of the State and the equitable basis of taxation. These inquiries take us to first principles, and to approach that part of our discussion it is desirable to carry further our sketch of the historic development of Liberalism in thought and action.

CHAPTER V

Gladstone and Mill

From the middle of the nineteenth century two great names stand out in the history of British Liberalism – that of Gladstone in the world of action, that of Mill in the world of thought. Differing in much, they agreed in one respect. They had the supreme virtue of keeping their minds fresh and open to new ideas, and both of them in consequence advanced to a deeper interpretation of social life as they grew older. In 1846 Gladstone ranked as a Conservative, but he parted from his old traditions under the leadership of Peel on the question of Free Trade, and for many years to come the most notable of his public services lay in the completion of the Cobdenite policy of financial emancipation. In the pursuit of this policy he was brought into collision with the House of Lords, and it was his active intervention in 1859–60 which saved the Commons from a humiliating surrender, and secured its financial supremacy unimpaired until 1909. In the following decade he stood for the extension of the suffrage, and it was his Government which, in 1884, carried the extension of the representative principle to the point at which it rested twenty-seven years later. In economics Gladstone kept upon the whole to the Cobdenite principles which he acquired in middle life. He was not sympathetically disposed to the 'New Unionism' and the semi-socialistic ideas that came at the end of the 'eighties, which, in fact, constituted a powerful cross current to the political work that he had immediately in hand. Yet in relation to Irish land he entered upon a new departure[12] which threw over freedom of contract in a leading

---

[12] The Irish Land Acts (1870 and 1881) were intended to protect vulnerable tenant farmers from powerful landowners. The earlier Act provided departing tenants with

49

case where the two parties were on glaringly unequal terms. No abstract thinker, he had a passion for justice in the concrete which was capable of carrying him far. He knew tyranny when he saw it, and upon it he waged unremitting and many-sided war.

But his most original work was done in the sphere of imperial relations. The maligned Majuba settlement[13] was an act of justice which came too late to effect a permanent undoing of mischief. All the greater was the courage of the statesman who could throw himself at that time upon the inherent force of national liberty and international fair dealing. In the case of Ireland Gladstone again relied on the same principles, but another force was necessary to carry the day, a force which no man can command, the force of time. In international dealings generally Gladstone was a pioneer. His principle was not precisely that of Cobden. He was not a non-interventionist. He took action on behalf of Greece, and would have done so on behalf of the Armenians, to save the national honour and prevent a monstrous wrong. The Gladstonian principle may be defined by antithesis to that of Machiavelli, and to that of Bismarck, and to the practice of every Foreign Office. As that practice proceeds on the principle that reasons of State justify everything, so Gladstone proceeded on the principle that reasons of State justify nothing that is not justified already by the human conscience. The statesman is for him a man charged with maintaining not only the material interests but the honour of his country. He is a citizen of the world in that he represents his nation, which is a member of the community of the world. He has to recognize rights and duties, as every representative of every other human organization has to recognize rights and duties. There is no line drawn beyond which human obligations cease. There is no gulf across which the voice of human suffering cannot be heard, beyond which massacre and torture cease to be execrable. Simply as a patriot, again, a man should recognize that a nation may become great not merely by painting the map red, or extending her commerce

a return for improvements made to the land, and compensation on eviction for causes other than non-payment of rent. The much more ambitious second Act allowed tenants to sell their leases, and established an administrative system which – upon application by tenant or landlord – would fix a 'fair' rent thereafter securing the tenant from eviction except on certain specific grounds.

[11] In 1881 the rebellious Boers defeated the British at the battle of Majuba Hill. The subsequent peace agreement recognized the Boers' right to self-government under the ultimate sovereignty of the Crown.

beyond all precedent, but also as the champion of justice, the succourer of the oppressed, the established home of freedom. From the denunciation of the Opium War, from the exposure of the Neapolitan prisons, to his last appearance on the morrow of the Constantinople massacre[14] this was the message which Gladstone sought to convey. He was before his time. He was not always able to maintain his principle in his own Cabinet, and on his retirement the world appeared to relapse definitely into the older ways. His own party gave itself up in large measure to opposite views. On the other hand, careful and unprejudiced criticism will recognize that the chief opponent of his old age, Lord Salisbury, had imbibed something of his spirit, and under its influence did much to save the country from the excesses of Imperialism, while his follower, Sir Henry Campbell-Bannerman, used the brief term of his power to reverse the policy of racial domination in South Africa and to prove the value of the old Gladstonian trust in the recuperative force of political freedom. It may be added that, if cynicism has since appeared to hold the field in international politics, it is the cynicism of terror rather than the cynicism of ambition. The Scare has superseded the Vision as the moving force in our external relations, and there are now signs that the Scare in turn has spent its force and is making room at last for Sense.

In other respects, Gladstone was a moral rather than an intellectual force. He raised the whole level of public life. By habitually calling upon what was best in men, he deepened the sense of public responsibility and paved the way, half unconsciously, for the fuller exercise of the social conscience. Mill was also a moral force, and the most persistent influence of his books is more an effect of character than of intellect. But, in place of Gladstone's driving power and practical capacity, Mill had the qualities of a life-long learner, and in his single person he spans the interval between the old and the new Liberalism. Brought up on the pure milk of the Benthamite word, he never definitely abandoned the first principles of his father. But he was perpetually bringing them into contact with fresh experience and new trains of thought, considering how they worked, and how they ought

[14] Britain fought the Opium War (1839–42) to prevent China from closing its borders to the opium trade; in 1851 Gladstone denounced the deplorable conditions in which prisoners were being held by the King of Naples; in 1897 he condemned the killing of Armenian Christians in territories under Turkish control.

to be modified in order to maintain what was really sound and valuable in their content. Hence, Mill is the easiest person in the world to convict of inconsistency, incompleteness, and lack of rounded system. Hence, also, his work will survive the death of many consistent, complete, and perfectly rounded systems.

As a utilitarian, Mill cannot appeal to any rights of the individual that can be set in opposition to the public welfare. His method is to show that the permanent welfare of the public is bound up with the rights of the individual. Of course, there are occasions on which the immediate expediency of the public would be met by ignoring personal rights. But if the rule of expediency were followed there would be neither right nor law at all. There would be no fixed rules in social life, and nothing to which men could trust in guiding their conduct. For the utilitarian, then, the question of right resolves itself into the question: What claim is it, in general and as a matter of principle, advisable for society to recognize? What in any given relation are the permanent conditions of social health? In regard to liberty Mill's reply turns on the moral or spiritual forces which determine the life of society. First, particularly as regards freedom of thought and discussion, society needs light. Truth has a social value, and we are never to suppose that we are in the possession of complete and final truth. But truth is only to be sought by experience in the world of thought, and of action as well. In the process of experimentation there are endless opportunities of error, and the free search for truth therefore involves friction and waste. The promulgation of error will do harm, a harm that might be averted if error were suppressed. But suppression by any other means than those of rational suasion is one of those remedies which cure the disease by killing the patient. It paralyses the free search for truth. Not only so, but there is an element of positive value in honest error which places it above mechanically accepted truth. So far as it is honest it springs from the spontaneous operation of the mind on the basis of some partial and incomplete experience. It is, so far as it goes, an interpretation of experience, though a faulty one, whereas the belief imposed by authority is no interpretation of experience at all. It involves no personal effort. Its blind acceptance seals the resignation of the will and the intellect to effacement and stultification.

The argument on this side does not rest on human fallibility. It appeals in its full strength to those who are most confident that they possess truth final and complete. They are asked to recognize that the way in which this truth must be communicated to others is not by material but by spiritual means, and that if they hold out physical threats as a deterrent, or worldly advantage as a means of persuasion, they are destroying not merely the fruits but the very root of truth as it grows within the human mind. Yet the argument receives additional force when we consider the actual history of human belief. The candid man who knows anything of the movements of thought will recognize that even the faith which is most vital to him is something that has grown through the generations, and he may infer, if he is reasonable, that as it has grown in the past so, if it has the vital seed within it, it will grow in the future. It may be permanent in outline, but in content it will change. But, if truth itself is an expanding circle of ideas that grows through criticism and by modification, we need say no more as to the rough and imperfect apprehension of truth which constitutes the dominant opinion of society at any given moment. It needs little effort of detachment to appreciate the danger of any limitation of inquiry by the collective will whether its organ be law or the repressive force of public opinion.

The foundation of liberty on this side, then, is the conception of thought as a growth dependent on spiritual laws, flourishing in the movement of ideas as guided by experience, reflection and feeling, corrupted by the intrusion of material considerations, slain by the guillotine of finality. The same conception is broadened out to cover the whole idea of personality. Social well-being cannot be incompatible with individual well-being. But individual well-being has as its foundation the responsible life of the rational creature. Manhood, and Mill would emphatically add womanhood too, rests on the spontaneous development of faculty. To find vent for the capacities of feeling, of emotion, of thought, of action, is to find oneself. The result is no anarchy. The self so found has as the pivot of its life the power of control. To introduce some unity into life, some harmony into thought, action and feeling, is its central achievement, and to realize its relation to others and guide its own life thereby, its noblest rule. But the essential of control is that it should be self-control. Compulsion may be necessary for the purposes of external order, but it adds nothing to the inward life that is the true being of man. It even threatens it with loss of authority and infringes the sphere of its responsibility. It is a means and not an end, and a means that readily becomes a danger to ends that are very vital. Under self-guidance individuals will diverge widely, and some of their eccentricities will be futile, others wasteful, others even painful and abhorrent to witness. But, upon the whole, it is good that they should differ. Individuality is an element of well-being, and that not only because it is the necessary consequence of self-government, but because, after all allowances for waste, the common life is fuller and richer for the multiplicity of types that it includes, and that go to enlarge the area of collective experience. The larger wrong done by the repression of women is not the loss to women themselves who constitute one half of the community but the impoverishment of the community as a whole, the loss of all the elements in the common stock which the free play of the woman's mind would contribute.

Similar principles underlie Mill's treatment of representative government. If the adult citizen, male or female, has a right to vote, it is not so much as a means to the enforcement of his claims upon society, but rather as a means of enforcing his personal responsibility for the actions of the community. The problem of character is the determining issue in the question of government. If men could be spoon-fed with happiness, a benevolent despotism would be the ideal system. If they are to take a part in working out their own salvation, they must be summoned to their share in the task of directing the common life. Carrying this principle further, Mill turned the edge of the common objection to the extension of the suffrage based on the ignorance and the irresponsibility of the voters. To learn anything men must practise. They must be trusted with more responsibility if they are to acquire the sense of responsibility. There were dangers in the process, but there were greater dangers and there were fewer elements of hope as long as the mass of the population was left outside the circle of civic rights and duties. The greatest danger that Mill saw in democracy was that of the tyranny of the majority. He emphasized, perhaps more than any Liberal teacher before him, the difference between the desire of the majority and the good of the community. He recognized that the different rights for which the Liberal was wont to plead might turn out in practice hard to reconcile with one another, that if personal liberty were fundamental it might only be imperilled by a so-called political liberty which would give to the majority unlimited powers of coercion. He was, therefore, for many years anxiously concerned with the means of securing a fair hearing and fair representation to minorities, and as a pioneer of the movement for Proportional Representation he sought to make Parliament the reflection not of a portion of the people, however preponderant numerically, but of the whole.

On the economic side of social life Mill recognized in principle the necessity of controlling contract where the parties were not on equal terms, but his insistence on personal responsibility made him chary in extending the principle to grown-up persons, and his especial attachment to the cause of feminine emancipation led him to resist the tide of feeling which was, in fact, securing the first elements of emancipation for the woman worker. He trusted at the outset of his career to the elevation of the standard of comfort as the best means of improving the position of the wage-earner, and in this elevation he regarded the limitation of the family as an essential condition. As he advanced in life, however, he became more and more dissatisfied with the whole structure of a system which left the mass of the population in the position of wage-earners, while the minority lived on rents, profits, and the interest on invested capital. He came to look forward to a co-operative organization of society in which a man would learn to 'dig and weave for his country', as he now is prepared to fight for it, and in which the surplus products of industry would be distributed among the producers. In middle life voluntary co-operation appeared to him the best means to this end, but towards the close he recognized that his change of views was such as, on the whole, to rank him with the Socialists, and the brief exposition of the Socialist ideal given in his Autobiography remains perhaps the best summary statement of Liberal Socialism that we possess.

CHAPTER VI

The Heart of Liberalism

The teaching of Mill brings us close to the heart of Liberalism. We learn from him, in the first place, that liberty is no mere formula of law, or of the restriction of law. There may be a tyranny of custom, a tyranny of opinion, even a tyranny of circumstance, as real as any tyranny of government and more pervasive. Nor does liberty rest on the self-assertion of the individual. There is scope abundant for Liberalism and illiberalism in personal conduct. Nor is liberty opposed to discipline, to organization, to strenuous conviction as to what is true and just. Nor is it to be identified with tolerance of opposed opinions. The Liberal does not meet opinions which he conceives to be false with toleration, as though they did not matter. He meets them with justice, and exacts for them a fair hearing as though they mattered just as much as his own. He is always ready to put his own convictions to the proof, not because he doubts them, but because he believes in them. For, both as to that which he holds for true and as to that which he holds for false, he believes that one final test applies. Let error have free play, and one of two things will happen. Either as it develops, as its implications and consequences become clear, some elements of truth will appear within it. They will separate themselves out; they will go to enrich the stock of human ideas; they will add something to the truth which he himself mistakenly took as final; they will serve to explain the root of the error; for error itself is generally a truth misconceived, and it is only when it is explained that it is finally and satisfactorily confuted. Or, in the alternative, no element of truth will appear. In that case the more fully the error is understood, the more patiently it is followed up in all the windings of its implications and consequences, the more thoroughly will it refute itself. The cancerous growth cannot be extirpated by the knife. The root is always left, and it is only the evolution of the self-protecting anti-toxin that works the final cure. Exactly parallel is the logic of truth. The more the truth is developed in all its implications, the greater is the opportunity of detecting any element of error that it may contain; and, conversely, if no error appears, the more completely does it establish itself as the whole truth and nothing but the truth. Liberalism applies the wisdom of Gamaliel in no spirit of indifference, but in the full conviction of the potency of truth. If this thing be of man, *i.e.* if it is not rooted in actual verity, it will come to nought. If it be of God, let us take care that we be not found fighting against God.

Divergences of opinion, of character, of conduct are not unimportant matters. They may be most serious matters, and no one is called on in the name of Liberalism to overlook their seriousness. There are, for example, certain disqualifications inherent in the profession of certain opinions. It is not illiberal to recognize such disqualifications. It is not illiberal for a Protestant in choosing a tutor for his son to reject a conscientious Roman Catholic who avows that all his teaching is centred on the doctrine of his Church. It would be illiberal to reject the same man for the specific purpose of teaching arithmetic, if he avowed that he had no intention of using his position for the purpose of religious propagandism. For the former purpose the divergence of religious opinion is an inherent disqualification. It negates the object propounded, which is the general education of the boy on lines in which the father believes. For the latter purpose the opinion is no disqualification. The devout Catholic accepts the multiplication table, and can impart his knowledge without reference to the infallibility of the Pope. To refuse to employ him is to impose an extraneous penalty on his convictions. It is not illiberal for an editor to decline the services of a member of the opposite party as a leader writer, or even as a political reviewer or in any capacity in which his opinions would affect his work. It is illiberal to reject him as a compositor or as a clerk, or in any capacity in which his opinions would not affect his work for the paper. It is not illiberal to refuse a position of trust to the man whose record shows that he is likely to abuse such a trust. It is illiberal – and this the 'moralist' has yet to learn – to punish a man who has done a wrong in one relation by excluding him from the performance of useful social functions for which he is perfectly fitted, by which he could at once serve society and re-establish his own self-respect. There may, however, yet come a time when Liberalism, already recognized as a duty in religion and in politics, will take its true place at the centre of our ethical conceptions, and will be seen to have its application not only to him whom we conceive to be the teacher of false opinions, but to the man whom we hold a sinner.

The ground of Liberalism so understood is certainly not the view that a man's personal opinions are socially indifferent, nor that his personal morality matters nothing to others. So far as Mill rested his case on the distinction between self-regarding actions and actions that affect others, he was still dominated by the older individualism. We should frankly recognize that there is no side of a man's life which is unimportant to society, for whatever he is, does, or thinks may affect his own well-being, which is and ought to be matter of common concern, and may also directly or indirectly affect the thought, action, and character of those with whom he comes in contact. The underlying principle may be put in two ways. In the first place, the man is much more than his opinions and his actions. Carlyle and Sterling did not differ 'except in opinion'. To most of us that is just what difference means. Carlyle was aware that there was something much deeper, something that opinion just crassly formulates, and for the most part formulates inadequately, that is the real man. The real man is something more than is ever adequately expressed in terms which his fellows can understand; and just as his essential humanity lies deeper than all distinctions of rank, and class, and colour, and even, though in a different sense, of sex, so also it goes far below those comparatively external events which make one man figure as a saint and another as a criminal. This sense of ultimate oneness is the real meaning of equality, as it is the foundation of social solidarity and the bond which, if genuinely experienced, resists the disruptive force of all conflict, intellectual, religious, and ethical.

But, further, while personal opinions and social institutions are like crystallized results, achievements that have been won by certain definite processes of individual or collective effort, human personality is that within which lives and grows, which can be destroyed but cannot be made, which cannot be taken to pieces and repaired, but can be placed under conditions in which it will flourish and expand, or, if it is diseased, under conditions in which it will heal itself by its own recuperative powers. The foundation of liberty is the idea of growth. Life is learning, but whether in theory or practice what a man genuinely learns is what he absorbs, and what he absorbs depends on the energy which he himself puts forth in response to his surroundings. Thus, to come at once to the real crux, the question of moral discipline, it is of course possible to reduce a man to order and prevent him from being a nuisance to his neighbours by arbitrary control and harsh punishment. This may be to the comfort of the neighbours, as is admitted, but regarded as a moral discipline it is a contradiction in terms. It is doing less than nothing for the character of the man himself. It is merely crushing him, and unless his will is killed the effect will be seen if ever the superincumbent pressure is by chance removed. It is also possible, though it takes a much higher skill, to teach the same man to discipline himself, and this is to foster the development of will, of personality, of self-control, or whatever we please to call that central harmonizing power which makes us capable of directing our own lives. Liberalism is the belief that society can safely be founded on this self-directing power of personality, that it is only on this foundation that a true community can be built, and that so established its foundations are so deep and so wide that there is no limit that we can place to the extent of the building. Liberty then becomes not so much a right of the individual as a necessity of society. It rests not on the claim of A to be let alone by B, but on the duty of B to treat A as a rational being. It is not right to let crime alone or to let error alone, but it is imperative to treat the criminal or the mistaken or the ignorant as beings capable of right and truth, and to lead them on instead of merely beating them down. The rule of liberty is just the application of rational method. It is the opening of the door to the appeal of reason, of imagination, of social feeling; and except through the response to this appeal there is no assured progress of society.

Now, I am not contending that these principles are free from difficulty in application. At many points they suggest difficulties both in theory and in practice, with some of which I shall try to deal later on. Nor, again, am I contending that freedom is the universal solvent, or the idea of liberty the sole foundation on which a true social philosophy can be based. On the contrary, freedom is only one side of social life. Mutual aid is not less important than mutual forbearance, the theory of collective action no less fundamental than the theory of personal freedom. But, in an inquiry where all the elements are so closely interwoven as they are in the field of social life, the point of departure becomes almost indifferent. Wherever we start we shall, if we are quite frank and consistent, be led on to look at the whole from some central point, and this, I think, has happened to us in working with the conception of 'liberty'. For, beginning with the right of the individual, and the antithesis between personal freedom and social control, we have been led on to a point at which we regard liberty as primarily a matter of social interest, as something flowing from the necessities of continuous advance in those regions of truth and of ethics which constitute the matters of highest social concern. At the same time, we have come to look for the effect of liberty in the firmer establishment of social solidarity, as the only foundation on which such solidarity can securely rest. We have, in fact, arrived by a path of our own at that which is ordinarily described as the organic conception of the relation between the individual and society – a conception towards which Mill worked through his career, and which forms the starting-point of T. H. Green's philosophy alike in ethics and in politics.

The term organic is so much used and abused that it is best to state simply what it means. A thing is called organic when it is made up of parts which are quite distinct from one another, but which are destroyed or vitally altered when they are removed from the whole. Thus, the human body is organic because its life depends on the functions performed by many organs, while each of these organs depends in turn on the life of the body, perishing and decomposing if removed therefrom. Now, the organic view of society is equally simple. It means that, while the life of society is nothing but the life of individuals as they act one upon another, the life of the individual in turn would be something utterly different if he could be separated from society. A great deal of him would not exist at all. Even if he himself could maintain physical existence by the luck and skill of a Robinson Crusoe, his mental and moral being would, if it existed at all, be something quite different from anything that we know. By language, by training, by simply living with others, each of us absorbs into his system the social atmosphere that surrounds us. In particular, in the matter of rights and duties which is cardinal for Liberal theory, the relation of the individual to the community is everything. His rights and his duties are alike defined by the common good. What, for example, is my right? On the face of it, it is something that I claim. But a mere claim is nothing. I might claim anything and everything. If my claim is of right it is because it is sound, well grounded, in the judgement of an impartial observer. But an impartial observer will not consider me alone. He will equally weigh the opposed claims of others. He will take us in relation to one another, that is to say, as individuals involved in a social relationship. Further, if his decision is in any sense a rational one, it must rest on a principle of some kind; and again, as a rational man, any principle which he asserts he must found on some good result which it serves or embodies, and as an impartial man he must take the good of every one affected into account. That is to say, he must found his judgement on the common good. An individual right, then, cannot conflict with the common good, nor could any right exist apart from the common good.

The argument might seem to make the individual too subservient to society. But this is to forget the other side of the original supposition. Society consists wholly of persons. It has no distinct personality separate from and superior to those of its members. It has, indeed, a certain collective life and character. The British nation is a unity with a life of its own. But the unity is constituted by certain ties that bind together all British subjects, which ties are in the last resort feelings and ideas, sentiments of patriotism, of kinship, a common pride, and a thousand more subtle sentiments that bind together men who speak a common language, have behind them a common history, and understand one another as they can understand no one else. The British nation is not a mysterious entity over and above the forty odd millions of living souls who dwell together under a common law. Its life is their life, its well-being or ill-fortune their well-being or ill-fortune. Thus, the common good to which each man's rights are subordinate is a good in which each man has a share. This share consists in realizing his capacities of feeling, of loving, of mental and physical energy, and in realizing these he plays his part in the social life, or, in Green's phrase, he finds his own good in the common good.

Now, this phrase, it must be admitted, involves a certain assumption, which may be regarded as the fundamental postulate of the organic view of society. It implies that such a fulfilment or full development of personality is practically possible not for one man only but for all members of a community. There must be a line of development open along which each can move in harmony with others. Harmony in the full sense would involve not merely absence of conflict but actual support. There must be for each, then, possibilities of development such as not merely to permit but actively to further the development of others. Now, the older economists conceived a natural harmony, such that the interest of each would, if properly understood and unchecked by outside interference, inevitably lead him in courses profitable to others and to society at large. We saw that this assumption was too optimistic. The conception which we have now reached does not assume so much. It postulates, not that there is an actually existing harmony requiring nothing but prudence and coolness of judgement for its effective operation, but only that there is a possible ethical harmony, to which, partly by discipline, partly by the improvement of the conditions of life, men might attain, and that in such attainment lies the social ideal. To attempt the systematic proof of this postulate would take us into the field of philosophical first principles. It is the point at which the philosophy of politics comes into contact with that of ethics. It must suffice to say here that, just as the endeavour to establish coherent system in the world of thought is the characteristic of the rational impulse which lies at the root of science and philosophy, so the impulse to establish harmony in the world of feeling and action – a harmony which must include all those who think and feel – is of the essence of the rational impulse in the world of practice. To move towards harmony is the persistent impulse of the rational being, even if the goal lies always beyond the reach of accomplished effort.

These principles may appear very abstract, remote from practical life, and valueless for concrete teaching. But this remoteness is of the nature of first principles when taken without the connecting links that bind them to the details of experience. To find some of these links let us take up again our old Liberal principles, and see how they look in the light of the organic, or, as we may now call it, the harmonic conception. We shall readily see, to begin with, that the old idea of equality has its place. For the common good includes every individual. It is founded on personality, and postulates free scope for the development of personality in each member of the community. This is the foundation not only of equal rights before the law, but also of what is called equality of opportunity. It does not necessarily imply actual equality of treatment for all persons any more than it implies original equality of powers.' It does, I think, imply that whatever inequality of actual treatment, of income, rank, office, consideration, there be in a good social system, it would rest, not on the interest of the favoured individual as such, but on the common good. If the existence of millionaires on the one hand and of paupers on the other is just, it must be because such contrasts are the result of an economic system which upon the whole works out for the common good, the good of the pauper being included therein as well as the good of the millionaire; that is to say, that when we have well weighed the good and the evil of all parties concerned we can find no alternative open to us which could do better for the good of all. I am not for the moment either attacking or defending any economic system. I point out only that this is the position which according to the organic or harmonic view of society must be made good by any rational defence of grave inequality in the distribution of wealth. In relation to equality, indeed, it appears, oddly enough, that the harmonic principle can adopt wholesale, and even expand, one of the 'Rights of Man' as formulated in 1789 – 'Social distinctions can only be founded upon common utility.' If it is really just that A should be superior to B in wealth or power or position, it is only because when the good of all concerned is considered, among whom B is one, it turns out that there is a net gain in the arrangement as compared with any alternative that we can devise.

If we turn from equality to liberty, the general lines of argument have already been indicated, and the discussion of difficulties in detail must be left for the next chapter. It need only be repeated here that on the harmonic principle the fundamental importance of liberty rests on the nature of the 'good' itself, and that whether we are thinking of the good of society or the good of the individual. The good is something attained by the development of the basal factors of personality, a development proceeding by the widening of ideas, the awakening of the imagination, the play of affection and passion, the strengthening and extension of rational control. As it is the development of these factors in each human being that makes his life worth having, so it is their harmonious interaction, the response of each to

' An absurd misconception fostered principally by opponents of equality for controversial purposes.

each, that makes of society a living whole. Liberty so interpreted cannot, as we have seen, dispense with restraint; restraint, however, is not an end but a means to an end, and one of the principal elements in that end is the enlargement of liberty.

But the collective activity of the community does not necessarily proceed by coercion or restraint. The more securely it is founded on freedom and general willing assent, the more it is free to work out all the achievements in which the individual is feeble or powerless while combined action is strong. Human progress, on whatever side we consider it, is found to be in the main social progress, the work of conscious or unconscious co-operation. In this work voluntary association plays a large and increasing part. But the State is one form of association among others, distinguished by its use of coercive power, by its supremacy, and by its claim to control all who dwell within its geographical limits. What the functions of such a form of association are to be we shall have to consider a little further in connection with the other questions which we have already raised. But that, in general, we are justified in regarding the State as one among many forms of human association for the maintenance and improvement of life is the general principle that we have to point out here, and this is the point at which we stand furthest from the older Liberalism. We have, however, already seen some reason for thinking that the older doctrines led, when carefully examined, to a more enlarged conception of State action than appeared on the surface; and we shall see more fully before we have done that the 'positive' conception of the State which we have now reached not only involves no conflict with the true principle of personal liberty, but is necessary to its effective realization.

There is, in addition, one principle of historic Liberalism with which our present conception of the State is in full sympathy. The conception of the common good as it has been explained can be realized in its fullness only through the common will. There are, of course, elements of value in the good government of a benevolent despot or of a fatherly aristocracy. Within any peaceful order there is room for many good things to flourish. But the full fruit of social progress is only to be reaped by a society in which the generality of men and women are not only passive recipients but practical contributors. To make the rights and responsibilities of citizens real and living, and to extend them as widely as the conditions of society allow, is thus an integral part of the organic conception of society, and the justification of the democratic principle. It is, at the same time, the justification of nationalism so far as nationalism is founded on a true interpretation of history. For, inasmuch as the true social harmony rests on feeling and makes use of all the natural ties of kinship, of neighbourliness, of congruity of character and belief, and of language and mode of life, the best, healthiest, and most vigorous political unit is that to which men are by their own feelings strongly drawn. Any breach of such unity, whether by forcible disruption or by compulsory inclusion in a larger society of alien sentiments and laws, tends to mutilate – or, at lowest, to cramp – the spontaneous development of social life. National and personal freedom are growths of the same root, and their historic connection rests on no accident, but on ultimate identity of idea.

Thus in the organic conception of society each of the leading ideas of historic Liberalism has its part to play. The ideal society is conceived as a whole which lives and flourishes by the harmonious growth of its parts, each of which in developing on its own lines and in accordance with its own nature tends on the whole to further the development of others. There is some elementary trace of such harmony in every form of social life that can maintain itself, for if the conflicting impulses predominated society would break up, and when they do predominate society does break up. At the other extreme, true harmony is an ideal which it is perhaps beyond the power of man to realize, but which serves to indicate the line of advance. But to admit this is to admit that the lines of possible development for each individual or, to use a more general phrase, for each constituent of the social order are not limited and fixed. There are many possibilities, and the course that will in the end make for social harmony is only one among them, while the possibilities of disharmony and conflict are many. The progress of society like that of the individual depends, then, ultimately on choice. It is not 'natural', in the sense in which a physical law is natural, that is, in the sense of going forward automatically from stage to stage without backward turnings, deflections to the left, or fallings away on the right. It is natural only in this sense, that it is the expression of deep-seated forces of human nature which come to their own only by an infinitely slow and cumbersome process of mutual adjustment. Every constructive social doctrine rests on the conception of human progress.

The heart of Liberalism is the understanding that progress is not a matter of mechanical contrivance, but of the liberation of living spiritual energy. Good mechanism is that which provides the channels wherein such energy can flow unimpeded, unobstructed by its own exuberance of output, vivifying the social structure, expanding and ennobling the life of mind.

CHAPTER VII

The State and the Individual

We have seen something of the principle underlying the Liberal idea and of its various applications. We have now to put the test question. Are these different applications compatible? Will they work together to make that harmonious whole of which it is easy enough to talk in abstract terms? Are they themselves really harmonious in theory and in practice? Does scope for individual development, for example, consort with the idea of equality? Is popular sovereignty a practicable basis of personal freedom, or does it open an avenue to the tyranny of the mob? Will the sentiment of nationality dwell in unison with the ideal of peace? Is the love of liberty compatible with the full realization of the common will? If reconcilable in theory, may not these ideals collide in practice? Are there not clearly occasions demonstrable in history when development in one direction involves retrogression in another? If so, how are we to strike the balance of gain and loss? Does political progress offer us nothing but a choice of evils, or may we have some confidence that, in solving the most pressing problem of the moment, we shall in the end be in a better position for grappling with the obstacles that come next in turn?,

I shall deal with these questions as far as limits of space allow, and I will take first the question of liberty and the common will upon which everything turns. Enough has already been said on this topic to enable us to shorten the discussion. We have seen that social liberty rests on restraint. A man can be free to direct his own life only in so far as others are prevented from molesting and interfering with him. So far there is no real departure from the strictest tenets of individualism. We have, indeed, had occasion to examine the application of the doctrine to freedom of contract on the one hand, and to the action of combinations on the other, and have seen reason to think that in either case nominal freedom, that is to say, the absence of legal restraint, might have the effect of impairing real freedom, that is to say, would allow the stronger party to coerce the weaker. We have also seen that the effect of combination may be double edged, that it may restrict freedom on one side and enlarge it on the other. In all these cases our contention has been simply that we should be guided by real and not by verbal considerations – that we should ask in every case what policy will yield effective freedom – and we have found a close connection in each instance between freedom and equality. In these cases, however, we were dealing with the relations of one man with another, or of one body of men with another, and we could regard the community as an arbiter between them whose business it was to see justice done and prevent the abuse of coercive power. Hence we could treat a very large part of the modern development of social control as motived by the desire for a more effective liberty. The case is not so clear when we find the will of the individual in conflict with the will of the community as a whole. When such conflict occurs, it would seem that we must be prepared for one of two things. Either we must admit the legitimacy of coercion, avowedly not in the interests of freedom but in furtherance, without regard to freedom, of other ends which the community deems good. Or we must admit limitations which may cramp the development of the general will, and perchance prove a serious obstacle to collective progress. Is there any means of avoiding this conflict? Must we leave the question to be fought out in each case by a balance of advantages and disadvantages, or are there any general considerations which help us to determine the true sphere of collective and of private action?

Let us first observe that, as Mill pointed out long ago, there are many forms of collective action which do not involve coercion.[15] The State may provide for certain objects which it deems good without compelling any one to make use of them. Thus it may maintain hospitals, though any one who can pay for them remains free to employ his own doctors and nurses. It may and does maintain a great educational system, while leaving every one free to maintain or to

<hr />

[15] John Stuart Mill, *Principles of Political Economy* (1848), Book V, chap. xi.

attend a private school. It maintains parks and picture galleries without driving any one into them. There is a municipal tramway service, which does not prevent private people from running motor 'buses along the same streets, and so on. It is true that for the support of these objects rates and taxes are compulsorily levied, but this form of compulsion raises a set of questions of which we shall have to speak in another connection, and does not concern us here. For the moment we have to deal only with those actions of State which compel all citizens, or all whom they concern, to fall in with them and allow of no divergence. This kind of coercion tends to increase. Is its extension necessarily an encroachment upon liberty, or are the elements of value secured by collective control distinct from the elements of value secured by individual choice, so that within due limits each may develop side by side?

We have already declined to solve the problem by applying Mill's distinction between self-regarding and other-regarding actions, first because there are no actions which may not directly or indirectly affect others, secondly because even if there were they would not cease to be matter of concern to others. The common good includes the good of every member of the community, and the injury which a man inflicts upon himself is matter of common concern, even apart from any ulterior effect upon others. If we refrain from coercing a man for his own good, it is not because his good is indifferent to us, but because it cannot be furthered by coercion. The difficulty is founded on the nature of the good itself, which on its personal side depends on the spontaneous flow of feeling checked and guided not by external restraint but by rational self-control. To try to form character by coercion is to destroy it in the making. Personality is not built up from without but grows from within, and the function of the outer order is not to create it, but to provide for it the most suitable conditions of growth. Thus, to the common question whether it is possible to make men good by Act of Parliament, the reply is that it is not possible to compel morality because morality is the act or character of a free agent, but that it is possible to create the conditions under which morality can develop, and among these not the least important is freedom from compulsion by others.

The argument suggests that compulsion is limited not by indifference – how could the character of its members be matter of indifference to the community? – but by its own incapacity to achieve its ends. The spirit cannot be forced. Nor, conversely, can it prevail by force. It may require social expression. It may build up an association, a church for example, to carry out the common objects and maintain the common life of all who are like-minded. But the association must be free, because spiritually everything depends not on what is done but on the will with which it is done. The limit to the value of coercion thus lies not in the restriction of social purpose, but in the conditions of personal life. No force can compel growth. Whatever elements of social value depend on the accord of feeling, on comprehension of meaning, on the assent of will, must come through liberty. Here is the sphere and function of liberty in the social harmony.

Where, then, is the sphere of compulsion, and what is its value? The reply is that compulsion is of value where outward conformity is of value, and this may be in any case where the non-conformity of one wrecks the purpose of others. We have already remarked that liberty itself only rests upon restraint. Thus a religious body is not, properly speaking, free to march in procession through the streets unless people of a different religion are restrained from pelting the procession with stones and pursuing it with insolence. We restrain them from disorder not to teach them the genuine spirit of religion, which they will not learn in the police court, but to secure to the other party the right of worship unmolested. The enforced restraint has its value in the action that it sets free. But we may not only restrain one man from obstructing another – and the extent to which we do this is the measure of the freedom that we maintain – but we may also restrain him from obstructing the general will; and this we have to do whenever uniformity is necessary to the end which the general will has in view. The majority of employers in a trade we may suppose would be willing to adopt certain precautions for the health or safety of their workers, to lower hours or to raise the rate of wages. They are unable to do so, however, as long as a minority, perhaps as long as a single employer, stands out. He would beat them in competition if they were voluntarily to undertake expenses from which he is free. In this case, the will of a minority, possibly the will of one man, thwarts that of the remainder. It coerces them, indirectly, but quite as effectively as if he were their master. If they, by combination, can coerce him no principle of liberty is violated. It is coercion against coercion, differing possibly in form and method, but not in principle or in spirit. Further, if the community as a whole sympathizes with the one side rather than the other, it can reasonably bring the law into play. Its object is not the moral education of the recusant individuals. Its object is to secure certain conditions which it believes necessary for the welfare of its members, and which can only be secured by an enforced uniformity.

It appears, then, that the true distinction is not between self-regarding and other-regarding actions, but between coercive and non-coercive actions. The function of State coercion is to override individual coercion, and, of course, coercion exercised by any association of individuals within the State. It is by this means that it maintains liberty of expression, security of person and property, genuine freedom of contract, the rights of public meeting and association, and finally its own power to carry out common objects undefeated by the recalcitrance of individual members. Undoubtedly it endows both individuals and associations with powers as well as with rights. But over these powers it must exercise supervision in the interests of equal justice. Just as compulsion failed in the sphere of liberty, the sphere of spiritual growth, so liberty fails in the external order wherever, by the mere absence of supervisory restriction, men are able directly or indirectly to put constraint on one another. This is why there is no intrinsic and inevitable conflict between liberty and compulsion, but at bottom a mutual need. The object of compulsion is to secure the most favourable external conditions of inward growth and happiness so far as these conditions depend on combined action and uniform observance. The sphere of liberty is the sphere of growth itself. There is no true opposition between liberty as such and control as such, for every liberty rests on a corresponding act of control. The true opposition is between the control that cramps the personal life and the spiritual order, and the control that is aimed at securing the external and material conditions of their free and unimpeded development.

I do not pretend that this delimitation solves all problems. The 'inward' life will seek to express itself in outward acts. A religious ordinance may bid the devout refuse military service, or withhold the payment of a tax, or decline to submit a building to inspection. Here are external matters where conscience and the State come into direct conflict, and where is the court of appeal that is to decide between them? In any given case the right, as judged by the ultimate effect on human welfare, may, of course, be on the one side, or on the other, or between the two. But is there anything to guide the two parties as long as each believes itself to be in the right and sees no ground for waiving its opinion? To begin with, clearly the State does well to avoid such conflicts by substituting alternatives. Other duties than that of military service may be found for a follower of Tolstoy, and as long as he is willing to take his full share of burdens the difficulty is fairly met. Again, the mere convenience of the majority cannot be fairly weighed against the religious convictions of the few. It might be convenient that certain public work should be done on Saturday, but mere convenience would be an insufficient ground for compelling Jews to participate in it. Religious and ethical conviction must be weighed against religious and ethical conviction. It is not number that counts morally, but the belief that is reasoned out according to the best of one's lights as to the necessities of the common good. But the conscience of the community has its rights just as much as the conscience of the individual. If we are convinced that the inspection of a convent laundry is required in the interest, not of mere official routine, but of justice and humanity, we can do nothing but insist upon it, and when all has been done that can be done to save the individual conscience the common conviction of the common good must have its way. In the end the external order belongs to the community, and the right of protest to the individual.

On the other side, the individual owes more to the community than is always recognized. Under modern conditions he is too much inclined to take for granted what the State does for him and to use the personal security and liberty of speech which it affords him as a vantage ground from which he can in safety denounce its works and repudiate its authority. He assumes the right to be in or out of the social system as he chooses. He relies on the general law which protects him, and emancipates himself from some particular law which he finds oppressive to his conscience. He forgets or does not take the trouble to reflect that, if every one were to act as he does, the social machine would come to a stop. He certainly fails to make it clear how a society would subsist in which every man should claim the right of unrestricted disobedience to a law which he happens to think wrong. In fact, it is possible for an over-tender conscience to consort with an insufficient sense of social responsibility. The combination is unfortunate; and we may fairly say that, if the State owes the utmost consideration to the conscience, its owner owes a corresponding debt to the State. With such mutual consideration, and with the development of the civic sense, conflicts between law and conscience are capable of being brought within very narrow limits, though their complete reconciliation will always remain a problem until men are generally agreed as to the fundamental conditions of the social harmony.

It may be asked, on the other hand, whether in insisting on the free development of personality we have not understated the duty of society to its members. We all admit a collective responsibility for children. Are there not grown-up people who stand just as much in need of care? What of the idiot, the imbecile, the feeble-minded or the drunkard? What does rational self-determination mean for these classes? They may injure no one but themselves except by the contagion of bad example. But have we no duty towards them, having in view their own good alone and leaving every other consideration aside? Have we not the right to take the feeble-minded under our care and to keep the drunkard from drink, purely for their own good and apart from every ulterior consideration? And, if so, must we not extend the whole sphere of permissible coercion, and admit that a man may for his own sake and with no ulterior object, be compelled to do what we think right and avoid what we think wrong?

The reply is that the argument is weak just where it seeks to generalize. We are compelled to put the insane under restraint for social reasons apart from their own benefit. But their own benefit would be a fully sufficient reason if no other existed. To them, by their misfortune, liberty, as we understand the term, has no application, because they are incapable of rational choice and therefore of the kind of growth for the sake of which freedom is valuable. The same thing is true of the feeble-minded, and if they are not yet treated on the same principle it is merely because the recognition of their type as a type is relatively modern. But the same thing is also in its degree true of the drunkard, so far as he is the victim of an impulse which he has allowed to grow beyond his own control; and the question whether he should be regarded as a fit object for tutelage or not is to be decided in each case by asking whether such capacity of self-control as he retains would be impaired or repaired by a period of tutelar restraint. There is nothing in all this to touch the essential of liberty which is the value of the power of self-governance where it exists. All that is proved is that where it does not exist it is right to save men from suffering, and if the case admits to put them under conditions in which the normal balance of impulse is most likely to be restored. It may be added that, in the case of the drunkard – and I think the argument applies to all cases where overwhelming impulse is apt to master the will – it is a still more obvious and elementary duty to remove the sources of temptation, and to treat as anti-social in the highest degree every attempt to make profit out of human weakness, misery, and wrong-doing. The case is not unlike that of a very unequal contract. The tempter is coolly seeking his profit, and the sufferer is beset with a fiend within. There is a form of coercion here which the genuine spirit of liberty will not fail to recognize as its enemy, and a form of injury to another which is not the less real because its weapon is an impulse which forces that other to the consent which he yields.

I conclude that there is nothing in the doctrine of liberty to hinder the movement of general will in the sphere in which it is really efficient, and nothing in a just conception of the objects and methods of the general will to curtail liberty in the performance of the functions, social and personal, in which its value lies. Liberty and compulsion have complementary functions, and the self-governing State is at once the product and the condition of the self-governing individual.

Thus there is no difficulty in understanding why the extension of State control on one side goes along with determined resistance to encroachments on another. It is a question not of increasing or diminishing, but of reorganizing, restraints. The period which has witnessed a rapid extension of industrial legislation has seen as determined a resistance to anything like the establishment of doctrinal religious teaching by a State authority,/ and the distinction is perfectly just. At bottom it is the same conception of liberty and the same conception of the common will that prompts the regulation of industry and the severence of religious worship and doctrinal teaching from the mechanism of State control.

So far we have been considering what the State compels the individual to do. If we pass to the question what the State is to do for the individual, a different but parallel question arises, and we have to note a corresponding movement of opinion. If the State does for

---

/ The objection most often taken to 'undenominationalism' itself is that it is in reality a form of doctrinal teaching seeking State endowment.

the individual what he ought to do for himself what will be the effect on character, initiative, enterprise? It is a question now not of freedom, but of responsibility, and it is one that has caused many searchings of heart, and in respect of which opinion has undergone a remarkable change. Thus, in relation to poverty the older view was that the first thing needful was self-help. It was the business of every man to provide for himself and his family. If, indeed, he utterly failed, neither he nor they could be left to starve, and there was the Poor Law machinery to deal with his case. But the aim of every sincere friend of the poor must be to keep them away from the Poor Law machine. Experience of the forty years before 1834[16] had taught us what came of free resort to public funds by way of subvention to inadequate wages. It meant simply that the standard of remuneration was lowered in proportion as men could rely on public aid to make good the deficiency, while at the same time the incentives to independent labour were weakened when the pauper stood on an equal footing with the hard-working man. In general, if the attempt was made to substitute for personal effort the help of others, the result would only sap individual initiative and in the end bring down the rate of industrial remuneration. It was thought, for example – and this very point was urged against proposals for Old Age Pensions – that if any of the objects for which a man will, if possible, provide were removed from the scope of his own activity, he would in consequence be content with proportionally lower wages; if the employer was to compensate him for accident, he would fail to make provision for accidents on his own account; if his children were fed by the ratepayers, he would not earn the money wherewith to feed them. Hence, on the one hand, it was urged that the rate of wages would tend to adapt itself to the necessities of the wage earner, that in proportion as his necessities were met from other sources his wages would fall, that accordingly the apparent relief would be in large measure illusory, while finally, in view of the diminished stimulus to individual exertion, the productivity of labour would fall off, the incentives to industry would be diminished, and the community as a whole would be poorer. Upon the other hand, it was conceived that,

[16] After 1795 there was a considerable extension in the provision of 'outdoor relief' – assistance paid to the poor without requiring the recipient to enter a workhouse. The practice was sharply curtailed after passage of the Poor Law Amendment Act of 1834.

however deplorable the condition of the working classes might be, the right way of raising them was to trust to individual enterprise and possibly, according to some thinkers, to voluntary combination. By these means the efficiency of labour might be enhanced and its regular remuneration raised. By sternly withholding all external supports we should teach the working classes to stand alone, and if there were pain in the disciplinary process there was yet hope in the future. They would come by degrees to a position of economic independence in which they would be able to face the risks of life, not in reliance upon the State, but by the force of their own brains and the strength of their own right arms.

These views no longer command the same measure of assent. On all sides we find the State making active provision for the poorer classes and not by any means for the destitute alone. We find it educating the children, providing medical inspection, authorizing the feeding of the necessitous at the expense of the ratepayers, helping them to obtain employment through free Labour Exchanges, seeking to organize the labour market with a view to the mitigation of unemployment, and providing old age pensions for all whose incomes fall below thirteen shillings a week, without exacting any contribution. Now, in all this, we may well ask, is the State going forward blindly on the paths of broad and generous but unconsidered charity? Is it and can it remain indifferent to the effect on individual initiative and personal or parental responsibility? Or may we suppose that the wiser heads are well aware of what they are about, have looked at the matter on all sides, and are guided by a reasonable conception of the duty of the State and the responsibilities of the individual? Are we, in fact – for this is really the question – seeking charity or justice?

We said above that it was the function of the State to secure the conditions upon which mind and character may develop themselves. Similarly we may say now that the function of the State is to secure conditions upon which its citizens are able to win by their own efforts all that is necessary to a full civic efficiency. It is not for the State to feed, house, or clothe them. It is for the State to take care that the economic conditions are such that the normal man who is not defective in mind or body or will can by useful labour feed, house, and clothe himself and his family. The 'right to work' and the right to a 'living wage' are just as valid as the rights of person or property. That is to say, they are integral conditions of a good social order. A society in which a single honest man of normal capacity is definitely unable to find the means of maintaining himself by useful work is to that extent suffering from malorganization. There is somewhere a defect in the social system, a hitch in the economic machine. Now, the individual workman cannot put the machine straight. He is the last person to have any say in the control of the market. It is not his fault if there is over-production in his industry, or if a new and cheaper process has been introduced which makes his particular skill, perhaps the product of years of application, a drug in the market.[17] He does not direct or regulate industry. He is not responsible for its ups and downs, but he has to pay for them. That is why it is not charity but justice for which he is asking. Now, it may be infinitely difficult to meet his demand. To do so may involve a far-reaching economic reconstruction. The industrial questions involved may be so little understood that we may easily make matters worse in the attempt to make them better. All this shows the difficulty in finding means of meeting this particular claim of justice, but it does not shake its position as a claim of justice. A right is a right none the less though the means of securing it be imperfectly known; and the workman who is unemployed or underpaid through economic malorganization will remain a reproach not to the charity but to the justice of society as long as he is to be seen in the land.

If this view of the duty of the State and the right of the workman is coming to prevail, it is owing partly to an enhanced sense of common responsibility, and partly to the teaching of experience. In the earlier days of the Free Trade era, it was permissible to hope that self-help would be an adequate solvent, and that with cheap food and expanding commerce the average workman would be able by the exercise of prudence and thrift not only to maintain himself in good times, but to lay by for sickness, unemployment, and old age. The actual course of events has in large measure disappointed these hopes. It is true that the standard of living in England has progressively advanced throughout the nineteenth century. It is true, in particular, that, since the disastrous period that preceded the Repeal of the Corn Laws and the passing of the Ten Hours' Act, social improvement has been real and marked. Trade Unionism and co-

---

[17] 'a drug in the market': 'a commodity which is no longer in demand, and so has lost its value or become unsaleable' (*OED*).

operation have grown, wages upon the whole have increased, the cost of living has diminished, housing and sanitation have improved, the death rate has fallen from about twenty-two to less than fifteen per thousand. But with all this improvement the prospect of a complete and lifelong economic independence for the average workman upon the lines of individual competition, even when supplemented and guarded by the collective bargaining of the Trade Union, appears exceedingly remote. The increase of wages does not appear to be by any means proportionate to the general growth of wealth. The whole standard of living has risen; the very provision of education has brought with it new needs and has almost compelled a higher standard of life in order to satisfy them. As a whole, the working classes of England, though less thrifty than those of some Continental countries, cannot be accused of undue negligence with regard to the future. The accumulation of savings in Friendly Societies, Trade Unions, Co-operative Societies, and Savings Banks shows an increase which has more than kept pace with the rise in the level of wages; yet there appears no likelihood that the average manual worker will attain the goal of that full independence, covering all the risks of life for self and family, which can alone render the competitive system really adequate to the demands of a civilized conscience. The careful researches of Mr Booth in London and Mr Rowntree in York, and of others in country districts, have revealed that a considerable percentage of the working classes are actually unable to earn a sum of money representing the full cost of the barest physical necessities for an average family; and, though the bulk of the working classes are undoubtedly in a better position than this, these researches go to show that even the relatively well-to-do gravitate towards this line of primary poverty in seasons of stress, at the time when the children are still at school, for example, or from the moment when the principal wage-earner begins to fail, in the decline of middle life. If only some ten per cent of the population are actually living upon the poverty line at any given time,[*] twice or three times that number, it is reasonable to suppose, must approach the line in one period or other of their lives. But when we ascend from the conception of a bare physical maintenance for an average family to such a wage as would provide the real

---

[*] I do not include those living in 'secondary poverty', as defined by Mr Rowntree, as the responsibility in this case is partly personal. It must, however, be remembered that great poverty increases the difficulty of efficient management.

minimum requirements of a civilized life and meet all its contingencies without having to lean on any external prop, we should have to make additions to Mr Rowntree's figure which have not yet been computed, but as to which it is probably well within the mark to say that none but the most highly skilled artisans are able to earn a remuneration meeting the requirements of the case. But, if that is so, it is clear that the system of industrial competition fails to meet the ethical demand embodied in the conception of the 'living wage'. That system holds out no hope of an improvement which shall bring the means of such a healthy and independent existence as should be the birthright of every citizen of a free state within the grasp of the mass of the people of the United Kingdom. It is this belief slowly penetrating the public mind which has turned it to new thoughts of social regeneration. The sum and substance of the changes that I have mentioned may be expressed in the principle that the individual cannot stand alone, but that between him and the State there is a reciprocal obligation. He owes the State the duty of industriously working for himself and his family. He is not to exploit the labour of his young children, but to submit to the public requirements for their education, health, cleanliness and general well-being. On the other side society owes to him the means of maintaining a civilized standard of life, and this debt is not adequately discharged by leaving him to secure such wages as he can in the higgling of the market.

This view of social obligation lays increased stress on public but by no means ignores private responsibility. It is a simple principle of applied ethics that responsibility should be commensurate with power. Now, given the opportunity of adequately remunerated work, a man has the power to earn his living. It is his right and his duty to make the best use of his opportunity, and if he fails he may fairly suffer the penalty of being treated as a pauper or even, in an extreme case, as a criminal. But the opportunity itself he cannot command with the same freedom. It is only within narrow limits that it comes within the sphere of his control. The opportunities of work and the remuneration for work are determined by a complex mass of social forces which no individual, certainly no individual workman, can shape. They can be controlled, if at all, by the organized action of the community, and therefore, by a just apportionment of responsibility, it is for the community to deal with them.

But this, it will be said, is not Liberalism but Socialism. Pursuing the economic rights of the individual we have been led to contemplate a Socialistic organization of industry. But a word like Socialism has many meanings, and it is possible that there should be a Liberal Socialism, as well as a Socialism that is illiberal. Let us, then, without sticking at a word, seek to follow out the Liberal view of the State in the sphere of economics. Let us try to determine in very general terms what is involved in realizing those primary conditions of industrial well-being which have been laid down, and how they consort with the rights of property and the claims of free industrial enterprise.

CHAPTER VIII

Economic Liberalism

There are two forms of Socialism with which Liberalism has nothing to do. These I will call the mechanical and the official. Mechanical Socialism is founded on a false interpretation of history. It attributes the phenomena of social life and development to the sole operation of the economic factor, whereas the beginning of sound sociology is to conceive society as a whole in which all the parts interact. The economic factor, to take a single point, is at least as much the effect as it is the cause of scientific invention. There would be no world-wide system of telegraphy if there was no need of world-wide inter-communication. But there would be no electric telegraph at all but for the scientific interest which determined the experiments of Gauss and Weber. Mechanical Socialism, further, is founded on a false economic analysis which attributes all value to labour, denying, con-founding or distorting the distinct functions of the direction of enter-prise, the unavoidable payment for the use of capital, the productivity of nature, and the very complex social forces which, by determining the movements of demand and supply actually fix the rates at which goods exchange with one another. Politically, mechanical Socialism supposes a class war, resting on a clear-cut distinction of classes which does not exist. Far from tending to clear and simple lines of cleavage, modern society exhibits a more and more complex inter-weaving of interests, and it is impossible for a modern revolutionist to assail 'property' in the interest of 'labour' without finding that half the 'labour' to which he appeals has a direct or indirect interest in 'property'. As to the future, mechanical Socialism conceives a logically developed system of the control of industry by government.

Of this all that need be said is that the construction of Utopias is not a sound method of social science; that this particular Utopia makes insufficient provision for liberty, movement, and growth; and that in order to bring his ideals into the region of practical discussion, what the Socialist needs is to formulate not a system to be substituted as a whole for our present arrangements but a principle to guide statesmanship in the practical work of reforming what is amiss and developing what is good in the actual fabric of industry. A principle so applied grows if it has seeds of good in it, and so in particular the collective control of industry will be extended in proportion as it is found in practice to yield good results. The fancied clearness of Utopian vision is illusory, because its objects are artificial ideas and not living facts. The 'system' of the world of books must be reconstructed as a principle that can be applied to the railway, the mine, the workshop, and the office that we know, before it can even be sensibly discussed. The evolution of Socialism as a practical force in politics has, in point of fact, proceeded by such a reconstruction, and this change carries with it the end of the materialistic Utopia.

Official Socialism is a creed of different brand. Beginning with a contempt for ideals of liberty based on a confusion between liberty and competition, it proceeds to a measure of contempt for average humanity in general. It conceives mankind as in the mass a helpless and feeble race, which it is its duty to treat kindly. True kindness, of course, must be combined with firmness, and the life of the average man must be organized for his own good. He need not know that he is being organized. The socialistic organization will work in the background, and there will be wheels within wheels, or rather wires pulling wires. Ostensibly there will be a class of the elect, an aristocracy of character and intellect which will fill the civil services and do the practical work of administration. Behind these will be committees of union and progress who will direct operations, and behind the committees again one or more master minds from whom will emanate the ideas that are to direct the world. The play of democratic government will go on for a time, but the idea of a common will that should actually undertake the organization of social life is held the most childish of illusions. The master minds can for the moment work more easily through democratic forms, because they are here, and to destroy them would cause an upheaval. But the essence of government lies in the method of capture. The ostensible leaders of democracy are ignorant creatures who can with a little management be set to walk in the way in which they should go, and whom the crowd will follow like sheep. The art of governing consists in making men do what you wish without knowing what they are doing, to lead them on without showing them whither until it is too late for them to retrace their steps. Socialism so conceived has in essentials nothing to do with democracy or with liberty. It is a scheme of the organization of life by the superior person, who will decide for each man how he should work, how he should live, and indeed, with the aid of the Eugenist, whether he should live at all or whether he has any business to be born. At any rate, if he ought not to have been born – if, that is, he comes of a stock whose qualities are not approved – the Samurai will take care that he does not perpetuate his race.

Now the average Liberal might have more sympathy with this view of life if he did not feel that for his part he is just a very ordinary man. He is quite sure that he cannot manage the lives of other people for them. He finds it enough to manage his own. But with the leave of the Superior he would rather do this in his own way than in the way of another, whose way may be much wiser but is not his. He would rather marry the woman of his own choice, than the one who would be sure to bring forth children of the standard type. He does not want to be standardized. He does not conceive himself as essentially an item in a census return. He does not want the standard clothes or the standard food, he wants the clothes which he finds comfortable and the food which he likes. With this unregenerate Adam in him, I fear that the Liberalism that is also within him is quite ready to make terms. Indeed, it incites him to go still further. It bids him consider that other men are, on the whole, very like himself and look on life in much the same way, and when it speaks within him of social duty it encourages him to aim not at a position of superiority which will enable him to govern his fellow creatures for their own good, but at a spirit of comradeship in which he will stand shoulder to shoulder with them on behalf of common aims.

If, then, there be such a thing as a Liberal Socialism – and whether there be is still a subject for inquiry – it must clearly fulfil two conditions. In the first place, it must be democratic. It must come from below, not from above. Or rather, it must emerge from the efforts of society as a whole to secure a fuller measure of justice, and a better organization of mutual aid. It must engage the efforts and respond to the genuine desires not of a handful of superior beings, but of great masses of men. And, secondly, and for that very reason, it must make its account with the human individual. It must give the average man free play in the personal life for which he really cares. It must be founded on liberty, and must make not for the suppression but for the development of personality. How far, it may be asked, are these objects compatible? How far is it possible to organize industry in the interest of the common welfare without either overriding the freedom of individual choice or drying up the springs of initiative and energy? How far is it possible to abolish poverty, or to institute economic equality without arresting industrial progress? We cannot put the question without raising more fundamental issues. What is the real meaning of 'equality' in economics? Would it mean, for example, that all should enjoy equal rewards, or that equal efforts should enjoy equal rewards, or that equal attainments should enjoy equal rewards? What is the province of justice in economics? Where does justice end and charity begin? And what, behind all this, is the basis of property? What is its social function and value? What is the measure of consideration due to vested interest and prescriptive right? It is impossible, within the limits of a volume, to deal exhaustively with such fundamental questions. The best course will be to follow out the lines of development which appear to proceed from those principles of Liberalism which have been already indicated and to see how far they lead to a solution.

We saw that it was the duty of the State to secure the conditions of self-maintenance for the normal healthy citizen. There are two lines along which the fulfilment of this duty may be sought. One would consist in providing access to the means of production, the other in guaranteeing to the individual a certain share in the common stock. In point of fact, both lines have been followed by Liberal legislation. On the one side this legislation has set itself, however timidly and ineffectively as yet, to reversing the process which divorced the English peasantry from the soil. Contemporary research is making it clear that this divorce was not the inevitable result of slowly operating economic forces. It was brought about by the deliberate policy of the enclosure of the common fields begun in the fifteenth century, partially arrested from the middle of the sixteenth to the eighteenth, and completed between the reigns of George II and Queen Victoria. As this process was furthered by an aristocracy, so there is every reason to hope that it can be successfully reversed by a democracy, and that it will be possible to reconstitute a class of independent peasantry as the backbone of the working population. The experiment, however, involves one form or another of communal ownership. The labourer can only obtain the land with the financial help of the State, and it is certainly not the view of Liberals that the State, having once regained the fee simple,[18] should part with it again. On the contrary, in an equitable division of the fruits of agriculture all advantages that are derived from the qualities or position of the soil itself, or from the enhancement of prices by tariffs would, since they are the product of no man's labour, fall to no man's share, or, what is the same thing, they should fall to every man, that is, to the community. This is why Liberal legislation seeks to create a class not of small landlords but of small tenants. It would give to this class access to the land and would reward them with the fruits of their own work – and no more. The surplus it would take to itself in the form of rent, and while it is desirable to give the State tenant full security against disturbance, rents must at stated periods be adjustable to prices and to cost. So, while Conservative policy is to establish a peasant proprietary which would reinforce the voting strength of property, the Liberal policy is to establish a State tenantry from whose prosperity the whole community would profit. The one solution is individualist. The other, as far as it goes, is nearer to the Socialist ideal.

But, though British agriculture may have a great future before it, it will never regain its dominant position in our economic life, nor are small holdings ever likely to be the prevalent form of agriculture. The bulk of industry is, and probably will be, more and more in the hands of large undertakings with which the individual workman could not compete whatever instruments of production were placed in his hands. For the mass of the people, therefore, to be assured of the means of a decent livelihood must mean to be assured of continuous employment at a living wage, or, as an alternative, of public assistance. Now, as has been remarked, experience goes to show that the wage of the average worker, as fixed by competition, is not and is not likely to become sufficient to cover all the fortunes and misfortunes of

[18] 'fee simple': 'an estate in land, etc. belonging to the owner and his heirs for ever, without limitation to any particular class of heirs' (*OED*).

life, to provide for sickness, accident, unemployment and old age, in addition to the regular needs of an average family. In the case of accident the State has put the burden of making provision on the employer. In the case of old age it has, acting, as I think, upon a sounder principle, taken the burden upon itself. It is very important to realize precisely what the new departure involved in the Old Age Pensions Act amounted to in point of principle. The Poor Law already guaranteed the aged person and the poor in general against actual starvation. But the Poor Law came into operation only at the point of sheer destitution. It failed to help those who had helped themselves. Indeed, to many it held out little inducement to help themselves if they could not hope to lay by so much as would enable them to live more comfortably on their means than they would live in the workhouse. The pension system throws over the test of destitution. It provides a certain minimum, a basis to go upon, a foundation upon which independent thrift may hope to build up a sufficiency. It is not a narcotic but a stimulus to self help and to friendly aid or filial support, and it is, up to a limit, available for all alike. It is precisely one of the conditions of independence of which voluntary effort can make use, but requiring voluntary effort to make it fully available.

The suggestion underlying the movement for the break up of the Poor Law is just the general application of this principle. It is that, instead of redeeming the destitute, we should seek to render generally available the means of avoiding destitution, though in doing so we should uniformly call on the individual for a corresponding effort on his part. One method of meeting these conditions is to supply a basis for private effort to work upon, as is done in the case of the aged. Another method is that of State-aided insurance, and on these lines Liberal legislators have been experimenting in the hope of dealing with sickness, invalidity, and one portion of the problem of unemployment. A third may be illustrated by the method by which the Minority of the Poor Law Commissioners[19] would deal with the case, at present

---

[19] The two reports issued by the members of Royal Commission on the Poor Laws (1905–9) were in substantial agreement as to the diagnosis of deficiencies in the administration of public assistance; however, while the majority called for a serious reform of the Poor Laws, the minority report (signed by Beatrice Webb and three other dissenting members) advocated abolition of the Poor Law system and the distribution of its functions to other agencies.

so often full of tragic import, of the widowed or deserted mother of young children. Hitherto she has been regarded as an object of charity. It has been a matter for the benevolent to help her to retain her home, while it has been regarded as her duty to keep 'off the rates' at the cost of no matter what expenditure of labour away from home. The newer conception of rights and duties comes out clearly in the argument of the commissioners, that if we take in earnest all that we say of the duties and responsibilities of motherhood, we shall recognize that the mother of young children is doing better service to the community and one more worthy of pecuniary remuneration when she stays at home and minds her children than when she goes out charing and leaves them to the chances of the street or to the perfunctory care of a neighbour. In proportion as we realize the force of this argument, we reverse our view as to the nature of public assistance in such a case. We no longer consider it desirable to drive the mother out to her charing work if we possibly can, nor do we consider her degraded by receiving public money. We cease, in fact, to regard the public money as a dole, we treat it as a payment for a civic service, and the condition that we are inclined to exact is precisely that she should not endeavour to add to it by earning wages, but rather that she should keep her home respectable and bring up her children in health and happiness.

In defence of the competitive system two arguments have been familiar from old days. One is based on the habits of the working classes. It is said that they spend their surplus incomes on drink, and that if they have no margin for saving, it is because they have sunk it in the public-house. That argument is rapidly being met by the actual change of habits. The wave of temperance which two generations ago reformed the habits of the well-to-do in England is rapidly spreading through all classes in our own time. The drink bill is still excessive, the proportion of his weekly wages spent on drink by the average workman is still too great, but it is a diminishing quantity, and the fear which might have been legitimately expressed in old days that to add to wages was to add to the drink bill could no longer be felt as a valid objection to any improvement in the material condition of the working population in our own time. We no longer find the drink bill heavily increasing in years of commercial prosperity as of old. The second argument has experienced an even more decisive fate. Down to my own time it was forcibly contended that any improvement in the material condition of the mass of the people would result in an increase of the birth rate which, by extending the supply of labour, would bring down wages by an automatic process to the old level. There would be more people and they would all be as miserable as before. The actual decline of the birth rate, whatever its other consequences may be, has driven this argument from the field. The birth rate does not increase with prosperity, but diminishes. There is no fear of over-population; if there is any present danger, it is upon the other side. The fate of these two arguments must be reckoned as a very important factor in the changes of opinion which we have noted.

Nevertheless, it may be thought that the system that I have outlined is no better than a vast organization of State charity, and that as such it must carry the consequences associated with charity on a large scale. It must dry up the sources of energy and undermine the independence of the individual. On the first point, I have already referred to certain cogent arguments for a contrary view. What the State is doing, what it would be doing if the whole series of contemplated changes were carried through to the end, would by no means suffice to meet the needs of the normal man. He would still have to labour to earn his own living. But he would have a basis to go upon, a substructure on which it would be possible for him to rear the fabric of a real sufficiency. He would have greater security, a brighter outlook, a more confident hope of being able to keep his head above water. The experience of life suggests that hope is a better stimulus than fear, confidence a better mental environment than insecurity. If desperation will sometimes spur men to exceptional exertion the effect is fleeting, and, for a permanence, a more stable condition is better suited to foster that blend of restraint and energy which makes up the tissue of a life of normal health. There would be those who would abuse their advantages as there are those who abuse every form of social institution. But upon the whole it is thought that individual responsibility can be more clearly fixed and more rigorously insisted on when its legitimate sphere is properly defined, that is to say, when the burden on the shoulders of the individual is not too great for average human nature to bear.

But, it may be urged, any reliance on external assistance is destructive of independence. It is true that to look for support to private philanthropy has this effect, because it makes one man dependent on the good graces of another. But it is submitted that a form of support on which a man can count as a matter of legal right has not necessarily the same effect. Charity, again, tends to diminish the value of independent effort because it flows in the direction of the failures. It is a compensation for misfortune which easily slides into an encouragement to carelessness. What is matter of right, on the other hand, is enjoyed equally by the successful and the unsuccessful. It is not a handicap in favour of the one, but an equal distance deducted from the race to be run against fate by both. This brings us to the real question. Are measures of the kind under discussion to be regarded as measures of philanthropy or measures of justice, as the expression of collective benevolence or as the recognition of a general right? The full discussion of the question involves complex and in some respects novel conceptions of economics and of social ethics to which I can hardly do justice within the limits of this chapter. But I will endeavour to indicate in outline the conception of social and economic justice which underlies the movement of modern Liberal opinion.

We may approach the subject by observing that, whatever the legal theory, in practice the existing English Poor Law recognizes the right of every person to the bare necessaries of life. The destitute man or woman can come to a public authority, and the public authority is bound to give him food and shelter. He has to that extent a lien on the public resources in virtue of his needs as a human being and on no other ground. This lien, however, only operates when he is destitute; and he can only exercise it by submitting to such conditions as the authorities impose, which when the workhouse test is enforced means loss of liberty. It was the leading 'principle of 1834' that the lot of the pauper should be made 'less eligible' than that of the independent labourer. Perhaps we may express the change of opinion which has come about in our day by saying that according to the newer principle the duty of society is rather to ensure that the lot of the independent labourer be more eligible than that of the pauper. With this object the lien on the common wealth is enlarged and reconstituted. Its exercise does not entail the penal consequence of the loss of freedom unless there is proved misfeasance or neglect on the part of the individual. The underlying contention is that, in a State so wealthy as the United Kingdom, every citizen should have full means of earning by socially useful labour so much material support as experience proves to be the necessary basis of a healthy, civilized existence. And if in the actual working of the industrial system the means are not in actual fact sufficiently available he is held to have a claim not as of charity but as of right on the national resources to make good the deficiency.

That there are rights of property we all admit. Is there not perhaps a general right *to* property? Is there not something radically wrong with an economic system under which through the laws of inheritance and bequest vast inequalities are perpetuated? Ought we to acquiesce in a condition in which the great majority are born to nothing except what they can earn, while some are born to more than the social value of any individual of whatever merit? May it not be that in a reasoned scheme of economic ethics we should have to allow a true right of property in the member of the community as such which would take the form of a certain minimum claim on the public resources? A pretty idea, it may be said, but ethics apart, what are the resources on which the less fortunate is to draw? The British State has little or no collective property available for any such purpose. Its revenues are based on taxation, and in the end what all this means is that the rich are to be taxed for the benefit of the poor, which we may be told is neither justice nor charity but sheer spoliation. To this I would reply that the depletion of public resources is a symptom of profound economic disorganization. Wealth, I would contend, has a social as well as a personal basis. Some forms of wealth, such as ground rents in and about cities, are substantially the creation of society, and it is only through the misfeasance of government in times past that such wealth has been allowed to fall into private hands. Other great sources of wealth are found in financial and speculative operations, often of distinctly anti-social tendency and possible only through the defective organization of our economy. Other causes rest in the partial monopolies which our liquor laws, on the one side, and the old practice of allowing the supply of municipal services to fall into private hands have built up. Through the principle of inherit-ance, property so accumulated is handed on; and the result is that while there is a small class born to the inheritance of a share in the material benefits of civilization, there is a far larger class which can say 'naked we enter, naked we leave'. This system, as a whole, it is maintained, requires revision. Property in this condition of things ceases, it is urged, to be essentially an institution by which each man can secure to himself the fruits of his own labour, and becomes an instrument whereby the owner can command the labour of others on terms which he is in general able to dictate. This tendency is held to be undesirable, and to be capable of a remedy through a concerted series of fiscal, industrial, and social measures which would have the effect of augmenting the common stock at the disposal of society, and so applying it as to secure the economic independence of all who do not forfeit their advantages by idleness, incapacity, or crime. There are early forms of communal society in which each person is born to his appropriate status, carrying its appropriate share of the common land. In destroying the last relics of this system economic individualism has laid the basis of great material advances, but at great cost to the happiness of the masses. The ground problem in economics is not to destroy property, but to restore the social conception of property to its right place under conditions suitable to modern needs. This is not to be done by crude measures of redistribution, such as those of which we hear in ancient history. It is to be done by distinguishing the social from the individual factors in wealth, by bringing the elements of social wealth into the public coffers, and by holding it at the disposal of society to administer to the prime needs of its members.

The basis of property is social, and that in two senses. On the one hand, it is the organized force of society that maintains the rights of owners by protecting them against thieves and depredators. In spite of all criticism many people still seem to speak of the rights of property as though they were conferred by Nature or by Providence upon certain fortunate individuals, and as though these individuals had an unlimited right to command the State, as their servant, to secure them by the free use of the machinery of law in the undisturbed enjoyment of their possessions. They forget that without the organized force of society their rights are not worth a week's purchase. They do not ask themselves where they would be without the judge and the policeman and the settled order which society maintains. The prosperous business man who thinks that he has made his fortune entirely by self help does not pause to consider what single step he could have taken on the road to his success but for the ordered tranquillity which has made commercial development possible, the security by road, and rail, and sea, the masses of skilled labour, and the sum of intelligence which civilization has placed at his disposal, the very demand for the goods which he produces which the general progress of the world has created, the inventions which he uses as a matter of course and which have been built up by the collective effort of generations of men of science and organizers of industry. If he dug to the foundations of his fortune he would recognize that, as it is society that maintains and guarantees his possessions, so also it is society which is an indispensable partner in its original creation.

This brings us to the second sense in which property is social. There is a social element in value and a social element in production. In modern industry there is very little that the individual can do by his unaided efforts. Labour is minutely divided; and in proportion as it is divided it is forced to be co-operative. Men produce goods to sell, and the rate of exchange, that is, price, is fixed by relations of demand and supply the rates of which are determined by complex social forces. In the methods of production every man makes use, to the best of his ability, of the whole available means of civilization, of the machinery which the brains of other men have devised, of the human apparatus which is the gift of acquired civilization. Society thus provides conditions or opportunities of which one man will make much better use than another, and the use to which they are put is the individual or personal element in production which is the basis of the personal claim to reward. To maintain and stimulate this personal effort is a necessity of good economic organization, and without asking here whether any particular conception of Socialism would or would not meet this need we may lay down with confidence that no form of Socialism which should ignore it could possibly enjoy enduring success. On the other hand, an individualism which ignores the social factor in wealth will deplete the national resources, deprive the community of its just share in the fruits of industry and so result in a one-sided and inequitable distribution of wealth. Economic justice is to render what is due not only to each individual but to each function, social or personal, that is engaged in the performance of useful service, and this due is measured by the amount necessary to stimulate and maintain the efficient exercise of that useful function. This equation between function and sustenance is the true meaning of economic equality.

Now to apply this principle to the adjustment of the claims of the community on the one hand and the producers or inheritors of wealth on the other would involve a discrimination of the factors of production which is not easy to make in all instances. If we take the case of urban land, referred to above, the distinction is tolerably clear. The value of a site in London is something due essentially to London, not to the landlord. More accurately a part of it is due to London, a part to the British empire, a part, perhaps we should say, to Western civilization. But while it would be impossible to disentangle these subsidiary factors, the main point that the entire increment of value is due to one social factor or another is sufficiently clear, and this explains why Liberal opinion has fastened on the conception of site value as being by right communal and not personal property. The monopoly value of licensed premises, which is the direct creation of laws passed for the control of the liquor traffic, is another case in point. The difficulty which society finds in dealing with these cases is that it has allowed these sources of wealth to pass out of its hands, and that property of these kinds has freely passed from one man to another in the market, in the belief that it stood and would stand on the same basis in law as any other. Hence, it is not possible for society to insist on the whole of its claim. It could only resume its full rights at the cost of great hardship to individuals and a shock to the industrial system. What it can do is to shift taxation step by step from the wealth due to individual enterprise to the wealth that depends on its own collective progress, thus by degrees regaining the ownership of the fruits of its own collective work.

Much more difficult in principle is the question of the more general elements of social value which run through production as a whole. We are dealing here with factors so intricately interwoven in their operation that they can only be separated by an indirect process. What this process would be we may best understand by imagining for a moment a thoroughgoing centralized organization of the industrial system endeavouring to carry out the principles of remuneration outlined above. The central authority which we imagine as endowed with such wisdom and justice as to find for every man his right place and to assign to every man his due reward would, if our argument is sound, find it necessary to assign to each producer, whether working with hand or brain, whether directing a department of industry or serving under direction, such remuneration as would stimulate him to put forth his best efforts and would maintain him in the condition necessary for the life-long exercise of his function. If we are right in considering that a great part of the wealth produced from year to year is of social origin, it would follow that, after the assignment of this remuneration, there would remain a surplus, and this would fall to the coffers of the community and be available for public purposes, for national defence, public works, education, charity, and the furtherance of civilized life.

Now, this is merely an imaginary picture, and I need not ask whether such a measure of wisdom on the part of a Government is practically attainable, or whether such a measure of centralization might not carry consequences which would hamper progress in other directions. The picture serves merely to illustrate the principles of equitable distribution by which the State should be guided in dealing with property. It serves to define our conception of economic justice, and therewith the lines on which we should be guided in the adjustment of taxation and the reorganization of industry. I may illustrate its bearing by taking a couple of cases.

One important source of private wealth under modern conditions is speculation. Is this also a source of social wealth? Does it produce anything for society? Does it perform a function for which our ideal administration would think it necessary to pay? I buy some railway stock at 110. A year or two later I seize a favourable opportunity and sell it at 125. Is the increment earned or unearned? The answer in the single case is clear, but it may be said that my good fortune in this case may be balanced by ill luck in another. No doubt. But, to go no further, if on balance I make a fortune or an income by this method it would seem to be a fortune or an income not earned by productive service. To this it may be replied that the buyers and sellers of stocks are indirectly performing the function of adjusting demand and supply, and so regulating industry. So far as they are expert business men trained in the knowledge of a particular market this may be so. So far as they dabble in the market in the hope of profiting from a favourable turn, they appear rather as gamblers. I will not pretend to determine which of the two is the larger class. I would point out only that, on the face of the facts, the profits derived from this particular source appear to be rather of the nature of a tax which astute or fortunate individuals are able to levy on the producer than as the reward which they obtain for a definite contribution on their own part to production. There are two possible empirical tests of this view. One is that a form of collective organization should be devised which should diminish the importance of the speculative market. Our principle would suggest the propriety of an attempt in that direction whenever opportunity offers. Another would be the imposition of a special tax on incomes derived from this source, and experience would rapidly show whether any such tax would actually hamper the process of production and distribution at any stage. If not, it would justify itself. It would prove that the total profit now absorbed by individuals exceeds, at least by the amount of the tax, the remuneration necessary to maintain that particular economic function.

The other case I will take is that of inherited wealth. This is the main determining factor in the social and economic structure of our time. It is clear on our principle that it stands in quite a different position from that of wealth which is being created from day to day. It can be defended only on two grounds. One is prescriptive right, and the difficulty of disturbing the basis of the economic order. This provides an unanswerable argument against violent and hasty methods, but no argument at all against a gentle and slow-moving policy of economic reorganization. The other argument is that inherited wealth serves several indirect functions. The desire to provide for children and to found a family is a stimulus to effort. The existence of a leisured class affords possibilities for the free development of originality, and a supply of disinterested men and women for the service of the State. I would suggest once again that the only real test to which the value of these arguments can be submitted is the empirical test. On the face of the facts inherited wealth stands on a different footing from acquired wealth, and Liberal policy is on the right lines in beginning the discrimination of earned from unearned income. The distinction is misconceived only so far as income derived from capital or land may represent the savings of the individual and not his inheritance. The true distinction is between the inherited and the acquired, and while the taxation of acquired wealth may operate, so far as it goes, to diminish the profits, and so far to weaken the motive springs, of industry, it is by no means self-evident that any increase of taxation on inherited wealth would necessarily have that effect, or that it would vitally derange any other social function. It is, again, a matter on which only experience can decide, but if experience goes to show that we can impose a given tax on inherited wealth without diminishing the available supply of capital and without losing any service of value, the result would be net gain. The State could never be the sole producer, for in production the personal factor is vital, but there is no limit set by the necessities of things to the extension of its control of natural resources, on the one hand, and the accumulated heritage of the past, on the other.

If Liberal policy has committed itself not only to the discrimination of earned and unearned incomes but also to a super-tax on large incomes from whatever source, the ground principle, again, I take to be a respectful doubt whether any single individual is worth to society by any means as much as some individuals obtain. We might, indeed, have to qualify this doubt if the great fortunes of the world fell to the great geniuses. It would be impossible to determine what we ought to pay for a Shakespere, a Browning, a Newton, or a Cobden. Impossible, but fortunately unnecessary. For the man of genius is forced by his own cravings to give, and the only reward that he asks from society is to be let alone and have some quiet and fresh air. Nor is he in reality entitled, notwithstanding his services, to ask more than the modest sufficiency which enables him to obtain those primary needs of the life of thought and creation, since his creative energy is the response to an inward stimulus which goads him on without regard to the wishes of any one else. The case of the great organizers of industry is rather different, but they, again, so far as their work is socially sound, are driven on more by internal necessity than by the genuine love of gain. They make great profits because their works reach a scale at which, if the balance is on the right side at all, it is certain to be a big balance, and they no doubt tend to be interested in money as the sign of their success, and also as the basis of increased social power. But I believe the direct influence of the lust of gain on this type of mind to have been immensely exaggerated; and as proof I would refer, first, to the readiness of many men of this class to accept and in individual cases actively to promote measures tending to diminish their material gain, and, secondly, to the mass of high business capacity which is at the command of the public administration for salaries which, as their recipient must be perfectly conscious, bear no relation to the income which it would be open to him to earn in commercial competition.

On the whole, then, we may take it that the principle of the super-tax is based on the conception that when we come to an income of some £5,000 a year we approach the limit of the industrial value of the individual.' We are not likely to discourage any service of genuine

---

' It is true that so long as it remains possible for a certain order of ability to earn £50,000 a year, the community will not obtain its services for £5,000. But if things

social value by a rapidly increasing surtax on incomes above that amount. It is more likely that we shall quench the anti-social ardour for unmeasured wealth, for social power, and the vanity of display.

These illustrations may suffice to give some concreteness to the conception of economic justice as the maintenance of social function. They serve also to show that the true resources of the State are larger and more varied than is generally supposed. The true function of taxation is to secure to society the element in wealth that is of social origin, or, more broadly, all that does not owe its origin to the efforts of living individuals. When taxation, based on these principles, is utilized to secure healthy conditions of existence to the mass of the people it is clear that this is no case of robbing Peter to pay Paul. Peter is not robbed. Apart from the tax it is he who would be robbing the State. A tax which enables the State to secure a certain share of social value is not something deducted from that which the taxpayer has an unlimited right to call his own, but rather a repayment of something which was all along due to society.

But why should the proceeds of the tax go to the poor in particular? Granting that Peter is not robbed, why should Paul be paid? Why should not the proceeds be expended on something of common concern to Peter and Paul alike, for Peter is equally a member of the community? Undoubtedly the only just method of dealing with the common funds is to expend them in objects which subserve the common good, and there are many directions in which public expenditure does in fact benefit all classes alike. This, it is worth noting, is true even of some important branches of expenditure which in their direct aim concern the poorer classes. Consider, for example, the value of public sanitation, not merely to the poorer regions which would suffer first if it were withheld, but to the richer as well who, seclude themselves as they may, cannot escape infection. In the old days judge and jury, as well as prisoners, would die of gaol fever. Consider, again, the economic value of education, not only to the worker, but to the employer whom he will serve. But when all this is allowed for it must be admitted that we have throughout contemplated a considerable measure of public expenditure in the elimina-

should be so altered by taxation and economic reorganization that £5,000 became in practice the highest limit attainable, and remained attainable even for the ablest only by effort, there is no reason to doubt that that effort would be forthcoming. It is not the absolute amount of remuneration, but the increment of remuneration in proportion to the output of industrial or commercial capacity, which serves as the needed stimulus to energy.

tion of poverty. The prime justification of this expenditure is that the prevention of suffering from the actual lack of adequate physical comforts is an essential element in the common good, an object in which all are bound to concern themselves, which all have the right to demand and the duty to fulfil. Any common life based on the avoidable suffering even of one of those who partake in it is a life not of harmony, but of discord.

But we can go further. We said at the outset that the function of society was to secure to all normal adult members the means of earning by useful work the material necessaries of a healthy and efficient life. We can see now that this is one case and, properly understood, the largest and most far reaching case falling under the general principle of economic justice. This principle lays down that every social function must receive the reward that is sufficient to stimulate and maintain it through the life of the individual. Now, how much this reward may be in any case it is probably impossible to determine otherwise than by specific experiment. But if we grant, in accordance with the idea with which we have been working all along, that it is demanded of all sane adult men and women that they should live as civilized beings, as industrious workers, as good parents, as orderly and efficient citizens, it is, on the other side, the function of the economic organization of society to secure them the material means of living such a life, and the immediate duty of society is to mark the points at which such means fail and to make good the deficiency. Thus the conditions of social efficiency mark the minimum of industrial remuneration, and if they are not secured without the deliberate action of the State they must be secured by means of the deliberate action of the State. If it is the business of good economic organization to secure the equation between function and maintenance, the first and greatest application of this principle is to the primary needs. These fix the minimum standard of remuneration beyond which we require detailed experiment to tell us at what rate increased value of service rendered necessitates corresponding increase of reward.

It may be objected that such a standard is unattainable. There are those, it may be contended, who are not, and never will be, worth a full efficiency wage. Whatever is done to secure them such a remuneration will only involve net loss. Hence it violates our standard of economic justice. It involves payment for a function of more than it is actually worth, and the discrepancy might be so great as to cripple society. It must, of course, be admitted that the population contains a certain percentage of the physically incapable, the mentally defective, and the morally uncontrolled. The treatment of these classes, all must agree, is and must be based on other principles than those of economics. One class requires punitive discipline, another needs life-long care, a third – the mentally and morally sound but physically defective – must depend, to its misfortune, on private and public charity. There is no question here of payment for a function, but of ministering to human suffering. It is, of course, desirable on economic as well as on broader grounds that the ministration should be so conceived as to render its object as nearly as possible independent and self-supporting. But in the main all that is done for these classes of the population is, and must be, a charge on the surplus. The real question that may be raised by a critic is whether the considerable proportion of the working class whose earnings actually fall short, as we should contend, of the minimum, could in point of fact earn that minimum. Their actual value, he may urge, is measured by the wage which they do in fact command in the competitive market, and if their wage falls short of the standard society may make good the deficiency if it will and can, but must not shut its eyes to the fact that in doing so it is performing, not an act of economic justice, but of charity. To this the reply is that the price which naked labour without property can command in bargaining with employers who possess property is no measure at all of the addition which such labour can actually make to wealth. The bargain is unequal, and low remuneration is itself a cause of low efficiency which in turn tends to react unfavourably on remuneration. Conversely, a general improvement in the conditions of life reacts favourably on the productivity of labour. Real wages have risen considerably in the last half century, but the income-tax returns indicate that the wealth of the business and professional man has increased even more rapidly. Up to the efficiency minimum there is, then, every reason to think that a general increase of wages would positively increase the available surplus whether that surplus goes to individuals as profits or to the State as national revenue. The material improvement of working-class conditions will more than pay its way regarded purely as an economic investment on behalf of society.

This conclusion is strengthened if we consider narrowly what elements of cost the 'living wage' ought in principle to cover. We are apt to assume uncritically that the wages earned by the labour of an adult man ought to suffice for the maintenance of an average family, providing for all risks. It ought, we think, to cover not only the food and clothing of wife and children, but the risks of sickness, accident, and unemployment. It ought to provide for education and lay by for old age. If it fails we are apt to think that the wage earner is not self-supporting. Now, it is certainly open to doubt whether the actual addition to wealth made by an unskilled labourer denuded of all inherited property would equal the cost represented by the sum of these items. But here our further principle comes into play. He ought not to be denuded of all inherited property. As a citizen he should have a certain share in the social inheritance. This share should be his support in the times of misfortune, of sickness, and of worklessness, whether due to economic disorganization or to invalidity and old age. His children's share, again, is the State-provided education. These shares are charges on the social surplus. It does not, if fiscal arrangements are what they should be, infringe upon the income of other individuals, and the man who without further aid than the universally available share in the social inheritance which is to fall to him as a citizen pays his way through life is to be justly regarded as self-supporting.

The central point of Liberal economics, then, is the equation of social service and reward. This is the principle that every function of social value requires such remuneration as serves to stimulate and maintain its effective performance; that every one who performs such a function has the right, in the strict ethical sense of that term, to such remuneration and to no more; that the residue of existing wealth should be at the disposal of the community for social purposes. Further, it is the right, in the same sense, of every person capable of performing some useful social function that he should have the opportunity of so doing, and it is his right that the remuneration that he receives for it should be his property, *i.e.* that it should stand at his free disposal enabling him to direct his personal concerns according to his own preferences. These are rights in the sense that they are conditions of the welfare of its members which a well-ordered State will seek by every means to fulfil. But it is not suggested that the way of such fulfilment is plain, or that it could be achieved at a stroke by a revolutionary change in the tenure of property or the system of industry. It is, indeed, implied that the State is vested with a certain overlordship over property in general and a supervisory power over industry in general, and this principle of economic sovereignty may be set side by side with that of economic justice as a no less fundamental conception of economic Liberalism. For here, as elsewhere, liberty implies control. But the manner in which the State is to exercise its controlling power is to be learnt by experience and even in large measure by cautious experiment. We have sought to determine the principle which should guide its action, the ends at which it is to aim. The systematic study of the means lies rather within the province of economics; and the teaching of history seems to be that progress is more continuous and secure when men are content to deal with problems piecemeal than when they seek to destroy root and branch in order to erect a complete system which has captured the imagination.

It is evident that these conceptions embody many of the ideas that go to make up the framework of Socialist teaching, though they also emphasize elements of individual right and personal independence, of which Socialism at times appears oblivious. The distinction that I would claim for economic Liberalism is that it seeks to do justice to the social and individual factors in industry alike, as opposed to an abstract Socialism which emphasizes the one side and an abstract Individualism which leans its whole weight on the other. By keeping to the conception of harmony as our clue we constantly define the rights of the individual in terms of the common good, and think of the common good in terms of the welfare of all the individuals who constitute a society. Thus in economics we avoid the confusion of liberty with competition, and see no virtue in the right of a man to get the better of others. At the same time we are not led to minimize the share of personal initiative, talent, or energy in production, but are free to contend for their claim to adequate recognition. A Socialist who is convinced of the logical coherence and practical applicability of his system may dismiss such endeavours to harmonize divergent claims as a half-hearted and illogical series of compromises. It is equally possible that a Socialist who conceives Socialism as consisting in essence in the co-operative organization of industry by consumers, and is convinced that the full solution of industrial problems lies in that direction, should in proportion as he considers the psychological factors in production and investigates the means of realizing his ideal, find himself working back along the path to a point where he will meet the men who are grappling with the problems of the day on the principles here suggested, and will find himself able to move forward in practice in the front ranks of economic Liberalism. If this is so, the growing co-operation of political Liberalism and Labour, which in the last few years has replaced the antagonism of the 'nineties, is no mere accident of temporary political convenience, but has its roots deep in the necessities of Democracy.

CHAPTER IX

The Future of Liberalism

The nineteenth century might be called the age of Liberalism, yet its close saw the fortunes of that great movement brought to their lowest ebb. Whether at home or abroad those who represented Liberal ideas had suffered crushing defeats. But this was the least considerable of the causes for anxiety. If Liberals had been defeated, something much worse seemed about to befall Liberalism. Its faith in itself was waxing cold. It seemed to have done its work. It had the air of a creed that is becoming fossilized as an extinct form, a fossil that occupied, moreover, an awkward position between two very active and energetically moving grindstones – the upper grindstone of plutocratic imperialism, and the nether grindstone of social democracy. 'We know all about you', these parties seemed to say to Liberalism; 'we have been right through you and come out on the other side. Respectable platitudes, you go maundering on about Cobden and Gladstone, and the liberty of the individual, and the rights of nationality, and government by the people. What you say is not precisely untrue, but it is unreal and uninteresting.' So far in chorus. 'It is not up to date', finished the Imperialist, and the Socialist bureaucrat. 'It is not bread and butter', finished the Social democrat. Opposed in everything else, these two parties agreed in one thing. They were to divide the future between them. Unfortunately, however, for their agreement, the division was soon seen to be no equal one. Whatever might be the ultimate recuperative power of Social Democracy, for the time being, in the paralysis of Liberalism, the Imperial reaction had things all to itself. The governing classes of England were to assert themselves. They were to consolidate the

Empire, incidentally passing the steam roller over two obstructive republics.[20] They were to 'teach the law' to the 'sullen new-caught peoples' abroad. They were to re-establish the Church at home by the endowment of doctrinal education. At the same time they were to establish the liquor interest – which is, after all, the really potent instrument of government from above. They were to bind the colonies to us by ties of fiscal preference, and to establish the great commercial interests on the basis of protection. Their government, as conceived by the best exponents of the new doctrine, was by no means to be indifferent to the humanitarian claims of the social conscience. They were to deal out factory acts, and establish wages boards. They were to make an efficient and a disciplined people. In the idea of discipline the military element rapidly assumed a greater prominence. But on this side the evolution of opinion passed through two well-marked phases. The first was the period of optimism and expansion. The Englishman was the born ruler of the world. He might hold out a hand of friendship to the German and the American, whom he recognized as his kindred and who lived within the law. The rest of the world was peopled by dying nations whose manifest destiny was to be 'administered' by the coming races, and exploited by their commercial syndicates. This mood of optimism did not survive the South African War. It received its death-blow at Colenso and Magersfontein,[21] and within a few years fear had definitely taken the place of ambition as the mainspring of the movement to national and imperial consolidation. The Tariff Reform movement[22] was largely inspired by a sense of insecurity in our commercial position. The half-patronizing friendship for Germany rapidly gave way, first to commercial jealousy, and then to unconcealed alarm for our national safety. All the powers of society were bent on lavish naval expenditure, and of imposing the idea of compulsory service on a reluctant people. The disciplined nation was needed no longer to dominate the world, but to maintain its own territory.

[20] The 'two obstructive republics' were the Boer republics, the Transvaal and the Orange Free State.

[21] British forces suffered serious defeats at Colenso and Magersfontein in 1899, during the early stages of the war with the Boer Republics.

[22] Starting in 1903, Tariff Reformers led by Joseph Chamberlain conducted a vigorous campaign in favour of a system of preferential tariffs to protect British industry and encourage Imperial unity. Tariff Reform became official Unionist policy in 1907, and remained at the centre of political argument until eclipsed by the Irish crisis in 1913.

Now, we are not concerned here to follow up the devious windings of modern Conservatism. We have to note only that what modern democracy has to face is no mere inertia of tradition. It is a distinct reactionary policy with a definite and not incoherent creed of its own, an ideal which in its best expression – for example, in the daily comments of the *Morning Post* – is certain to exercise a powerful attraction on many generous minds – the ideal of the efficient, disciplined nation, centre and dominating force of a powerful, self-contained, militant empire. What concerns us more particularly is the reaction of Conservative development upon the fortunes of democracy. But to understand this reaction, and, indeed, to make any sound estimate of the present position and prospects of Liberalism, we must cast a rapid glance over the movement of progressive thought during the last generation. When Gladstone formed his second Government in 1880 the old party system stood secure in Great Britain. It was only a band of politicians from the other side of St George's Channel[23] who disowned both the great allegiances. For the British political mind the plain distinction of Liberal and Conservative held the field, and the division was not yet a class distinction. The great Whig families held their place, and they of the aristocratic houses divided the spoil. But a new leaven was at work. The prosperity which had culminated in 1872 was passing away. Industrial progress slowed down; and, though the advance from the 'Hungry 'Forties' had been immense, men began to see the limit of what they could reasonably expect from retrenchment and Free Trade. The work of Mr Henry George awakened new interest in problems of poverty, and the idealism of William Morris gave new inspiration to Socialist propaganda. Meanwhile, the teaching of Green and the enthusiasm of Toynbee were setting Liberalism free from the shackles of an individualist conception of liberty and paving the way for the legislation of our own time. Lastly, the Fabian Society brought Socialism down from heaven and established a contact with practical politics and municipal government. Had Great Britain been an island in the mid-Pacific the onward movement would have been rapid and undeviating in its course. As it was, the new ideas were reflected in the parliament and the cabinet of 1880–5, and the Radicalism of Birmingham barely kept on terms with the Whiggery of the clubs. A redistribution of social forces which would amalgamate the interests of 'property' on

<hr />

[23] St George's Channel: the strait which separates Ireland from Wales.

the one side and those of democracy on the other was imminent, and on social questions democracy reinforced by the enfranchisement of the rural labourers in 1884 stood to win. At this stage the Irish question came to a head. Mr Gladstone declared for Home Rule, and the party fissure took place on false lines. The upper and middle classes in the main went over to Unionism, but they took with them a section of the Radicals, while Mr Gladstone's personal force retained on the Liberal side a number of men whose insight into the needs of democracy was by no means profound. The political fight was for the moment shifted from the social question to the single absorbing issue of Home Rule, and the new Unionist party enjoyed twenty years of almost unbroken supremacy. Again, had the Home Rule issue stood alone it might have been settled in 1892, but meanwhile in the later 'eighties the social question had become insistent. Socialism, ceasing to be a merely academic force, had begun to influence organized labour, and had inspired the more generous minds among the artisans with the determination to grapple with the problem of the unskilled workmen. From the Dockers' strike of 1889 the New Unionism became a fighting force in public affairs, and the idea of a Labour party began to take shape. On the new problems Liberalism, weakened as it already had been, was further divided, and its failure in 1892 is to be ascribed far more to this larger cause than to the dramatic personal incident of the Parnell divorce.[24] In office without legislative power from 1892 to 1895, the Liberal party only experienced further loss of credit, and the rise of Imperialism swept the whole current of public interest in a new direction. The Labour movement itself was paralysed, and the defeat of the Engineers in 1897 put an end to the hope of achieving a great social transformation by the method of the strike. But, in the meanwhile, opinion was being silently transformed. The labours of Mr Charles Booth and his associates had at length stated the problem of poverty in scientific terms. Social and economic history was gradually taking shape as a virtually new branch of knowledge. The work of Mr and Mrs Sidney Webb helped to clear up the relations between the organ-

---

[24] Co-operation between the Liberals and the Irish Nationalists was disrupted when Charles Parnell – the Irish leader – became embroiled in public scandal after he was named as co-respondent in divorce proceedings Captain William O'Shea had instituted against his wife Kitty.

ized efforts of workmen and the functions of the State. The discerning observer could trace the 'organic filaments' of a fuller and more concrete social theory.

On the other hand, in the Liberal ranks many of the most influential men had passed, without consciousness of the transition, under the sway of quite opposite influences. They were becoming Imperialists in their sleep, and it was only as the implications of Imperialism became evident that they were awakened. It was with the outbreak of the South African War that the new development of Conservative policy first compelled the average Liberal to consider his position. It needed the shock of an outspoken violation of right to stir him; and we may date the revival of the idea of justice in the party as an organized force from the speech in the summer of 1901 in which Sir Henry Campbell-Bannerman set himself against the stream of militant sentiment and challenged in a classic phrase the methods of the war. From the day of this speech, which was supposed at the time to have irretrievably ruined his political career, the name of the party-leader, hitherto greeted with indifference, became a recognized signal for the cheers of a political meeting, and a man with no marked genius but that of character and the insight which character gave into the minds of his followers acquired in his party the position of a Gladstone. This was the first and fundamental victory, the reinstatement of the idea of Right in the mind of Liberalism. Then, as the Conservative attack developed and its implications became apparent, one interest after another of the older Liberalism was rudely shaken into life. The Education Act of 1902 brought the Non-conformists into action.[25] The Tariff Reform movement put Free Trade on its defence, and taught men to realize what the older economics of Liberalism had done for them. The Socialists of practical politics, the Labour Party, found that they could by no means dispense with the discipline of Cobden. Free Trade finance was to be the basis of social reform. Liberalism and Labour learned to co-operate in resisting delusive promises of remedies for unemployment and in maintaining the right of free international exchange. Meanwhile, Labour itself had experienced the full brunt of the attack. It had come not from

[25] The Education Act of 1902 streamlined the administration of public education, but was opposed by Non-conformists because it increased state subsidies payable to voluntary Church of England and Roman Catholic schools.

the politicians but from the judges,[26] but in this country we have to realize that within wide limits the judges are in effect legislators, and legislators with a certain persistent bent which can be held in check only by the constant vigilance and repeated efforts of the recognized organ for the making and repeal of law. In destroying the old position of the Trade Unions, the judges created the modern Labour party and cemented its alliance with Liberalism.[27] Meanwhile, the aftermath of Imperialism in South Africa was reaped, and Conservative disillusionment unlocked the floodgates for the advancing tide of the Liberal revival.

The tide has by no means spent itself. If it no longer rushes in an electoral torrent as in 1906 it flows in a steady stream towards social amelioration and democratic government. In this movement it is now sufficiently clear to all parties that the distinctive ideas of Liberalism have a permanent function. The Socialist recognizes with perfect clearness, for example, that popular government is not a meaningless shibboleth, but a reality that has to be maintained and extended by fighting. He is well aware that he must deal with the House of Lords and the Plural vote[28] if he is to gain his own ends. He can no longer regard these questions as difficulties interposed by half-hearted Liberals to distract attention from the Social problem. He is aware that the problem of Home Rule and of devolution generally is an integral part of the organization of democracy. And, as a rule, he not merely acquiesces in the demand of women for a purely political right, but only quarrels with the Liberal party for its tardiness in meeting the demand. The old Liberal idea of peace and retrenchment again is recognized by the Socialistic, and indeed by the whole body of social

---

[26] In 1901, ruling on a suit brought by the Taff Vale Railway company against the Amalgamated Railway Servants' Society following a strike, the High Court determined that a trade union could be held liable in civil law for acts committed by its officers and members. The decision, upheld by the House of Lords on appeal, contradicted the general understanding of the immunities granted to trade unions in 1871, and made strike action virtually impossible. Desire to modify the law on which the Taff Vale decision was based encouraged the labour movement to become more directly involved in political action.

[27] From 1903, Labour and the Liberals co-operated to prevent three-cornered constituency races from splitting the anti-Conservative vote. After 1914 this collaboration broke down.

[28] Under British law some electors had the right to vote in several constituencies. The remaining vestiges of this practice ended when a Labour Government passed the Representation of the People Act of 1948, which abolished the twelve university seats and the business premises franchise.

reformers, as equally essential for the successful prosecution of their aims. Popular budgets will bring no relief to human suffering if the revenues that they secure are all to go upon the most expensive ship that is the fashion of the moment, nor can the popular mind devote itself to the improvement of domestic conditions while it is distracted either by ambitions or by scares. On the other side, the Liberal who starts from the Gladstonian tradition has in large measure realized that if he is to maintain the essence of his old ideas it must be through a process of adaptation and growth. He has learnt that while Free Trade laid the foundations of prosperity it did not erect the building. He has to acknowledge that it has not solved the problems of unemployment, of underpayment, of overcrowding. He has to look deeper into the meaning of liberty and to take account of the bearing of actual conditions on the meaning of equality. As an apostle of peace and an opponent of swollen armaments, he has come to recognize that the expenditure of the social surplus upon the instruments of progress is the real alternative to its expenditure on the instruments of war. As a Temperance man he is coming to rely more on the indirect effect of social improvement on the one hand and the elimination of monopolist profit on the other, than on the uncertain chances of absolute prohibition.

There are, then, among the composite forces which maintained the Liberal Government in power through the crisis of 1910, the elements of such an organic view as may inspire and direct a genuine social progress. Liberalism has passed through its Slough of Despond, and in the give and take of ideas with Socialism has learnt, and taught, more than one lesson. The result is a broader and deeper movement in which the cooler and clearer minds recognize below the differences of party names and in spite of certain real cross-currents a genuine unity of purpose. What are the prospects of this movement? Will it be maintained? Is it the steady stream to which we have compared it, or a wave which must gradually sink into the trough?

To put this question is to ask in effect whether democracy is in substance as well as in form a possible mode of government. To answer this question we must ask what democracy really means, and why it is the necessary basis of the Liberal idea. The question has already been raised incidentally, and we have seen reason to dismiss both the individualist and the Benthamite argument for popular government as unsatisfactory. We even admitted a doubt whether some of the concrete essentials of liberty and social justice might not, under certain conditions, be less fully realized under a widely-extended suffrage than under the rule of a superior class or a well-ordered despotism. On what, then, it may be asked, do we found our conception of democracy? Is it on general principles of social philosophy, or on the special conditions of our own country or of contemporary civilization? And how does our conception relate itself to our other ideas of the social order? Do we assume that the democracy will in the main accept these ideas, or if it rejects them are we willing to acquiesce in its decision as final? And in the end what do we expect? Will democracy assert itself, will it find a common purpose and give it concrete shape? Or will it blunder on, the passive subject of scares and ambitions, frenzies of enthusiasm and dejection, clay in the hands of those whose profession it is to model it to their will?

First as to the general principle. Democracy is not founded merely on the right or the private interest of the individual. This is only one side of the shield. It is founded equally on the function of the individual as a member of the community. It founds the common good upon the common will, in forming which it bids every grown-up, intelligent person to take a part. No doubt many good things may be achieved for a people without responsive effort on its own part. It may be endowed with a good police, with an equitable system of private law, with education, with personal freedom, with a well-organized industry. It may receive these blessings at the hands of a foreign ruler, or from an enlightened bureaucracy or a benevolent monarch. However obtained, they are all very good things. But the democratic theory is that, so obtained, they lack a vitalizing element. A people so governed resembles an individual who has received all the external gifts of fortune, good teachers, healthy surroundings, a fair breeze to fill his sails, but owes his prosperous voyage to little or no effort of his own. We do not rate such a man so high as one who struggles through adversity to a much less eminent position. What we possess has its intrinsic value, but how we came to possess it is also an important question. It is so with a society. Good government is much, but the good will is more, and even the imperfect, halting, confused utterance of the common will may have in it the potency of higher things than a perfection of machinery can ever attain.

But this principle makes one very large assumption. It postulates the existence of a common will. It assumes that the individuals whom it would enfranchise can enter into the common life and contribute to the formation of a common decision by a genuine interest in public transactions. Where and in so far as this assumption definitely fails, there is no case for democracy. Progress, in such a case, is not wholly impossible, but it must depend on the number of those who do care for the things that are of social value, who advance knowledge or 'civilize life through the discoveries of art', or form a narrow but effective public opinion in support of liberty and order. We may go further. Whatever the form of government progress always does in fact depend on those who so think and live, and on the degree in which these common interests envelop their life and thought. Now, complete and wholehearted absorption in public interests is rare. It is the property not of the mass but of the few, and the democrat is well aware that it is the remnant which saves the people. He subjoins only that if their effort is really to succeed the people must be willing to be saved. The masses who spend their toilsome days in mine or factory struggling for bread have not their heads for ever filled with the complex details of international policy or industrial law. To expect this would be absurd. What is not exaggerated is to expect them to respond and assent to the things that make for the moral and material welfare of the country, and the position of the democrat is that the 'remnant' is better occupied in convincing the people and carrying their minds and wills with it than in imposing on them laws which they are concerned only to obey and enjoy. At the same time, the remnant, be it never so select, has always much to learn. Some men are much better and wiser than others, but experience seems to show that hardly any man is so much better or wiser than others that he can permanently stand the test of irresponsible power over them. On the contrary, the best and wisest is he who is ready to go to the humblest in a spirit of inquiry, to find out what he wants and why he wants it before seeking to legislate for him. Admitting the utmost that can be said for the necessity of leadership, we must at the same time grant that the perfection of leadership itself lies in securing the willing, convinced, open-eyed support of the mass.

Thus individuals will contribute to the social will in very varying degrees, but the democratic thesis is that the formation of such a will, that is, in effect, the extension of intelligent interest in all manner of public things, is in itself a good, and more than that, it is a condition qualifying other good things. Now the extension of interest is not to be created by democratic forms of government, and if it neither exists nor can be brought into existence, democracy remains an empty form and may even be worse than useless. On the other hand, where the capacity exists the establishment of responsible government is the first condition of its development. Even so it is not the sole condition. The modern State is a vast and complex organism. The individual voter feels himself lost among the millions. He is imperfectly acquainted with the devious issues and large problems of the day, and is sensible how little his solitary vote can affect their decision. What he needs to give him support and direction is organization with his neighbours and fellow workers. He can understand, for example, the affairs of his trade union, or, again, of his chapel. They are near to him. They affect him, and he feels that he can affect them. Through these interests, again, he comes into touch with wider questions – with a Factory Bill or an Education Bill – and in dealing with these questions he will now act as one of an organized body, whose combined voting strength will be no negligible quantity. Responsibility comes home to him, and to bring home responsibility is the problem of all government. The development of social interest – and that is democracy – depends not only on adult suffrage and the supremacy of the elected legislature, but on all the intermediate organizations which link the individual to the whole. This is one among the reasons why devolution and the revival of local government, at present crushed in this country by a centralized bureaucracy, are of the essence of democratic progress.

The success of democracy depends on the response of the voters to the opportunities given them. But, conversely, the opportunities must be given in order to call forth the response. The exercise of popular government is itself an education. In considering whether any class or sex or race should be brought into the circle of enfranchisement, the determining consideration is the response which that class or sex or race would be likely to make to the trust. Would it enter effectively into the questions of public life, or would it be so much passive voting material, wax in the hands of the less scrupulous politicians? The question is a fair one, but people are too ready to answer it in the less favourable sense on the ground of the actual indifference or ignorance which they find or think they find among the unenfranchised. They forget that in that regard enfranchisement itself may be precisely the stimulus needed to awaken interest, and while they are impressed with the danger of admitting ignorant and irresponsible, and perhaps corruptible voters to a voice in the government, they are apt to overlook the counterbalancing danger of leaving a section of the community outside the circle of civic responsibility. The actual work of government must affect, and also it must be affected by, its relation to all who live within the realm. To secure good adaptation it ought, I will not say to reflect, but at least to take account of, the dispositions and circumstances of every class in the population. If any one class is dumb, the result is that Government is to that extent uninformed. It is not merely that the interests of that class may suffer, but that, even with the best will, mistakes may be made in handling it, because it cannot speak for itself. Officious spokesmen will pretend to represent its views, and will obtain, perhaps, undue authority merely because there is no way of bringing them to book. So among ourselves does the press constantly represent public opinion to be one thing while the cold arithmetic of the polls conclusively declares it to be another. The ballot alone effectively liberates the quiet citizen from the tyranny of the shouter and the wire-puller.

I conclude that an impression of existing inertness or ignorance is not a sufficient reason for withholding responsible government or restricting the area of the suffrage. There must be a well-grounded view that political incapacity is so deep-rooted that the extension of political rights would tend only to facilitate undue influence by the less scrupulous sections of the more capable part of the people. Thus where we have an oligarchy of white planters in the midst of a coloured population, it is always open to doubt whether a general colour-franchise will be a sound method of securing even-handed justice. The economic and social conditions may be such that the 'coloured' man would just have to vote as his master told him, and if the elementary rights are to be secured for all it may be that a semi-despotic system like that of some of our Crown colonies is the best that can be devised. On the other side, that which is most apt to frighten a governing class or race, a clamour on the part of an unenfranchised people for political rights, is to the democrat precisely the strongest reason that he can have in the absence of direct experience for believing them fit for the exercise of civic responsibility. He welcomes signs of dissatisfaction among the disfranchised as the best proof of awakening interest in public affairs, and he has none of those fears of ultimate social disruption which are a nightmare to bureaucracies because experience has sufficiently proved to him the healing power of freedom, of responsibility, and of the sense of justice. Moreover, a democrat cannot be a democrat for his own country alone. He cannot but recognize the complex and subtle interactions of nation upon nation which make every local success or failure of democracy tell upon other countries. Nothing has been more encouraging to the Liberalism of Western Europe in recent years than the signs of political awakening in the East. Until yesterday it seemed as though it would in the end be impossible to resist the ultimate 'destiny' of the white races to be masters of the rest of the world. The result would have been that, however far democracy might develop within any Western State, it would always be confronted with a contrary principle in the relation of that State to dependencies, and this contradiction, as may easily be seen by the attentive student of our own political constitutions, is a standing menace to domestic freedom. The awakening of the Orient, from Constantinople to Pekin, is the greatest and most hopeful political fact of our time, and it is with the deepest shame that English Liberals have been compelled to look on while our Foreign Office has made itself the accomplice in the attempt to nip Persian freedom in the bud, and that in the interest of the most ruthless tyranny that has ever crushed the liberties of a white people.[29]

The cause of democracy is bound up with that of internationalism. The relation is many-sided. It is national pride, resentment, or ambition one day that sweeps the public mind and diverts it from all interest in domestic progress. The next day the same function is performed no less adequately by a scare. The practice of playing on popular emotions has been reduced to a fine art which neither of the great parties is ashamed to employ. Military ideals possess the mind, and military expenditure eats up the public resources. On the other side, the political economic and social progress of other nations reacts on our own. The backwardness of our commercial rivals in industrial legislation was long made an argument against further advances

---

[29] In March 1909 Russia invaded northern Persia to support Mohammed Ali Shah who had been deposed after he repressed the constitutional regime which had been established in the wake of the (1906) Persian Revolution. According to the terms of an Anglo-Russian Entente of 1907, Britain recognized north Persia as a Russian sphere of interest in return for Russian acknowledgement of British primacy in south Persia and the Gulf.

among ourselves. Conversely, when they go beyond us, as now they often do, we can learn from them. Physically the world is rapidly becoming one, and its unity must ultimately be reflected in political institutions. The old doctrine of absolute sovereignty is dead. The greater States of the day exhibit a complex system of government within government, authority limited by authority, and the world-state of the not impossible future must be based on a free national self-direction as full and satisfying as that enjoyed by Canada or Australia within the British Empire at this moment. National emulation will express itself less in the desire to extend territory or to count up ships and guns, and more in the endeavour to magnify the contribution of our own country to civilized life. Just as in the rebirth of our municipal life we find a civic patriotism which takes interest in the local university, which feels pride in the magnitude of the local industry, which parades the lowest death rate in the country, which is honestly ashamed of a bad record for crime or pauperism, so as Englishmen we shall concern ourselves less with the question whether two of our Dreadnoughts[30] might not be pitted against one German, and more with the question whether we cannot equal Germany in the development of science, of education, and of industrial technique. Perhaps even, recovering from our present artificially induced and radically insincere mood of national self-abasement, we shall learn to take some pride in our own characteristic contributions as a nation to the arts of government, to the thought, the literature, the art, the mechanical inventions which have made and are re-making modern civilization.

Standing by national autonomy and international equality, Liberalism is necessarily in conflict with the Imperial idea as it is ordinarily presented. But this is not to say that it is indifferent to the interests of the Empire as a whole, to the sentiment of unity pervading its white population, to all the possibilities involved in the bare fact that a fourth part of the human race recognizes one flag and one supreme authority. In relation to the self-governing colonies the Liberal of today has to face a change in the situation since Cobden's time not unlike that which we have traced in other departments. The Colonial Empire as it stands is in substance the creation of the older Liberalism. It is founded on self-government, and self-government is the root from which the existing sentiment of unity has sprung. The

[30] 'Dreadnoughts': heavily armed battleships.

problem of our time is to devise means for the more concrete and living expression of this sentiment without impairing the rights of self-government on which it depends. Hitherto the 'Imperialist' has had matters all his own way and has cleverly exploited Colonial opinion, or an appearance of Colonial opinion, in favour of class ascendancy and reactionary legislation in the mother country. But the colonies include the most democratic communities in the world. Their natural sympathies are not with the Conservatives, but with the most Progressive parties in the United Kingdom. They favour Home Rule, they set the pace in social legislation. There exist accordingly the political conditions of a democratic alliance which it is the business of the British Liberal to turn to account. He may hope to make his country the centre of a group of self-governing, democratic communities, one of which, moreover, serves as a natural link with the other great commonwealth of English-speaking people. The constitutional mechanism of the new unity begins to take shape in the Imperial Council, and its work begins to define itself as the adjustment of interests as between different portions of the Empire and the organization of common defence. Such a union is no menace to the world's peace or to the cause of freedom. On the contrary, as a natural outgrowth of a common sentiment, it is one of the steps towards a wider unity which involves no backstroke against the ideal of self-government. It is a model, and that on no mean scale, of the International State.

Internationalism on the one side, national self-government on the other, are the radical conditions of the growth of a social mind which is the essence, as opposed to the form, of democracy. But as to form itself a word must, in conclusion, be said. If the forms are unsuitable the will cannot express itself, and if it fails of adequate expression it is in the end thwarted, repressed and paralysed. In the matter of form the inherent difficulty of democratic government, whether direct or representative, is that it is government by majority, not government by universal consent. Its decisions are those of the larger part of the people, not of the whole. This defect is an unavoidable consequence of the necessities of decision and the impossibility of securing universal agreement. Statesmen have sought to remedy it by applying something of the nature of a brake upon the process of change. They have felt that to justify a new departure of any magnitude there must be something more than a bare majority. There must either be a large majority, two-thirds or three-fourths of the electorate, or there must be some friction to be overcome which will serve to test the depth and force as well as the numerical extent of the feeling behind the new proposal. In the United Kingdom we have one official brake, the House of Lords, and several unofficial ones, the civil service, the permanent determined opposition of the Bench[31] to democratic measures, the Press, and all that we call Society. All these brakes act in one way only. There is no brake upon reaction – a lack which becomes more serious in proportion as the Conservative party acquires a definite and constructive policy of its own. In this situation the Liberal party set itself to deal with the official brake by the simple method of reducing its effective strength, but, to be honest, without having made up its mind as to the nature of the brake which it would like to substitute. On this question a few general remarks would seem to be in place. The function of a check on the House of Commons is to secure reconsideration. Conservative leaders are in the right when they point to the accidental elements that go to the constitution of parliamentary majorities. The programme of any general election is always composite, and a man finds himself compelled, for example, to choose between a Tariff Reformer whose views on education he approves, and a Free Trader whose educational policy he detests. In part this defect might be remedied by the Proportional system to which, whether against the grain or not, Liberals will find themselves driven the more they insist on the genuinely representative character of the House of Commons. But even a Proportional system would not wholly clear the issues before the electorate. The average man gives his vote on the question which he takes to be most important in itself, and which he supposes to be most likely to come up for immediate settlement. But he is always liable to find his expectations defeated, and a Parliament which is in reality elected on one issue may proceed to deal with quite another. The remedy proposed by the Parliament Bill was a two years' delay, which, it was held, would secure full discussion and considerable opportunity for the manifestation of opinion should it be adverse. This proposal had been put to the constituencies twice over, and had been ratified by them if any legislative proposal ever was ratified. It should enable the House of Commons, as the representatives of the people, to decide freely on

---

[31] 'the Bench': the judiciary.

the permanent constitution of the country. The Bill itself, however, does not lay down the lines of a permanent settlement. For, to begin with, in leaving the constitution of the House of Lords unaltered it provides a one-sided check, operating only on democratic measures which in any case have to run the gauntlet of the permanent officials, the judges, the Press, and Society. For permanent use the brake must be two-sided. Secondly, it is to be feared that the principle of delay would be an insufficient check upon a large and headstrong majority. What is really needed is that the people should have the opportunity of considering a proposal afresh. This could be secured in either of two ways: (1) by allowing the suspensory veto of the Second Chamber to hold a measure over to a new Parliament; (2) by allowing the House of Commons to submit a bill in the form in which it finally leaves the House to a direct popular vote. It is to my mind regrettable that so many Liberals should have closed the door on the Referendum. It is true that there are many measures to which it would be ill suited. For example, measures affecting a particular class or a particular locality would be apt to go by the board. They might command a large and enthusiastic majority among those primarily affected by them, but only receive a languid assent elsewhere, and they might be defeated by a majority beaten up for extraneous purposes among those without first-hand knowledge of the problems with which they are intended to deal. Again, if a referendum were to work at all it would only be in relation to measures of the first class, and only, if the public convenience is to be consulted, on very rare occasions. In all ordinary cases of insuperable difference between the Houses, the government of the day would accept the postponement of the measure till the new Parliament. But there are measures of urgency, measures of fundamental import, above all, measures which cut across the ordinary lines of party and with which, in consequence, our system is impotent to deal, and on these the direct consultation of the people would be the most suitable method of solution.[*]

What we need, then, is an impartial second chamber distinctly

[*] I need hardly add that financial measures are entirely unsuited to a referendum. Financial and executive control go together, and to take either of them out of the hands of the majority in the House of Commons is not to reform our system but to destroy it root and branch. The same is not true of legislative control. There are cases in which a government might fairly submit a legislative measure to the people without electing to stand or fall by it.

subordinate to the House of Commons, incapable of touching finance and therefore of overthrowing a ministry, but able to secure the submission of a measure either to the direct vote of the people or to the verdict of a second election – the government of the day having the choice between the alternatives. Such a chamber might be instituted by direct popular election. But the multiplication of elections is not good for the working of democracy, and it would be difficult to reconcile a directly elected house to a subordinate position. It might, therefore, as an alternative, be elected on a proportional system by the House of Commons itself, its members retaining their seat for two Parliaments. To bridge over the change half of the chamber for the present Parliament might be elected by the existing House of Lords, and their representatives retiring at the end of this Parliament would leave the next House of Commons and every future House of Commons with one-half of the chamber to elect. This Second Chamber would then reflect in equal proportions the existing and the last House of Commons, and the balance between parties should be fairly held." This chamber would have ample power of securing reasonable amendments and would also have good ground for exercising moderation in pressing its views. If the public were behind the measure it would know that in the end the House of Commons could carry it in its teeth, whether by referendum or by a renewed vote of confidence at a general election. The Commons, on their side, would have reasons for exhibiting a conciliatory temper. They would not wish to be forced either to postpone or to appeal. As to which method they would choose they would have absolute discretion, and if they went to the country with a series of popular measures hung up and awaiting their return for ratification, they would justly feel themselves in a strong position.

So far as to forms. The actual future of democracy, however, rests upon deeper issues. It is bound up with the general advance of civilization. The organic character of society is, we have seen, in one sense, an ideal. In another sense it is an actuality. That is to say, nothing of any import affects the social life on one side without setting up reactions all through the tissue. Hence, for example, we cannot

---

" Probably the best alternative to these proposals is that of a small directly elected Second Chamber, with a provision for a joint session in case of insuperable disagreement, but with no provision for delay. This proposal has the advantage, apparently, of commanding a measure of Conservative support.

maintain great political progress without some corresponding advance on other sides. People are not fully free in their political capacity when they are subject industrially to conditions which take the life and heart out of them. A nation as a whole cannot be in the full sense free while it fears another or gives cause of fear to another. The social problem must be viewed as a whole. We touch here the greatest weakness in modern reform movements. The spirit of specialism has invaded political and social activity, and in greater and greater degree men consecrate their whole energy to a particular cause to the almost cynical disregard of all other considerations. 'Not such the help, nor these the defenders' which this moment of the world's progress needs. Rather we want to learn our supreme lesson from the school of Cobden. For them the political problem was one, manifold in its ramifications but undivided in its essence. It was a problem of realizing liberty. We have seen reason to think that their conception of liberty was too thin, and that to appreciate its concrete content we must understand it as resting upon mutual restraint and value it as a basis of mutual aid. For us, therefore, harmony serves better as a unifying conception. It remains for us to carry it through with the same logical cogency, the same practical resourcefulness, the same driving force that inspired the earlier Radicals, that gave fire to Cobden's statistics, and lent compelling power to the eloquence of Bright. We need less of the fanatics of sectarianism and more of the unifying mind. Our reformers must learn to rely less on the advertising value of immediate success and more on the deeper but less striking changes of practice or of feeling, to think less of catching votes and more of convincing opinion. We need a fuller co-operation among those of genuine democratic feeling and more agreement as to the order of reform. At present progress is blocked by the very competition of many causes for the first place in the advance. Here, again, devolution will help us, but what would help still more would be a clearer sense of the necessity of co-operation between all who profess and call themselves democrats, based on a fuller appreciation of the breadth and the depth of their own meaning. The advice seems cold to the fiery spirits, but they may come to learn that the vision of justice in the wholeness of her beauty kindles a passion that may not flare up into moments of dramatic scintillation, but burns with the enduring glow of the central heat.

OTHER WRITINGS

Government by the People

The growth of representative institutions is one of the outstanding features of modern history. The movement, like all others, has its ebb and flow, but on a wide view the set of the current is unmistakable. Throughout the civilized world, including now not merely the peoples of Europe and of European descent, but the leading examples of Eastern civilization, we find the principle of self-government germinating where it had hitherto been unknown, and ripening where it had only been immature. In our own country, where alone among great nations Parliamentary institutions had enjoyed continuous vitality from a remote past, the advance took the form, first of consolidating the primacy of the popular House, and secondly of broadening the basis of representation. Of these two processes the first has, it is true, received a check. The vast and growing power of organized wealth has found in an irresponsible Chamber a handy instrument of obstruction. But in so doing it has only raised a constitutional issue of which the final settlement can neither be distant nor doubtful. The second process has been advanced by three great measures of reform, and has now to be completed by a fourth, which will extend the area of representation to the entire adult population.

The movement towards self-government is not to be understood if studied in isolation. It is part of a more comprehensive effort to broaden the basis of civilization, to break down artificial barriers of birth, nationality and sex, to raise the masses of the people from a condition of subservience and tutelage, to give them their share in the common heritage and their part to play in the common life. The movement is not exclusively political. It is reflected equally in religion, in ethics, in literature and in art. In one form or another it has engaged nearly all the best minds of the modern world outside the realm of pure science. Nor is it concerned with political rights alone, but with the entire mass of economic and social conditions on which the effective freedom of men and women and the harmony of the social order depend. Nevertheless, within the movement the struggle for the political franchise occupies an essential place.

There are, of course, those who disparage merely 'political' reforms and attach little value to the franchise. It may even be that this tendency has rather grown than diminished with experience of the partial systems of popular government which now exist. For those who live under them, all the blemishes of popular institutions come into sharp relief, while the deeper vices of older methods are softened by the haze of distance. Meanwhile, some of the old arguments for political equality have fallen into discredit. Thus the modern critic derides the 'Rights of Man' on which the early democrats took their stand. There are, indeed, types of political opinion to which the very idea of any kind of 'right' is, for obvious reasons, repugnant. On the point of form, however, we may agree. The franchise is no matter of 'abstract right'. It is not, that is to say, a right which holds good and is entitled to observance without any regard to other considerations. No right holds good in such a sense. A right is a claim founded on justice, and justice is that arrangement which an impartial judgement would decide to be the best possible for the whole group of those whom it affects. It may not be the best for anyone considered by himself, but it is the best for the whole to which he belongs. Any other principle must lead to an insoluble contradiction between what it is right to do and what it is good to do. If this is so the true 'rights' of the individual are just the fundamental conditions of good social organization. And, as with other rights, so with the right to vote. It is not a claim to which the social welfare must bow, but a claim which the deeper consideration of the social welfare makes good.

But is it the fact that universal suffrage can be justified on this ground? Here again some critics would tell us that the traditional argument of English democrats in particular is belied by experience. Thinkers like Bentham, they say, who discarded all abstract rights as 'anarchical' fallacies, rested the claims of democracy on a set of principles which are equally worn threadbare. Bentham held that the object of society was to promote 'the greatest happiness of the greatest number', and he inferred that if all men – and at one time he was for adding all women, too – had a right to shape the course of government, the interests of the greater number would always prevail. This simple deduction has been riddled with criticism. It assumes, first, that men are guided by a rational conception of their own interests, which is not true, because men are neither so selfish nor so intelligent as it supposes them to be. It assumes, secondly, that public questions are much more simple than they really are. If every question of public policy stood by itself and were voted on by itself, and if on each question every elector could see that one kind of answer would agree with his personal desires, and the opposite answer would conflict with them, then Bentham's argument might hold. Every decision would be taken on its own merits, and would accord with the interests of the majority, at any rate as understood by the majority itself. But these, the critic will insist, are the politics of cloudland. 'Actual politics', he will say, 'present us with a whole tangle of issues, in which prejudice and interests, patriotism and class feeling, public and personal considerations are blended together, and the end of any General Election leaves politicians and journalists wrangling about what the constituencies have really meant. Many of the questions raise issues so subtle and involved that only an expert can pretend to a judgement upon them. What is the real incidence of a tax, what will be the legal effect of a proposed amendment, how some alteration in the fiscal system will affect the course of trade, are questions to which one may give years of dispassionate study without arriving at certainty. Yet', the critic goes on, 'the plain man whose whole daily life is taken up with other matters is once in every four or five years suddenly called on to give a judgement on these questions, and not even then, as a rule, on one question alone, but on a mass of them all jumbled together in what is presented to him as the "record" of the Government or the alternative programme of the Opposition. It is even worse than this. He is not properly called on for a judgement at all. He is pestered to give a vote to Mr A or Mr B, and to let them answer the questions for him. His own responsibility in the matter is very dim to him. He is momentarily roused from the absorption in cricket or football, which is the normal occupation of his leisure, and reluctantly dragged to the meeting and the polling-booth. Whatever he does he may well doubt whether his action makes much difference. He is, perhaps, one of five or six thousand who will vote for Mr A, who last time had a majority of 1,200; Mr A will probably get in without his help, and when he does so will again only be one of 670 people on whose conduct affairs will actually depend. The political rights which were to make our "plain man" a free and responsible citizen come down to a many-thousandth "share of one member of the talking-shop".' Thus for the idealist picture of the patriotic citizen performing a public function with a responsible sense of his duty to the community; for the prosaic account of the individual casting his vote for a clear balance of personal advantage, the critic will substitute the reality of a confused individual voting with little sense of any consequences at all, perhaps caught by some impulse of the crowd, perhaps coaxed by a persuasive canvasser, perhaps badgered till he is glad to be done with it.

But all this is in reality a very one-sided presentment of the facts. The forty millions of us were once unkindly described as mostly fools. It would probably be fairer as well as kinder to suppose among us forty million gradations of wisdom and folly, public spirit and selfishness. There are in all classes plenty of men and women who take a constant and intelligent interest in public matters, and though doubtless they are a minority they have a close and personal influence on their friends and neighbours. But the truth is that this whole line of criticism on popular government founds itself on the very same mistake which it criticizes in Bentham. It looks too much at the individual. Each single man or woman is a very puny atom in the social mass, and if he felt himself alone might well ask what his vote was worth. But he does not stand alone. He is normally an item in the numerical voting strength of some definite group. He goes to make up the sum of the Irish vote in his constituency, or the Nonconformist vote, or the trade union vote, as the case may be, and this vote has a tangible strength which party managers measure and seek to attract to their side. It has also very often a definite and intelligent direction given to it by its leading representatives. Whatever definitely touches any one of these collective or group interests gets a speedy response, favourable or unfavourable, at the polls; and the same is true on a still larger scale of anything that appeals definitely and forcibly to the nation as a whole, that touches its pride or its compunction. Thus when we look back again from the individual to society, to the groups into which the population is divided, the varied interests which appeal to masses of men, we get a new sense of the value of representative government. The right of the individual to vote enables all the 'interests' to make themselves felt; and by interests we mean not merely the selfish desires of a class or a combination, but all that touches the feeling, the imagination, the enthusiasm of any important group of voters. All these in their degree make themselves heard in the struggle, and stand to win some share, small or great, in the representative Chamber, and thereby affect the decisions of government.

The charge that representative government is not a reality fails when we ask what it is that is represented. The sounder criticism is that the interests which are best organized are apt to obtain an undue influence. The representative system does not act automatically in such a way as to make a perfect record of the people's will. In point of fact it is only now and again on some great and simple issue that the people, as a whole, can be said to have a will. The more normal condition is that there are many wills of diverse parties, class interests, trade interests, religious interests and the like, and a General Election is a tussle among all of these in which those with the clearest views, the ablest leaders, the strongest organization, and the greatest political ability get their way. Hence in particular the enormous influence of wealth, as commanding the means of organization in a representative system. This is an influence which does not grow less. The machinery of political education becomes more and more costly. The Press, once an independent organ of opinion and an impartial channel for the dissemination of news, becomes more and more the exclusive property of a few men of colossal wealth. Every platform agitation and every Parliamentary candidature costs money, and in spite of legislation it is probable that expenditure grows. A candid upholder of democracy must admit a grave doubt whether the oligarchy of wealth has not consolidated its position and increased its influence in the quarter of a century that has passed since the last great extension of the franchise.

For such difficulties, in fact, the representative system in itself provides no remedy. What it does offer, as soon as it is carried to completion, is a fair field for all parties. It is no magic formula by which trade interests, class prejudices, religious bigotries are readily dissolved. On the contrary, political constitutions, be they what they may, are, in the main, dominated in their actual working by the great social and economic forces that prevail among a people. There can hardly be true political equality as long as the economic tendency sets strongly towards overwhelming inequalities of wealth. A representative system does not of itself correct this tendency or secure equal consideration for all interests. On the other hand, it does open the avenues of political expression to all who are sufficiently intelligent, resolute, and energetic to organize themselves for concerted political action. It does none of the work for them, but it makes it possible for them to do it for themselves. The popular parties can gain no victory by merely trusting to unorganized numbers, but as soon as the representative system is perfect they have at least an organ. It remains for them to learn how to make use of it.

Our system, however, is very far from perfect. By the device of plural voting it adds a make-weight of no small importance to the side of wealth. By its complicated and dilatory methods of registration it indirectly but effectively secures the disenfranchisement of large numbers of the working class, and by the sex disqualification it entirely denies representation to one of the great 'interests'. It shuts out women from all direct influence on the conduct of affairs. Now, whatever may be said for or against a representative system in the abstract, this at least seems clear: if we accept the principle at all, we should seek to carry it through. If government is by representation, then a limited representation means government of one part of the people by another, and any inequality of representation means the same thing less nakedly expressed. Now, it is easy to understand the ideal of government by an official autocracy, raised above all classes alike, emancipated from the necessity of cajoling an electorate, and rendered impartial by its superiority. For such an ideal under certain social conditions there is something to be said, though experience has shown that it is liable to perversions which throw the blemishes of democracy into the shade. But neither on the score of impartiality nor on that of efficiency is there anything to be said for a Government which rests on certain portions of the people, whether selected in accordance with birth, property or sex, to the exclusion of others. As to the male suffrage in this country, the anomalies and restrictions that were suffered to remain in 1884 are destitute of all basis in reason. They do not restrict the suffrage to any particular class. They do not impose any generic test of citizenship or any standard of intelligence. They are simple remnants of the older system of property* qualification, and far from acting as a balance to undue influence they only accentuate the undue influence of wealth, which is the principal danger of democracy.

With regard to the larger question of the representation of women, the case may be judged by the arguments used against it, which in principle are precisely those that have been urged against every extension of the suffrage to men. 'Women', we are told, 'have on the average less practical capacity and less knowledge of affairs than men'. The same argument was used against the working classes. 'Men alone have a stake in the great issues of war and peace', and so of old landowners alone had a stake in the country. 'Women are represented by their menfolk', and so formerly the workman was invited to trust his interests to his landlord or employer. 'More will be done by the chivalry of men for women than could be done by women for themselves.' Similarly, landlords and employers were to do more for their dependants than their dependants could do for themselves. 'Women can influence opinion indirectly without a vote', and so workmen were assured that a Parliament of their rulers would never turn a deaf ear to any expression of their real needs. 'Government rests on force, and force is in the hands of men'; just as in the argument against manhood suffrage, government must lie with those who have effective power, and effective power is with the owners of property and directors of industry. 'What, again, does the individual woman want with the vote? Her business is in the home; she wants steady wages and regular work for her husband, health and happiness for her children. What are public affairs to her?' And, similarly, what

---

* The special representation of property may be justified (*a*) on the ground that 'property' has a greater 'stake in the country'. To this it may be replied that the conduct of government affects all classes alike, but that if any class is better able than others to protect itself against the effects of bad legislation it is not the poor. (*b*) On the ground that property pays the bill. This is hardly the argument of property itself, which, when threatened with taxation, declares that it is the poor who will ultimately bear the cost. Nor does it conform to the facts, at least, of our fiscal system. Nor would it be to the interests of democracy to accumulate taxes on property unless the form of taxation were such as to leave the springs of industry unimpaired; and if this condition be observed, it may be denied that there is room for injustice. (*c*) On the ground that 'property' is in a minority and requires protection. But experience shows that property, possessing the means of organization, has a power quite disproportioned to the numbers of those who enjoy it. (*d*) On the ground that property and intelligence go together. This is a statement which commends itself more to 'property' than to 'intelligence'.

had the workman to do with the fate of empires? He wanted a good day's work and a fair day's wage. What mattered it to him who was in or out? There are no new arguments against the suffrage, and whatever ground there may be for admitting the representative principle is a good ground for carrying the principle to its logical conclusion.

But what of the principle itself? Be it admitted that representation is, after all allowances are made, more of a reality than appears to the critic. Be it admitted that if certain interests or social groupings are to have their say, all alike can claim the same right. Might it not still be better that we should seek rather to escape altogether from the government of the crowd, and look for salvation to the wise and good? An excellent solution of all difficulties, no doubt, but as a principle of politics somewhat lacking in the means of application. There is a certain figure in Carlyle's *French Revolution*: 'Whom we discern bawling for the space of an hour at all intervals, "Je demande l'arrestation des coquins et des lâches."' 'Really', comments Carlyle, 'one of the most comprehensive petitions ever put up; which indeed to this hour includes all that you can reasonably ask Constitution of Year One, Rotten Borough, Ballot-Box, or other miraculous political Ark of the Covenant to do for you to the end of the world! I also demand arrestment of the Knaves and Dastards, and nothing more whatever.' So, too, we all desire government by the wise and good, but the question how to get it and maintain it is less simple. Now, representative government has in it no magic that works infallibly to bring the best men to the head of affairs. On the contrary, the conditions of public life are such as to exclude many men of the highest quality who lack a certain physical elasticity and toughness of hide. But if we look closely into the working of any alternative system known to history we find corresponding drawbacks. The Minister of an absolute monarch must be a master of court intrigue, and throughout his career he has to rely less on his own efforts than on the favour of others. Our system, with its many alternative careers for men of strong public interests, has probably a wider field of selection than any other yet devised. But representative government has a deeper foundation than this. It is often spoken of as 'free government'. The phrase is cavilled at because no system of government liberates the individual from the social order. But it has a deeper meaning. The movement towards representation has been part, as has been said, of a much more comprehensive effort towards liberty – liberty as against arbitrary power, liberty as against national oppression, liberty as against territorial domination or commercial exploitation, liberty of speech, of writing and of worship. Now, representative government is no absolute security for these liberties, but it is the best, one may say the only tangible security in the shape of positive institutions that experience has yet suggested. What may be said of liberty may be said of any rights common to all classes. There can be no absolute guarantee that what one age has won another will maintain. The only final security is in the spirit of the people. But, so far as institutions go, popular representation is the natural guardian of popular rights. A democracy may tyrannize, but when it does so it sins against its own principle and tends to paralyse itself. Whatever of healthy life there is left in its members will protest. Further, as opposed to the best government 'from above', any representative system that is more than a form presents three great advantages. The first of these is government by public discussion, the second is the responsibility of the lawgiver and administrator, and the third is the adequate expression of the larger social forces.

(1) If we take any public question by itself, particularly any question of some complexity, a trained official will probably know much better than anyone else how it ought to be solved. If we could make him temporary dictator, he would carry out perhaps a perfect scheme, whereas when he has to convince a Cabinet Minister and persuade him to draft a Bill, when this Bill has to be carried through Parliament and run the gauntlet of criticism in the Press, it will emerge shorn of much of its logical glory, maimed by concessions on the right hand and on the left, a makeshift which returns to the trained official to do with as best he can. Looking at the single case, the popular element appears responsible for all the loss and the expert mind for all the gain. On the other side, we have to bear in mind that the expert is not infallible. The very training which has endowed him with a knowledge of housing questions or of local taxation above his fellows has also compelled him to concentrate attention on his own question to the exclusion of others. He is a specialist, and as such has no occasion to study the wider aspects of the social problems. He works in an office where things go by routine, and the elements of human reason and unreason, even of human joy and sorrow, are of no account unless they can be reduced to figures and arranged in pigeon

holes. The criticism that his Bill undergoes in Parliament is some
reflection of the actions and reactions that it would have set in motion
if he had been able to impose it by a ukase,[1] but one result of the
representative method is that these forces are reckoned with before
and not after the Bill becomes law. Thus discussion is not merely a
check on the misuse of arbitrary power, but, reasonably employed, is
an instrument in the hands of a statesman who is interested not in
paper legislation, but in the practical efficacy of his proposals.

(2) But we must look beyond the single measure. The development
of an admirable Civil Service in our own time[2] seems to have led
some people to conceive of the upright, incorruptible, efficient,
public-spirited administrator as a gift of the gods on whose gracious
aid suffering humanity may always count if it will be only wise enough
to employ it. They forget that this Civil Service is itself the creation
of the representative system, replacing one that was by no means so
impeccable nor so readily open to the best talents of all classes, and
they perhaps ignore the effect of responsibility in maintaining the
standard that was so difficult to reach. But, in point of fact, there is
human nature in an office as well as outside of it, and the official
mind has its little characteristic weaknesses no less than the political
mind or the journalistic. For such weaknesses no more wholesome
corrective has been found than the fresh air of criticism, the sense
of responsibility, the necessity of convincing other minds of very different antecedents and predispositions.

(3) Lastly, though something be lost through the necessity of convincing the public, something is also gained. Representative government does not always secure the best decisions, but, so far as it is
effectual, it does secure some relation between the acts of government
and the large social forces at work in the nation. Now, there may be
cases few and far between where a great man has succeeded in
imposing a new ideal upon a nation, and has thereby actually raised
it a stage in the scale of civilization. But it is safe to say that the
normal type of autocrat who has left his mark on history has been he
who without representative forms has through wisdom and insight

[1] 'ukase': 'an order or regulation of a final or arbitrary nature' (*OED*).
[2] Following the Northcote-Trevelyan Report (1854) a series of reforms gradually eliminated political patronage from the British civil service. By 1870 a system of public
examinations, and open competition for appointments, extended throughout the
Home Civil Service.

worked on the representative principle and has embodied and given shape to the best of the social forces that were striving for expression. Well-meaning rulers of equal capacity, but less heedful of the conditions of success, have more often served to point the moral of the instability of human greatness. In fact, when the wise bear rule, it is part of their wisdom to temper itself to the needs of the time and the possibilities of the social order, to recognize the limits of their power and to renounce the attempt to go beyond the point to which the people will follow them. Effectively they are limited by the prevailing social forces. Now, what the representative principle does is to let these forces measure themselves and express themselves. It does not secure the wisest or most just decisions on every question, but, so far as it is effective, it does secure that close relation between the acts of a people and the real forces constituting the life of the people which makes for sure and stable growth. It imposes in reality few limits or restraints on good government that are not already there independently of all constitutional forms inherent in the laws of social life. But it compels the enthusiast for progress to take the right method of bringing it about, which is that of convincing the world that he has a message worth the hearing.

Among the social forces of our own time not the least is the deepening sense of social responsibility which lies at the base of the effort towards progress. This effort finds itself thwarted often enough by its entanglement with the controversies of public life. Yet without the representative principle the diffused feeling on which it rests would be without a central organ, and much that is rightly done by a people for itself through its chosen representatives would wear a different aspect if done for it from above by a beneficent autocrat. No objection to social legislation is more frequently heard than the complaint that it is an interference with liberty and tends to sap the sense of personal responsibility. Whether it is a proposal for the feeding of school children, or of pensions for the aged, or assistance for the unemployed, these considerations are persistently urged, and rightly or wrongly sway many minds. With the merits of any of these questions we are not here concerned. But one point is very relevant. The common reply to the criticism of the 'individualist' is that the community has a certain collective responsibility for its members which is no less important than the personal responsibility of the individual for his own support or that of his children. Thus, it is maintained, in 'social legislation' we are not sapping the general sense of responsibility, but rather strengthening it: only we are taking on our shoulders collectively burdens that have been too heavy for the individual while standing alone. This line of reply has something more than an academic value. It strikes deep into the principles of a representative system, but except under a representative system it is wholly inapplicable. When any new public function is set on foot as the upshot of a prolonged course of public education with the deliberate assent of the average citizen and the concurrence of the main forces of opinion, it is no concatenation of empty words, but is bare and literal truth to describe it as the deliberate assumption of a new responsibility by the community as a whole. When it is simply the *fiat* of an autocrat or the ordinance of an official acting without regard to the general sense of what is just and desirable, it wears a very different appearance. It calls for no corresponding effort on the part of those whom it benefits, and so far as it supersedes such effort may check the more democratic development of the principle of mutual aid. Such a result was certainly a part of the intention of some of the Continental schemes of 'State Socialism'. Whether it has been their effect time must show. All that we would emphasize here is that the extension of public responsibility under a representative system is one thing; under any other system it is open to quite another set of objections.

But this argument again involves that the representation should be complete. The greater the sphere covered by such action the more necessary it is that all citizens of the State should be consulted before action is taken. In particular, in assuming a closer responsibility than of old for the health of children and for the condition of women workers, the State is placing itself under a direct obligation to consult its women citizens. There is a reciprocal obligation in these matters. As long as the business of government was confined in the main to the maintenance of public order and national defence the concern of the average man or woman in it was limited. Now that it enters more and more into the working of everyday life its control becomes a matter of active concern to every man and woman. In particular the regulation of women's work is a matter which may be approached from more than one point of view, and women have a right to judge whether any given regulation is conceived in the interest of their sex or in that, perhaps, of masculine monopoly. On this side social legislation will be increasingly hampered in the future until women are frankly admitted into the representative system, and that on terms which will give to working women a weight proportioned to their numbers.

Towards the close of the last century we used sometimes to hear that the work of political emancipation was now substantially complete, and that the time for social emancipation had arrived. The assurance that a piece of work is done is often the prelude to the discovery that it has to be done again. In fact, a certain stage had been reached which opened out new hopes, but they were hopes destined to disappointment. The representative principle had been carried far, but it was crippled by antiquated forms and stultified by the exclusion of an entire sex. The attempt in the present day to carry it to its logical conclusion has been born of the needs of the time, and is in line with the whole effort towards social progress. Democracy may be nothing but an experiment, and of the results of an experiment time alone can judge. But it is an experiment worth the making in a world where no alternative mode of government holds out equal hopes of social progress. In any case before it can be judged the experiment must be complete, and it can be completed only by the removal of every artificial barrier of sex, property, or the chicanery of complex laws, to the exercise of the rights of citizenship.

The Growth of the State

To answer the questions proposed at the end of the last lecture would be to write a book in many volumes. The task of measuring the actual movement of civilization becomes manageable only by a division of labour. I have attempted elsewhere to deal with it from the point of view of ethics[1] – a point of view which necessarily involves something of the development of religion and something of the development of jurisprudence within its scope. Recently Dr Müller Lyer, in his *Phasen der Kultur*,[2] has applied a similar treatment to the development of industry. Enough has been done to indicate some of the difficulties that beset this method of treatment, and also to suggest certain results. These I will endeavour to indicate to you by taking one side of social life, and tracing development on this side as we pass from the simplest to the most advanced modern societies. As some compensation for the limitations of the enquiry, I will take one of the fundamental problems. I will ask you to consider the nature of the social bond, to examine what is common to all societies and what is distinctive, and I shall try to show that what is distinctive in the nature of the social bond forms a fundamental principle of classification in any social morphology, and serves as one of the measuring rods which helps us to determine the nature of the movement which has made modern civilization what it is. From one point of view, as has been seen, social progress may be regarded as development of the principle of union, order, co-operation, harmony among human beings. This

[1] *Morals in Evolution* (London, 1906).
[2] F. Müller-Lyer, *Phasen der Kultur und Richtungslinien des Fortschritts* (Jena, 1908).

136

development may be traced in the first instance by means of a classification of the main types of social organization in accordance with the distinctive nature of the social bond.

Now there are, as has been hinted, some forces making for union which are common to the life of all society from the lowest to the highest. There is, for example, a certain mutual interest of a complex kind, which, from the lowest group of savages to the most highly developed civilized structure, tends to keep men together and maintain a certain kind of cooperation. This mutual interest,[a] moreover, is not entirely of a selfish character. It is not only that men have need of one another for mutual defence, or, at a higher stage, for cooperation in industry or in science; there is also the interest in another sense which we take in one another as human beings, and which is a wider thing than sympathy and a less purely moral thing than altruism or unselfishness. The solitary life is, for all but the most exceptional of individuals, the least tolerable of all. We choose – like Alexander Selkirk – 'to dwell in the midst of alarms' rather than to reign in a horrible place of solitude. Those we hate are preferable as companions to the desert and the seas. This mutuality of interests, so to speak, is something underlying all human, perhaps even all animal, association. It does not therefore serve as a distinguishing principle in social classifications. Doubtless it undergoes changes of degree and even of kind; as society progresses, the interest widens and deepens. On the whole, in the higher societies its more benevolent aspects tend to predominate; but we could not, I think, from these changes of degree make a universal basis of classification.

What we need for our purposes is to find certain principles of union, which serve as bonds for human society, and each of which may at successive stages be regarded as the *leading force* which gives its character to the social union. It is not necessary at a higher stage that the bond operating at a lower should disappear. On the contrary, we shall see that it is still maintained in its own place. But the different forces which I shall distinguish may, I think, be regarded as the dominant forces, each in certain great classes of human society.

[a] Which corresponds, I take it, broadly to what Professor Giddings called the Consciousness of Kind. [In *The Elements of Sociology* (New York, 1898), F. H. Giddings defined 'consciousness of kind' as 'that pleasurable state of mind which includes organic sympathy, the perception of resemblance, conscious or reflective sympathy, affection, and the desire for recognition' (p. 66).]

These forces may be grouped under three main heads, which may be called the leading principles of social union. They are the principles, first, of kinship; secondly, of authority; and thirdly, of citizenship. It should, of course, at once be explained that a most important bond, distinguished in a way from all these three, is that of a common religion; but it will be seen, as our examination advances, that the element of religion is common to all forms of society, and is to be regarded not so much as a distinct basis of social union, but rather from this point of view as an element involved in the social consciousness itself and as a factor strengthening its hold upon the minds of men.

What, then, are the different forms of society that we find based upon these three main principles? To begin with kinship. The lower forms of society appear to rest in a special way upon the tie of blood, and the way in which this tie is conceived, the extent to which it is recognized, and the manner in which it is extended, whether by fictitious forms or in other ways, gives the key to the social order of the greater part of the uncivilized world. In all the varieties that we find, the one permanent element – as it is, in the order of nature, the most indestructable element – is the relation of mother and children. When some thinkers conceived primitive man as possibly living, isolated, in a state of nature, they forgot one simple and well-established generalization – that all men have mothers; and whatever may be said of the inferior parent, it is at least the universal property of mothers to tend their children, feed, protect and shelter them as they grow up. This primitive group, which is constituted by the mother and children, runs alike through all forms of primitive and advanced society. It gives rise in the uncivilized world to two main forms of the social structure, which differ in accordance with the position of the husband and father. The husband may form a permanent union with the mother of such a kind that upon marriage a new family group is formed, which will consist not of mother and children alone, but of parents and children. In this case – speaking generally – the position of the father dominates the life of the family; the father remains in his own clan and the wife joins him, and the new group is added to the paternal clan. If we conceive such a family growing up and the sons taking to themselves fresh wives, we can imagine each new family forming a part of the larger household, a family within a family, a part within a whole. We can conceive the grandfather continuing to bear rule, and on his death handing over his authority, perhaps to his eldest son, perhaps to the son pointed out by natural gifts and attainments for the post of honour. If such a stock is fruitful and multiplies, we have a model of the patriarchate, the form of early society familiar to the first anthropological inquirers from the Book of Genesis, from the Roman law, and from what was known of our own Teutonic ancestors. It was a very natural inference to be drawn in the early stage of anthropology that this was in fact the primaeval form of human society, but a little further investigation shows that there is another possibility, which has actually been realized over a large part of the earth. The primitive group of mother and children might be formed into a larger society upon a different principle. The connection of husband and wife might be of a less intimate kind. A husband might remain a member of his own clan or of his own group, while the mother and her children remained associated with the group in which she was born; and descent, upon this principle, would continue in the female line, the daughters in their turn obtaining husbands from without, the sons remaining attached to the group, but finding themselves wives in another family. This is the system of maternal kinship in which descent goes, as it is termed, by mother-right. Whether this is the primitive system or not, the evidence is not sufficient to decide, but it is widely diffused in the uncivilized world, and traces of it are to be found in forms, both of civilized and uncivilized society, which have adopted the patriarchate.

The two forms of grouping are permeated by two different conceptions of kinship. In the one, kinship through the female is all-important, and in extreme cases is the only kind of kinship that counts. In the other, kinship through the male is the predominant factor, and kinship through the mother is secondary, is not as a rule reckoned so far and does not carry the same legal consequences. These differences are particularly important in relation to a further development of kinship which is now to be mentioned. It is to be observed that direct descent is not the only form of kinship known either to primitive or to advanced societies. It is certainly conceivable that a single patriarchal family, such as we have first described, might, if it be fruitful and multiply with exceptional success, develop into a clan and even into a large society; but such multiplication could only be very exceptional. In point of fact, another cause of growth has always to be taken into account. Whether kinship be reckoned through one parent alone or through both, it is the almost universal rule that the son or daughter should find a mate from outside the kin, as the kin are reckoned. This is an application of what is known as the principle of exogamy – a principle common to the Chinese, who forbid marriage between all persons of the same name, to the Red Indian, who forbids it to all of the same totem, and to ourselves, who do not allow it within what are known as the 'forbidden degrees'. Enormously as rules of exogamy differ, the total failure of any prohibition is exceedingly rare, if it is to be found at all, in human society, and the general result of exogamy is clear. It compels a union of distinct families, and in so far as kinship is a basis of co-operation, mutual defence, and so forth, it tends to connect certain families for these purposes. Thus when we speak of kinship as a basis of society we must bear in mind that kinship involves two distinct lines of interconnection – the line of descent and the line of intermarriage. Hence such a society is not limited to one family, but rather implies some association between several stocks.

But limiting, and in a sense counteracting, the rule of exogamy is the hardly less general rule of endogamy, which enjoins marriage within a certain group, and it can easily be seen that while this principle would tend to isolate the group to which it applies, it would equally strengthen the bonds of connection within that group. Endogamy within the clan, for example, would tend to intensify clan life and at the same time tend to seperate the clan from the rest of the world. So when the clan develops into a wider society, or when different clans come into association and begin to form a state, the process is frequently marked by a break-down of endogamous rules. In Rome, for example, marriage seems to have been originally limited to the *gens*. Then the patrician *gentes* came together and formed a circle of intermarrying clans, from which the *plebs* was excluded. The *plebs* obtained the *jus connubii* in 445 BC, and the same right was at an early period extended to the Latins. With the extension of Latin rights, and subsequently of full Roman rights, the possible circle of legal marriage was widened until it included the whole vast Roman world.

So much may be said in common of the principle of kinship, whether it be based on the blood of the father, or of the mother, or of both parents. But there is one important sociological difference between the two cases. Where mother-right prevails, the natural family, that is to say, the union of father, mother, and children, is never complete. The tie between the children and the mother's relations is one thing, and the tie between them and the father and his kin is another thing. The two cut across one another, so that normally under this system the child looks to his maternal relatives for support and protection rather than to his father. So too – as in the case of the Iroquois – the totemic bond cuts across the tribal, and each man is subject, as it were, to two allegiances. It can readily be seen that this does not form so firm a basis for a solid social structure as the paternal family, which makes direct descent always the closest and most substantial relationship and constitutes the natural family a unit, which cannot be dissolved by its relation to other families, though it may count upon these relations for mutual support. Hence it came about that the paternal family yielded the more solid basis for the larger social order of the civilized peoples. But whichever the principle adopted – and there are many gradations between the two, many cases in which elements of father-right and mother-right are blended and which may be regarded as transitional from one system to another – these forms of society resting upon kinship may be regarded as in a sense natural and primitive. They come about in the ordinary course of nature from the family instinct and the successive results which it engenders. We may conceive early society as constituted by ramifications of direct descent and intermarriage from the primordial group of mother and children, the relation of husband and wife being the variable factor giving rise where it is relatively loose to the maternal, where it is closer to the patriarchal system.

The growth of society brings new principles into play. In a primitive group there are, as a rule, few social distinctions. There is generally a leading member or head-man, but the powers of the chief are often but little developed, and are mainly dependent upon his personal prowess. It is true that when the patriarchal clan is highly developed and has grown into a body of many families, acknowledging a common descent from an ancestor who has already become mythical, his eldest male representative begins to wield despotic powers – as, for example, in a Highland clan – and his immediate relations, or perhaps his favourites and followers, begin to form a kind of aristocracy. But supposing such a clan, well-organized and disciplined under an ambitious chieftain, to betake itself to a military life, a new order of things comes into play. It will soon find occasion of quarrel with its neighbours – neighbours have a wonderful facility of giving 'just' causes of offence to those who are powerful – and the stronger clan starts upon a warlike career. A double series of results ensues. On the one hand, the weaker surrounding peoples are probably reduced to a dependent position. At the lowest stage perhaps their stronger neighbours may merely raid them for their cattle, but as soon as there is some progress in the arts of life their subjection takes a more permanent form. They may become tributary to the conquering people, who continue to live at a distance, or the conquerors may themselves enter into possession of their territory and reduce them either to a feudal vassalage or to slavery, and the distinction of conqueror and conquered will turn into that between lord and slave, or into that of upper and lower caste. Within the conquering people themselves, again, changes occur which affect the whole social order. For successful war discipline is needed, for discipline more powers must be given to the chief. Sometimes in barbaric societies this is pushed so far that the chief becomes absolute master of the persons and property of his subjects. In some of the West African States, like Dahomey and Ashanti, for example, he was the master of the person and property of every man and woman in his dominions. Any man might be made his slave, any woman be taken into his harem. Usually this exaltation of the chief is accompanied and fostered by religious or magical conceptions. The chief is a man-god; his person is sacred; it is even dangerous to his subjects to approach and look upon him. As in Ancient Egypt and in Babylon, his sanctity is carried to such a point that he has to be hedged round by minute ceremonial, his doings intimately affect the fortunes of the people, he becomes responsible for the weather and the crops, and finally, he is hedged in with so many taboos that from being absolute master he becomes a slave – the slave of his own courtiers and the priests; and if he does not manage the weather and the crops aright, it may be the worse for him, not, of course, for his royal spirit – *that* is sacred and immortal – but for the mere body in which it is housed it is another question.

But turning from the religious to the political side of the process, the actual power of a king, it may be observed, is limited by the narrowness of human capacity. The remark is attributed – upon what authority I do not know – to Nicholas I, the most autocratic of the czars, that 'Russia was governed by ten thousand clerks.' The remark, at any rate, was true, as subsequent czars have probably realized. One man cannot ever govern a great empire. The exceptions of Julius Caesar and Napoleon exist only to prove the rule, and the greater the empire, the wider the authority, the more it must be delegated. The followers and dependants of the king are naturally favoured in the distribution of territory when land is conquered, and they rise to the position of feudal lords, to aspire to some independence where distance tends in their favour. You may remember the story given by Tacitus of the provincial governor who explained to the Emperor Tiberius that it would be better not to raise the question of his removal. He had a large army under his immediate command, and they might (this nominal dependant went on) form a kind of treaty by which the one should be thoroughly loyal and a most obedient subject, but the other should entertain no question of removing him from his command. True or not, this story, dating from the beginnings of the Empire, gives a significant hint of the troubles that recurred throughout the imperial history whenever the hand at the centre weakened in its grasp, and which finally led to disruption and decay.

Conquest is originally based on force, but unadulterated force is never a permanent basis of social life. The ruler must at least clothe himself with the garb of justice or utility. He finds possibly a religious title, whether in the sanctity of his line or in the ordinance of God. In the lower order of such societies, as we have seen, he is himself God, or of the lineage of God, like the Pharaohs. At a higher remove, as with the absolute monarchs of western civilization, he is God's Anointed, he rules by Divine Right. It is rarely the case, as in India, that a priestly caste maintains the supremacy and guarantees the authority of the king, as it were, from above and not from below. But under whatever form, the tendency of this kind of social order is to transmute force into authority. The king governs, it may be – as in the Chinese theory – for the good of his subjects, but it is he who knows what is for their good. He is the fountain of justice, the pillar of the social order, the source of every law and ordinance.

The ideas underlying the social fabric are modified in correspondence with this conception. In the primitive community custom was sacred because it was custom, and because of certain sanctions, religious and magical, attending on its violation. In the more elaborate and advanced societies the rule of primitive custom is in some measure broken up. Law is no longer the direct, naive expression of the popular life. It is in truth at this stage, what some jurists have mistakenly supposed it to be in its essential nature, a command imposed by a superior upon an inferior and enforced by him through the medium of punishment. And it should be understood that the principle of subordination is not confined to the relation of governing and governed; it may run through the whole social life. We may have a feudal hierarchy of lord and vassal, descending from the king to the lowest subject. We may have a hierarchy of castes, as in India, or we may have an industrial system based on the relation of master and slave, or in the more mitigated form of that of lord and serf, and we may have this principle of subordination maintaining itself in the midst of higher social life in the more or less modified forms familiar to ourselves, in distinctions of class and in conceptions of social, political, or economic inferiority.

At the same time it should be noted that the transmutation of force into authority may have its good side. The absolute monarch may be in fact as well as in name the father of his people. He can often secure a better social order, and even a higher degree of justice, than can be achieved in the primitive society of the kindred. The very fact that he is raised above the body of his subjects may enable him to deal with them impartially; while by the same supremacy he may overcome the discords of nobles, suppress feudal strife, and weld a great people into a single nation. In such a nation there is a sense of solidarity which allows a higher principle to come into being, of which we shall speak a little later on.

But observe first that the authoritarian order has its own moral code, a code which is not perfect, but by no means to be despised. If the superior has privileges, he has also duties. According to the Chinese teachers, the emperor is the last person in the state to be considered. In Ancient Babylon a nobleman, who was tormented by evil spirits, was asked by the exorciser among other things, whether he had done his duty to his dependants, whether he had bound men who should have been free, or left those in prison whom he should have liberated. In Ancient Egypt kings and governors never fail to take credit to themselves in funeral inscriptions for their beneficence and kindness of heart to those whom they had ruled. Of the duties that are inculcated under this head by the higher religions it is needless to speak. All that must be said is that, excellent as these qualities are, they are relative to a social system which creates the necessity for them by its own inherent defects. Benevolence is beautiful, but it is not based on justice, nor is the 'Lady Bountiful' the last word of progress in ethics and civilization. Religion and ethics, like government, have their 'authoritarian' phase – the phase in which they are conceived as imposed from above and embodied in a hierarchy, and in which their most characteristic teaching is to inculcate the virtues of meekness and obedience on the one side, and on the other gentleness and forbearance in the use of that power which they consecrate with lawful authority.

The Principle of Citizenship

The authority of the superior is not the only method of organizing a large territory and maintaining order and harmony among a large population. There is an alternative known to the civilized, though hardly to the savage and barbarian world, in which the relation of government and governed are in a manner inverted. The people, or at any rate the citizens, are the state. The government is their servant rather than their master, and its members are as much bound by law as the humblest subject of the state. The social bond in this case may often be reinforced by a somewhat vague and extended sense of relationship, by a common language, and by all the complex relations, so difficult to define and analyse, that constitute a common nationality. But the civic bond as such is not the same thing as the link of language or nationality. It consists essentially in a certain reciprocity of obligation as between the individual members of the state, and also as between the state and its members. In some respects the state – to give that name to the social union based on citizenship – resembles the earlier commune. Its government, its laws and customs, come again into close relation with the actual life and character of the people. Law is no longer a command imposed by a superior, but an expression of the will of those who will obey it. So far as the principle of citizenship is carried through, there is a return to a certain equality among members of the state, replacing the hierarchical order of the authoritarian society, and recalling the equality of primitive times. But the resemblances are analogical rather than morphological. There is all the difference in the world between an equality which rests on a recognition of reciprocal obligations overriding pre-eminence of power, and one which subsists merely because no power has risen to an eminence which could disturb it. There is no less difference between a body of custom which expresses the life and character of a society – in the sense that it forms the framework subsisting unchanged through ages into which each new generation fits itself automatically, accepting what it finds without question – and the laws which a changing and developing society makes and remakes with a conscious sense of its needs. There is no less difference between the member of a clan whose rights and responsibilities are fixed by his place in the clan and the individual who can shape his own life and whose rights and responsibilities are determined principally by his own actions and agreements. The fully responsible individual, on the one side, and the legislative government expressing the will of the majority, on the other, are the characteristics of the state.

Now the principle of citizenship may be carried out with very varying degrees of thoroughness. It is complicated by questions of kinship, race, and nationality, and it is in practice blended in greater or lesser degree with the principle of authority. Further, the life of the state depends a good deal on the area which it covers, and is gravely affected by its external relations. These considerations go far to determine the actual character, the forms, and the life of the state as we see them in history. The earliest form of the state known to us is the city state of ancient Greece. Here the typical state was a fortified town of moderate and often of very small dimensions according to our standards, occupying a strong position in a strip of territory belonging to and cultivated by its citizens. But even in this small community the principle of citizenship was not pushed through. In most states a considerable part of the population were either slaves, as at Athens, or formed a servile caste like the Helots at Sparta, and whatever rights were secured to the slaves by law, custom, or religion, they were certainly in no sense citizens.

So far the despotic principle remained vigorous and living within the system of the free community. But in many states there were further gradations among the free men themselves. There were close oligarchies, like those of Thebes and Sparta, to whose members alone the privileges of government were confined, while the rest of the population, though personally free, like the Spartan Perioeci, or the

Roman plebs, were citizens only in the passive sense. Yet we should not deny the name of state to these oligarchical republics. The difference that separated them from the slave-holding democracy of Athens was more one of degree than of principle. The circle of the aristocracy formed internally a true state, but a state which had dependants which it governed despotically. The breaking down of class barriers and the extension of political and civic rights which makes up a large part of the history of Athens, of Rome, and of modern European nations is simply a development of the principle of citizenship at the expense of the principle of authority, until ideally it is extended to all permanent residents in the territory.

The city state of the ancients proved incapable of expansion. Democratic Athens governed her short-lived empire with reckless despotism, and the jealousies and resentments which she excited ruined the noblest city of Greece. The extension of the Roman suffrage as Rome consolidated her conquest was a beneficent admission of a wide circle to civic rights, but reduced the constitutional machinery of Rome to a farce. Citizens from all parts of Italy could not meet in the forum to elect consuls or pass a law, and the representative method was not thought of till the Republic was already dead. I will not speak here of the mediaeval city states, with their checkered but often glorious history, but will pass at once to the country states of the modern world, and will confine myself to noting two points of difference. Through the principle of representation, and often aided by the consolidation previously effected by an absolute monarchy, the modern state has largely solved the problem of uniting large areas and great populations on the basis of common citizenship; and owing to the disappearance of slavery and serfdom among white peoples has had no such sharp demarcations of free and unfree to overcome. Hence within its borders the principle of citizenship is in a fair way to be carried to its conclusion. Yet the old problems revive it in a new form. On the one hand, modern economic conditions engender inequalities of wealth and foster forms of industrial organization which constantly threaten to reduce political and civic equality to a meaningless form of words. On the other hand, within its borders the state through its very size finds itself frequently confronted with problems of race and nationality, which sometimes threaten its fundamental principles, while without it is usually encumbered with dependencies, to which it seldom scruples to add when occasion serves. Of the economic problems I shall speak later, but on the question of dependencies and of nationality a word must be said as bearing directly on the principles of government.

The conquest of a territory by force and its retention without regard to the wishes of the inhabitants is of course in flat contradiction with all the principles of citizenship. The democratic state which sends an autocratic governor to rule a great dependency is employing two distinct methods of rule, one for use at home, the other for use abroad. My own country may be regarded internally as a qualified democracy. The British Empire as a whole is as much an oligarchy as Sparta. The Indians are its Perioeci, and perhaps the Kaffirs its Helots. The government of white people by this method has, however, been abandoned. It was virtually destroyed by the American Revolution, and the renewed experiment in this direction may be said to have been brought to a conclusion when autonomy was extended to the Transvaal and the Orange Colony. The despotic principle tends now to coincide with the colour line, and much of the future of the modern state, particularly of my own country, must depend on the relation of the white to the coloured and non-European races. Until the rise of Japan as a modern power, it was almost universally believed that the characteristics of European civilization were a monopoly of race, and that whether we liked it or not, non-European peoples were forever destined to a type of civilization and a form of government totally different from ours. Probably the greatest social change now in progress in the world is the rise of a new spirit in the East which altogether repudiates this view, and the reaction of these changes upon the West will, I am convinced, if met in a statesmanlike spirit, be bracing and beneficial. We are not, however, concerned with speculation as to the future. We have only to note the fact that as it stands the principle of citizenship is crossed in the empire states of our own time with that of the authoritative government of dependencies, and that this fact has important reaction on our own domestic constitution. We cannot deny principles of liberty to Orientals, or for that matter to Zulus, and yet maintain them with the same fervour and conviction for the benefit of any one who may be oppressed among ourselves. We cannot foster a great bureaucratic class without being impregnated at home by its views of government. We cannot protect a great dependency from without except by remaining a great military and naval power; and to all these necessities our own body social must accommodate itself.

Mutatis mutandis, the same remarks apply to the foreign relations of the modern state. More and more, as means of communication multiply, the fate of each state is bound up with that of others, and the attitude of hostility still characteristic of the modern world threatens the healthy internal development of each member of the community of nations. If a nation may sometimes be consolidated by fear of an aggressor, it is consolidated as an armed camp, and its military organization tends to bring it back to the authoritarian form; the taxable resources of the community are expended on the means of defence or aggression; and the interests of the public are diverted from the improvement of social relations, not by wars, but by ever-renewed rumours of war. On this side, then, the development of the civic principle seems bound up with internationalism, and with a readjustment in the great empires of the relation of governing state and dependencies.

Within the state is apt to arise the even more difficult problem of nationality. It is in this form that the principle of kinship is mainly to be reckoned with as a political force in the modern world. Nationality, indeed, is not properly a matter of race. Most of the bodies of people which feel themselves to be nations are of highly complex racial origin. Yet the sentiment of nationality is confessedly analogous to that of kinship: it is a natural unity stronger in the fact than in the logical analysis, a composite effect of language, tradition, religion, and manners which makes certain people feel themselves at one with each other and apart from the rest of the world. Pride and self-respect are closely bound up with it, and to destroy a nationality is in a degree to wound the pride and lower the manhood of those who adhere to it. Analyse it away as we may, it remains a great force, and those states which are rooted in national unity have in them a great living power which will carry them through much adversity. But few states are fortunate enough to be one in nationality, and the problem of dealing with the minority nation is the hardest that statesmen have to solve. Clearly it is not achieved by equality of franchise. The smaller nationality does not merely want equal rights with others. It stands out for a certain life of its own. The endeavour to suppress it ends invariably in the withholding of some of the general civic rights

which are fundamental to the state system, and in this sense unrecon-
ciled nationalities are a standing danger to the civic principle. To
find the place for national rights within the unity of the state, to give
scope to national differences without destroying the organization of
a life which has somehow to be lived in common, is therefore the
problem which the modern state has to solve if it is to maintain itself.
It has not only to generalize the common rights of citizenship as
applied to individuals, but to make room for diversity and give scope
for collective sentiments which in a measure conflict with one
another. How far it will succeed is again matter of speculation, and
as such beyond the subject of our immediate inquiry, the object of
which is merely to indicate to what extent the principle of citizenship
has in fact been carried in the modern world and what are its principal
limitations.

If we put together the heads of this necessarily rough sketch, we
can, I think, trace the lines of a significant development. At the basis
we have the ties of kinship engendering the close association of the
small local group and at a higher stage of the firmly knit clan, within
the somewhat larger but looser unity of the tribe. Such associations
may have much vital force, compactness, and endurance, but they
are narrow and in proportion to their strength tend to be hard, self-
contained, and mutually hostile. They are, moreover, adapted only
to rude economic conditions and a rudimentary condition of the arts
of life. Hence, they yield with advancing civilization to the rule of
force by which, in the guise of kingly authority, far larger aggregations
of men can be held together and a more regular order can be maintained. In this change there is loss and gain, gain in the development
of order, loss in the suppression of much that is essential to humanity.
On the other hand, the principle of citizenship renders possible a
form of union as vital, as organic, as the clan and as wide as the
empire, while it adds a measure of freedom to the constituent parts
and an elasticity to the whole which are peculiarly its own. Further,
when pushed to its conclusion, it reveals the possibility of a world
state in which the constituent groups, as well as the constituent individuals, would have legitimate scope for self-development. To say
that such a state is actually in the making would be rather to give
utterance to a sanguine view than to rehearse the indubitable facts
which are the subject matter of science. But to say that the modern
world as it stands affords the conditions rendering such a state pos-

sible, and that there are important factors in the social mind working towards it is to keep within the limit of fact. Now we cannot say of humanity as a whole that it began with the system of kinship, passed into that of authority, and ended with that of citizenship. At most this might be said of certain societies, and of these the civic societies of antiquity lost their pre-eminence and fell into decay. What we can say is that the system of kinship is dominant in the lower and earlier stages of culture, that the system of authority is characteristic of the advance towards civilization, and that of citizenship of the higher civilization. It is, of course, possible that the civic systems of the present day may decay like those of antiquity, but taking it as it stands, the characteristic modern state, with all its imperfections, exhibits the most complete reconciliation yet achieved on the large scale of social co-operation with the freedom and spontaneity of the component individuals, localities, and nationalities.

The Individual and the State

Our task today is to examine the movement of opinion which has been outlined, in the light of social theory. We held that social progress consists in a harmonious development, and we further defined this conception as including a harmony in the development of the personal life of the members of society, and in the working out and fulfilment of the various and at first sight divergent elements of value which constitute the well-being of the social order. In the movement of opinion we have seen a certain conflict of ideals and our question is whether, if we probe deeper, a basis of reconstruction can be found. To find an answer let us take up the question afresh. Let us start with the conception of the social order which the principle of harmonious development would suggest. Let us consider to what view of the functions of the state and the rights of the individual it would lead and let us, in order to observe the limitations of time, deal with the question with special reference to the problem of liberty.

To begin with, the general theory of society indicated by the ideal of harmonious development is clearly one of co-operation. We may say, with Aristotle, that society is an association of human beings with a view to the good life. The social life is essentially a co-operation in the working out of common objects, and the best organized society will be that in which the co-operation is most perfect and complete; but in saying this, two distinctions have to be kept in view. In the first place co-operation has its negative as well as its positive side. Mutual aid is essential to social life; mutual forbearance is equally necessary; indeed, as a condition of living together, at least of living a harmonious life together, it is even the more fundamental of the two, and also perhaps the more difficult to secure. In thinking, then, of social life as a form of co-operation we must lay stress not only upon the activities which it cultivates in common, but on the idiosyncrasies which it tolerates, the privacy which it allows, the divergent developments of personality which it fosters.

Secondly, in speaking of the ideal of society, we must remember that social life and the life of the state are not one and the same thing. From the principle that social life is a mode of co-operation we cannot infer offhand that the function of the state is to foster co-operation of the same kind and in the same degree. To determine what functions the state itself has to perform within the co-operative social life, we have to ask ourselves, first, what are the special characteristics of the state as a form of society, and how these special characteristics affect its function. Two characteristics which affect all state action occur to us at once as bearing upon the question of its legitimate sphere. These are, in the first place, that the life of the state is crystallized into the form of definite institutions, that its ordinances have to be incorporated in laws and rules of universal application, that it must deal with men in masses and with problems in accordance with what is general and not with what is particular. Hence it is with difficulty adapted to the individuality of life; it is a clumsy instrument, as it were, for handling human variation. It is inadequate, to adapt Bacon's phrase, to the subtlety of human nature. Its sphere is the normal, the prosaic, the commonplace; its business is to solidify the substructure of society rather than to pursue its adornment. It can handle the matters upon which ordinary people usually agree better than those upon which there is variety of opinion.

In the second place, the state is a compulsory form of association. Its laws have force behind them, and not only so, but the state does not leave it open to the inhabitants of its territory to decide whether they will remain members of the association or not. In a voluntary association there are rules compulsory upon all those who remain members, but the ultimate liberty is reserved to individuals to part from the association if they please. In the case of the state, this ultimate liberty can only be exercised by quitting the state territory altogether, and even that privilege has been at various times denied to the subjects of the community, and is today not unhampered with difficulties for the poor. Now it is true that there are important functions which the state can perform without the direct use of compulsion. When government conducts a business enterprise it does not necessarily compel any one to avail himself of its services, nor does it necessarily suppress competition. On this side the question as between the state and the individual is not one of the limits of liberty, but of responsibility." But ordinarily the intervention of the state action does involve some sort of compulsion upon the individual and in what follows we will confine our attention to cases of this kind. It is not difficult to see that functions may be useful and salutary when freely performed which would be useless and even injurious when imposed on reluctant people. In a sense this may be said to be true of all moral and spiritual functions in so far as they are moral and spiritual, because when performed under compulsion they lose their moral and spiritual value. It is not to be inferred from this that the state has no moral or spiritual functions. Indeed, its action in certain capacities may be one way, and possibly the best way, of expressing the moral and spiritual interests of its members. It does suggest that its action as a spiritual body can only have value in as far as it is expressing the will of its members, and not imposing a law upon them which they do not freely and voluntarily accept.

It follows further that the legitimate functions of the state must depend upon the whole circumstances of the society which is under consideration. The kind of compulsion that is necessary, the degree of success with which compulsion can be applied, and the reflex consequences of its employment upon the general life of society will depend essentially upon the composition of the community and the relation of the government to its subjects. For example, in a very homogeneous society, where all the people are of one race, one allegiance, and one religion, there will be a general adherence to the same customs, a general sympathy with the same ideals of life, and there will be little difficulty in maintaining laws which could only be imposed upon an alien race by means of extreme severity. In such a society, then, the sphere of the state can quite usefully be extended to functions which, in a complex empire governing men of different nationalities and rival religions, will produce confusion and the breaking-up of laws. One cannot, then, lay down general rules as to the functions of the state which will apply to all times and places. Our only general rule will be that, seeing that the state is a form of

" See p. 162.

association and is limited by the fact that its functions have to be crystallized in definite institutions, expressed in universal laws and in large measure carried out by the use of compulsion, their sphere must be determined by considering how far the objects of social co-operation can be furthered by methods of this kind, or how far, on the other hand, the nature of the methods necessary will itself conflict with the ends desired.

In this discussion we have said nothing as yet of the rights of the individual as such, or of the ideal of liberty as itself a fundamental barrier to certain kinds of state action. In fact, this antithesis between the rights of the individual and the welfare of the state, between liberty as such and restraint as such, appears to be a false antithesis. To begin with, if liberty is a social conception, there can be no liberty without social restraint. For any one person, indeed, there might be a maximum of liberty if all social restraints were removed. Where physical strength alone prevails the strongest man has unlimited liberty to do what he likes with the weaker; but clearly, the greater the freedom of the strong man the less the freedom of the weaker. What we mean by liberty as a social conception is a right to be shared by all members of society, and very little consideration suffices to show that, in the absence of restraints enforced on and accepted by all members of a society, the liberty of some must involve the oppression of others. Just as the liberty of the strong man to assail the weak destroys the liberty of the weak man to call his body his own, so – to take an instance from our own contemporary experience – the liberty of the motor-car to use the roads may, and often does, go so far as to impair the liberty of any other class of vehicle or the liberty of pedestrians to use the same road for their purposes. Excess of liberty contradicts itself. In short, there is no such thing; there is only liberty for one and restraint for another. If liberty then be regarded as a social ideal, the problem of establishing liberty must be a problem of organizing restraints; and thus the conception of a liberty which is to set an entire people free from its government appears to be a self-contradictory ideal. Like other contradictory ideals, it has in fact an historical explanation. A community as a whole may cherish the ideal of freedom, and by freedom may mean escape from the whole system of government under which it lives, when that system of government is imposed by an alien power. Thus a subject nationality or a subject class may claim freedom in a quite general sense, but it is freedom, if properly understood, not from government altogether but from alien government, not from law as such, but from the particular laws alien to the good of the subject people, which are imposed upon them from without. In a self-governing people, unless the machinery of democracy is very sadly out of gear, so complete a want of touch between governing and governed can hardly be apprehended. Law and government in such a case must in the main express the character, on the whole forward the collective purpose of at least the majority of the individuals constituting the community. And here arises an important corollary to what has been said above of the ethical basis of state functions. So far as self-government is genuinely realized, state action expresses the combined will of individuals. The desires of the individual citizen may effectuate themselves most fully through state machinery, and in so far as the law and the administration are carrying out the moral will of the majority, so far their action has just as much moral value as though it were performed by the individuals themselves through the agency of a voluntary association. Hence when we trace the growing confidence in state action to the advance of democratic institutions we touch a deeper principle than that of the mere political control of the legislative and administrative machine. As long as law could be fairly regarded as a rule imposed by a superior there was a serious meaning in the antithesis between that which the law did for people and that which people did for themselves. There was point in the demand for self-help and the voluntary organization of mutual aid as something intrinsically superior to the parental interference of a superior authority. There was a ground for saying that the former method fostered a manly independence and a 'living' sense of social responsibility, while the latter was a species of charity which might sap these qualities. But when the reform of the law depends on the deliberate resolve of the people themselves, when it is won at the cost of a hard-fought political struggle, by the appeal to reason, by a contest involving widespread earnestness, some self-sacrifice, much serious attention to some social problem and the means of solving it, then the law is no magician's wand helping people out of trouble with no effort of their own. It is the reward of effort. It is the expression of a general resolve. It embodies a collective sense of responsibility. It is, in a word, something that a mass of people have achieved by their combined efforts for their common ends, just as a well-organized trade-union or a friendly society is an achievement won by combined effort for common ends. Now this, it may be objected, is an idealized picture of the working of democracy, and I am far from ignoring the seamier side. Nevertheless in so far as popular government succeeds, it does realize some elements of this ideal, and just so far the older objection to the extension of the sphere of the law which rests on the danger of weakening the moral fibre loses its strength.

But we can carry the argument a step further. If liberty is among other things the right of self-expression, this is a right which masses of men may claim when they want the same thing. Majorities will claim it as well as minorities, and they will seek to use the means that lie to hand for effectuating their claim. Now it may be that legal .nachinery is the only efficient means for the purpose, and if the members of a majority are debarred from the use of such machinery, their will is to that extent frustrated and their right so far denied. Now there may be good grounds for this denial. It may be better that a majority should be prevented in any given instance from exercising its will. The objections to the use of coercion in some directions may be, and for my part I should agree that they are, so great that it is better that the majority should fail to get its way. But do not let us shut our eyes to the fact that to insist on this in any case, whether for good and sufficient or for bad and insufficient reasons, is alike to put a restraint on self-expression, and to that extent upon liberty. The liberty of the minority in such a case is (as always) a restraint upon the majority.

Two questions, it will be seen, arise from this discussion. The first is, what are those matters in which the majority can only find self-expression through the machinery of law? The second is, what are those considerations which may legitimately restrain the majority from exercising their power even when as a result their *prima facie* right of self-expression is defeated?

The reply to the first question is in principle simple enough. Experience shows us that there are many things that can be done by individual initiative and by voluntary association, but that there are also many things in which these two agencies fail. A man may worship God as his own feelings dictate without compelling others to worship with him. He may associate himself with those who are like-minded. He may form a church where all may worship together after the fashion upon which they are agreed; and their worship, if it is a worship in spirit and in truth, is none the less hearty, none the less spiritually effective because of the existence of others who frequent different churches or who frequent no church at all. The effective formation of religious organization then does not depend upon universal adhesion, and in carrying out their common will, the members of a church have not to depend on securing the co-operation of those who differ from them. Hence, for this reason if for no other, the religious life of a community may be pursued with vigour without calling on the state for support.

On the other hand, there are many cases in which co-operation, if not universal, is altogether ineffective. Take, as an instance, the question of the early closing of shops. The great majority of employers in a given district may desire to close early, both for their own sake and for the good of those in their employment; but, as every one knows, in the world of competition the refusal of a handful of men, and perhaps even of a single tradesman, to agree to the common desire may wreck the whole intention. Unless the minority can be compelled to come in, the majority cannot get their way. In such case it would seem that an end, which the community holds valuable and which the majority of those affected by it desire, is a fair subject for enforcement by the common law with its compulsory powers.

Again, paradoxical as it seems at first sight, it is nevertheless profoundly true that there are cases in which the interest not of one man only or of some men, but of all considered individually and temporarily, is opposed to the interest of all considered collectively and permanently. Thus it is the interest of any individual at any moment to buy what he wants as cheaply as he can. But it is quite possible that a system of free competition catering for the temporary needs of each individual purchaser should have the effect of gradually and imperceptibly lowering the standard of production by substituting cheapness for quality. If so, the process set up by each man following his immediate interest may result in a general deterioration of standard whereby in the end the interest of each is less effectively served. Nor can the individual stand alone against this process by exercising a more far-sighted view. He cannot resist the tendency set in motion and constantly propelled by the pressure of immediate interests. It is only concerted action that is effective against the pressure of the mass, and if by such action a higher standard of quality can be permanently maintained, all are in the end the gainers. To take a slightly different illustration: any man driving a motor-car wants to get on as quickly as he can. The same man when walking may be annoyed or endangered by the speed of other people's cars, but by driving carefully himself he cannot force others to do the same. He can secure his safety only by supporting legislative and general control. Once again: it may be the interest of any particular employer to buy labour as cheaply as possible. He cannot, unless he has exceptional organizing capacity, pay more than others. But it is not to the interest of employers as a whole that the classes from whom their work-people are drawn should deteriorate in efficiency and lose in purchasing power through low wages and bad industrial conditions. Hence collectively they may be ready to accept regulations which individually they would be powerless to put in force.

The principal sphere of the state then appears to be in securing those common ends in which uniformity or, more generally, concerted action, is necessary. On the other hand, purposes which can be secured without compelling the adhesion of those who do not accept them fall naturally within the sphere of individual enterprise and voluntary co-operation. The function of the state then is to secure the common ends which recommend themselves to the general will and which cannot be secured without compulsion. But at this point our second question emerges: Is the general will, supposing that its ends cannot be secured without compulsion, to be entirely unfettered, or are there some general considerations which might still exercise a restraint in favour of the liberty of the individual?

This brings us to the question on what that liberty is based. We have seen that each man's liberty involves a restraint upon others, and we are asked to conceive it now as a restraint upon society as a whole. On what grounds is this restraint to be justified? In ordinary phraseology, it would depend upon the rights of the individual, and we have here to ask what is meant by a right. A right is generally said to be the correlative of a duty. If I have a right against you, you have some duty towards me. The duty may be quite general and purely negative in its character. For instance, I have a right to walk along the street without being pushed off the pavement into the mud, and your duty is merely to give me reasonable room. But, whether general or special, we may agree that the rights and duties of citizens form together a system making up as a whole the moral order recognized by society. In this order each duty is, broadly speaking, that which is expected of the individual; and each right is that which the individual expects of some other person or of society at large. Generically, therefore, a right is a kind of expectation; but it is not only an expectation, but an expectation held to be justified; and the important question is, on what grounds this justification is based. In the first place, it may be a legal right, and the justification then lies in an appeal to law. But, in addition, there are, or there may be, rights which the law does not recognize and which the moral consciousness holds ought to be recognized. These are the moral or ethical rights of men. The older thinkers spoke of them as 'natural rights', but to this phrase, if uncritically used, there is the grave objection that it suggests that such rights are independent of society, whereas, if our arguments hold, there is no moral order independent of society and therefore no rights which, apart from the social consciousness, would be recognized at all. Our analysis of the term 'right' goes to show that a right is nothing but an expectation which will appeal to an impartial person. A may make a claim on B, and B may refuse the claim. The claim only becomes recognized as a right if some impartial third person (C) upholds A in making it, and on what ground can C as an impartial being base his judgement? As impartial, he is looking at A and B just as two persons equally members of the community with himself. If there exists a rule recognized by the community which covers the case, no question arises. But we are looking at the case in which no rule exists, and C has to frame his decision on first principles. To what in such a case can he look except the common good? If he maintains as a right a general principle of action incompatible with the good of the community, he must hold that what is right is one thing and what is good another, and that not merely by the accidental circumstances of a peculiar case but as a matter of principle. Unless then we are to suppose such deep-seated conflict in the ethical order we must regard the common good as the foundation of all personal rights. If that is so, the rights of man are those expectations which the common good justify him in entertaining, and we may even admit that there are natural rights of man if we conceive the common good as resting upon certain elementary conditions affecting the life of society, which hold good whether people recognize them or not. Natural rights, in that case, are those expectations which it would be well for a society to guarantee to its members, whether it does or does not actually guarantee them. If this view is accorded, the more developed the conception of the common good the more completely will a society guarantee the natural rights of its individual members. To extend the conception of the rights of the individual will be one of the objects of statesmanship; to define and maintain the rights of its members will be the ever extending function of government.

Any genuine right then is one of the conditions of social welfare, and the conception of harmonious development suggests that there will be many such conditions governing the various sides of social life. If so the general conception of harmony implies that these conditions, properly understood, must mutually define and limit one another; not only so, it implies that in proportion as they are properly understood they will be found not to conflict with one another but to support and in the end even necessitate one another. Now it is conceivable that all individual rights, *e.g.* of person and property, might be brought under the general conception of liberty. But we need not press this point. We may assume that there will be various rights of the individual, of the family, and so forth, which owe their validity to the functions they perform in the harmonious development of society. It is clear too that the effective exercise of the common will is also for some purposes – though for what purpose in particular may be a matter on which opinion differs – a condition of the same object. Now in general the problem of social philosophy is to define in principle, and of statesmanship to adjust in practice the bearing of these several conditions. This bearing is to be understood by considering their social value, and thus it remains to state in quite general terms the basis of the value of personal liberty on the one hand and of social control on the other. As to liberty in general, since society is made up of persons, we prove its necessity sufficiently if we show that a measure of liberty is essential to the development of personality. And since personality consists in rational determination by clear-sighted purpose as against the rule of impulse on the one side or external compulsion on the other, it follows that liberty of choice is the condition of its development. The central condition of such development is self-guidance. We should not oppose self-guidance to guidance by others for the contact with other minds is an integral part of the growth, intellectual or moral, of each mind. But we must oppose it to coercion by external sanctions, which ousts all genuinely ethical considerations and closes the door on rational choice. Liberty then is the condition of mental and moral expansion, and of all forms of associated as well as personal life that rest for their value on spontaneous feeling and the sincere response of the intellect and of the will. It is therefore the foundation not only of all that part of life which rests on personal affection, but also of science and philosophy, of religion, art, and morals.

To recognize liberty on this side is the duty of the state, but to recognize liberty is by no means to abolish restraint. On the contrary, it is only by an organized system of restraints that such liberty is made available for all members of society, for the unpopular opinions as well as the popular ones, for those whose views of life are eccentric as well as for the normal and the commonplace. Even in regard to matters of conscience it is only opinion and persuasion that can be absolutely free, and even here it must be admitted that there are forms of persuasion that are in fact coercive, and it is fair for the state to consider how far the liberty of the younger or weaker must be protected against forms of temptation which overcome the will. Apart from this when opinion leads, however conscientiously, to action, such action may coerce others, and this would bring the state into play in the name of liberty itself. It may, more generally, infringe any right and it is the business of social control to adjust one right to another.

This adjustment is simply one part, though one of the most important parts, of the general function of social control. This function may now be defined in general terms as that of securing the best conditions for the common life (*a*) so far as these are best obtained by the use of public resources and governmental machinery, (*b*) so far as such conditions are only obtainable by the use of compulsion; that is to say, where action is frustrated if it is not universal, and again where in the absence of regulation one man can directly or indirectly constrain another, infringe his rights, obstruct his rational choice, or take advantage of his weakness or ignorance. The first object includes the organization of public services by the state[*] and the provision for all its members of the external conditions of a healthy and efficient civic life. To build on this foundation is the work of the individual,

---

[*] This, as remarked above (pp. 153–4), does not necessarily involve compulsion, and so far does not affect the question of the limits of liberty. It does, however, intimately concern the cognate question of the limits of personal and collective responsibility.

and the scope of personality is increased in proportion as the conditions of its effective development are made universal. The extension of the functions of the state in this direction, accordingly, is due not to a diminished sense of personal responsibility but to a heightened sense of collective responsibility. The second case includes the laying down of certain rules, as in the adoption of general holidays, where in the absence of legal control a general desire might be thwarted by individual and perhaps quite selfish objections. It covers, again, the regulation of contract where experience has shown that the weaker party to a bargain may be forced to consent to that which, if he stood on equal terms, he would never accept. In both cases as has been shown but particualrly in the latter the purpose of control is rather to define and enlarge the sphere of liberty than to restrict it. There remains the question of those who are incapable of rational choice – the feeble-minded or the habitual drunkard – for whom the value of liberty does not exist. To them society owes the duties of a guardian, and in their case the policy of constraining a man for his own good is no self-contradiction, for the 'good' of which they are capable is not that of personal development through the spontaneous action of thought and feeling and will, but the negative one of immunity from the dangers into which their helplessness might lead them. This is the exception proving the rule that a normal human being is not to be coerced for his own good, because as a rational being his good depends on self-determination, and is impaired or destroyed by coercion.

Thus liberty and control are not as such opposed. There are borderland cases where honest thinkers must allow conflict to be possible, *e.g.* the conscientious refusal of a Friend[1] to render military service judged to be necessary for the safety of the community. But the value of liberty is to build up the life of the mind, while the value of state control lies in securing the external conditions, including the mutual restraint, whereby the life of the mind is rendered secure. In the former sphere compulsion only defeats itself. In the latter liberty defeats itself. Hence in the main the extension of control does not impair liberty, but on the contrary is itself the means of extending liberty and may and should be conceived with that very object in view. Thus it is that upon the whole we see a tendency to the removal

---

[1] 'Friend': a Quaker, a member of the religious 'Society of Friends'.

of restraints in the sphere in which whatever there is of value to mankind depends on spontaneity of impulse, free interchange of ideas, and voluntary co-operation going along with the tendency to draw tighter the bonds which restrain men from acting directly or indirectly to the injury of their fellows and to enlarge the borders of the action of the state in response to a developing sense of collective responsibility. We are dealing with two conditions of harmonious development apparently opposed and requiring themselves to be rendered harmonious by careful appreciation of their respective functions, and the general direction in which harmony is to be sought may be expressed by saying that the further development of the state lies in such an extension of public control as makes for the fuller liberty of the life of the mind.

The problem of liberty is not the only one raised by the movement of opinion which has been traced. There are far-reaching questions of economics involved, to discuss which would take us to the foundation of the right of property. Having, for reasons of time, to confine myself to one aspect of the question, I choose that of the relation of liberty to collective control because it lies at the root of the harmonic conception of society. If we are right in thinking that social evolution has brought us to a point at which the future movement of society may be subjected to rational control, it becomes at once vital to determine how far that control is to be reconciled with the old ideal of freedom.

If the above argument is just, we may conclude that the development of the common life, the collective effort, which has already been in progress in my country for a generation or more, is not adverse to the freedom, the responsibility, or the dignity of the individual. On the contrary it has in the past assisted and may in the future be expected to further the development of these essential features of a good social order. A more real freedom, a more general and more complete personal independence, a more stable because a more free family life are among the prime objects of the extension of social control. It is here that we realize the concrete meaning of the idea of harmony as the touchstone of social development. All one-sided progress cramps as much in one direction as it liberates in another. True development is not in metaphor but in essentials comparable to organic growth – the opening out of each element furthering instead of retarding that of others. Such a development, lastly, it has been my endeavour to show is not in conflict with immovable laws of evolution but is continuous with the line of advance which educed the higher from the lower animal forms, which evolved the human out of the animal species and civilized from barbaric society. The essential condition of this change was not the struggle for existence but the rise and growth of a principle of organic harmony or co-operation which from the first rise of parental care begins to mitigate and finally to restrict the field of struggle. Merely to point to the existence of this tendency was not, we admitted, sufficient to justify it, but we urged that its existence and success suffice to prove the feasibility of the conscious effort to carry through the harmonic principle in social life, and that this is in fact the guiding principle of a rational social philosophy. To apply such a principle, we admitted, is a matter of infinite practical difficulty, but it nowhere founders on any theoretic objections, for no essential element of social value has to be purchased at the expense of the fundamental and irrevocable loss of any other element of essential value. Its emergence constitutes a turning-point to which all previous progress leads up, and from which further progress will proceed with a new directness of aim and steadiness of tread. The keenest critics of the feasibility of social progress we saw rest their case on the tendency of the higher social ethics to preserve inferior types and so lead to racial deterioration. But on this point we saw that if it is true, which is not yet proved, that selection remains essential to social progress, the solution of the difficulty is to be found in the replacement of natural by social selection. At many points in the argument limitations of time have forced me to confine myself to mere illustrations of method in place of the full and lengthy statement of evidence which is requisite for proof. Those methods I would hope that some of you would follow out for yourselves, so as to verify or correct the conclusion to which I have sought to lead you. That conclusion I may be allowed to state provisionally and it is simply this: that the conception of social progress as a deliberate movement towards the reorganization of society in accordance with ethical ideas is not vitiated by any contradiction. It is free from any internal disharmony. Its possibility rests on the facts of evolution, of the higher tendencies of which it is indeed the outcome. It embodies a rational philosophy, it gives scope and meaning to the best impulses of human nature, and a new hope to the suffering among mankind.

Irish Nationalism and Liberal Principle

All through the nineteenth century the cause of subject nationalities was a constant stimulus to British Liberalism. Successive generations hoped and feared, wept and rejoiced with the rebels of Greece, of Italy, of Hungary, of Poland, of the Balkans. Their successes and failures were events of moment in the calendar of British Liberalism, for they were recognized as essential parts of the democratic movement, and the democratic cause was in that century looked upon as one all the world over. Nor was this sentiment ineffective. The moral support of England was in those days recognized as an asset to a cause. Individuals gave direct and tangible assistance, and there were even times when diplomacy moved. Nationalism, therefore, lay close to the heart of Liberalism. Yet there was all the time one nationality whose claims were not so readily understood as those of Greek or Italian, Pole or Bulgar. Ireland was raising a cry, protesting against grievances, formulating demands, which to impartial ears sounded very like those of other subject peoples. Here it seemed was an oppressed nationality at the British Liberal's own door, with grievances which he could redress by his own efforts if he would. Conscious – perhaps a little too conscious – of the rectitude of his intentions, the British Liberal had some difficulty in seeing himself in the light of an oppressor. But under Mr Gladstone's leadership he learned his lesson in two stages. He began by learning that there were very real grievances to be redressed, grievances resulting from the political subordination of Ireland, in particular the grievances of the Church Establishment and of the land system. But in the course of his remedial efforts he learned further that though oppressive government may do much to hold a nationality together, the redress of grievances does not necessarily loosen the bonds of national unity. While the Government of 1880–5 still oscillated between concession and coercion, the more adventurous minds began to realize that what they had preached for Italy, Hungary, and Poland must in its due measure, and with all reasonable regard to variation of circumstances, be offered to the Irish people. They were ready for the second stage upon which Mr Gladstone entered at the end of 1885, and in which, after a brief and memorable struggle, he carried with him the bulk of the Liberal Party. They had learned that the solution of the Irish question lay not in repressing Irish nationality, but in trusting it with the responsibility of self-government.

The Unionist leaders who defeated Mr Gladstone had nevertheless learnt from him the first of these two lessons. They acquired by degrees a working knowledge of the material grievances of Ireland, and bit by bit they dealt with them, confident that by so doing they would undermine the foundations of the national demand. They reached the first stage of Liberal education, but refused to advance beyond it. Time, however, has declared against them. The twenty years of resolute government which Lord Salisbury once demanded have gone by, broken only by the three years in the 'nineties, when Liberals held office without legislative power. Ireland is orderly, and, by comparison with the past, prosperous. But Ireland is still National-ist. The result is to leave the main arguments for Home Rule standing, while several of the old arguments against it are weakened or brought to naught. The Irish community is economically more vigorous, and so far more capable of self-support than it was in 1886. It is no longer a society which can be represented as honeycombed with conspiracies, or given up to disorder. It is no longer in the grip of a land system which necessitated an agrarian revolution, either as the precursor or as the first act of a self-governing Parliament. It is no longer so overtaxed that to maintain the fiscal balance with Great Britain would be to impose a permanent tribute on the smaller and poorer island. But it remains Nationalist, and the unsatisfied national sentiment of Ireland remains not only a reproach to British Liberal-ism, but a flaw in the fabric of our national security.

I dwell on the permanence of Irish nationalism, because in dealing with nationality, we are confronted with one of those political forces which may be very real and very stubborn, but which yet are neither measurable in statistics nor easily compressed into the four corners of a rigid definition. What precisely is a nationality, it may be asked, and why should it be so much a matter of concern to Liberals? Liberalism is for self-government, it is true, but, provided that all parts of a country or of an empire are equally represented on a democratic franchise in the governing assembly of the whole, what has the principle of liberty to say further in the matter? Why should it be on the side of division or against unity? It is not ever so. On the contrary, national jealousies, rival patriotisms are constantly thwarting another branch of Liberal endeavour. It must be frankly recognized that the development of nationality in Europe is in large measure responsible for the modern recrudescence of militarism. As a policy of peace and international goodwill, Liberalism has to make some sacrifices, and take some risks in upholding nationality. What does it gain in return? If its ideal is humanitarian, why must it countenance the national idea, self-centred and intolerant as the idea too often becomes?

The answer to this question is written in the history of the dealings of Governments with subject nationalities, Irish or other. The primary object of political Liberalism is to found Government on freedom. This end is not compassed at a stroke by the simple method of establishing a well-oiled representative machine. It involves, to deal with externals only, freedom of speech, of writing, of meeting, of organization. It involves the security of personal rights as much against the Executive Government as against any private aggression. But when a larger nation forcibly incorporates a smaller one in its system it is easy to see the difficulty of maintaining order on these lines. A free government in the full sense of the term must be founded on the voluntary adhesion of the mass of the people. This adhesion is not necessarily impaired by the conflicts of interest or conviction which are the inevitable incidents of public life in any community, and which compel now one section and now another to submit to laws or acts of government which it resents. As long as each class feels that its claims, even if overborne in the end, will not be rejected without adequate understanding and fair consideration, there exist the elements of government by consent. But a smaller nation forcibly incorporated in a larger one does not feel this. The very constitution which is the pride of its masters is the badge of its own subjection. It may have equality of franchise, but its representatives are in a permanent minority. By history, by sentiment, perhaps by religion, race, or language, it has acquired differences of tone and habit. It regards public questions from a different angle. Its emphasis is different, its essentials are trifles to other people, and their essentials are its trifles. Its problems, even when on the surface they appear the same, have a different historic background, are interwoven with special associations, complicated with local and peculiar sympathies and animosities. With these nuances the smaller nation can never hope that the majority will deal, because the majority can never understand them. Not only so but the smaller people will have a pride, memory, and hope of its own. It may have a larger patriotism if its self-respect is first consulted, but as long as its independent being is ignored its only collective ambition will be to assert itself. Thus in the subject people the milk of social feeling is turned to gall. All that leads a free people to respect law, to support Government, to take pride in public prosperity, to sacrifice personal to common interest, will work in this case only towards discord and civil strife, and the best men become in a sense the worst citizens. At least they become the most resolute opponents of the established order. The more opposition develops, and this means the more life flourishes in the subject people, the more the tension increases. Presently definite obstructions arise in the machinery of Government and the ruling democracy, however liberal in its original intentions, is driven into 'exceptional' legislation. Constitutional rights are curtailed. Legal securities are suspended, freedom of speech is withheld. These disabilities may either be confined to the disaffected people, in which case the principle of equal rights disappears, or to save appearances as to equality they are made universal, in which case general liberty is impaired. In either event this original condition is set at naught. The essentials of political liberty are violated. Wise and moderate statesmanship may mitigate the mischief. Reactionary statesmanship may inflame it. But the seeds of trouble will always be there as long as the foreign body is embedded in the organic tissues.

But it may be asked, are we always to give way to sectional feeling? History has interwoven many races and they must surely learn to live together. What of French and British in Canada, or of British and Dutch in South Africa? What again of Ulster? If Ireland is a nation, does the nation include the Protestant half of Ulster or does it not? If yes, how can any of our tests of unity stand? If not, how can we recognize Ireland as one nation and not as two? Let us take these questions in turn, and let us consider first the measure and importance to be attached to national sentiment. We are dealing here, it has been admitted, with a force which it is impossible to measure *a priori* by any external tests. We seem able to judge it only by the event. If in fact Irish nationalism had yielded to the redress of definite grievances, if it had been practically possible to kill Home Rule by kindness, Unionist statesmanship would have been justified. I do not say justified by success, for success is not a judge giving decision by rules of equity. It would have been justified rather in the sense that it would have been experimentally proved to have been founded on a true interpretation of the case. The Unionist case – at its best – was that Irish nationalism was a passing and superficial sentiment. At its core were certain real grievances, but it was swollen into a mass of imposing appearances, but of loose and flabby texture. The plan was to remove the grievances with one hand, while with the other every ebullition of sentiment into unruly speech or action was steadily repressed. Had the plan succeeded it would have shown that Irish nationality was an illusion, or at best a thin and insubstantial product of a passing historical phase. In so far as it has failed it has shown that Irish nationality is a reality, deep rooted in the past, and to be reckoned with permanently in the future. In a word the test of nationality lies in history. If the life of one people can be absorbed into that of another so that free Government can proceed unimpeded, not violated by the habitual resort to 'exceptional legislation', the union is justified by the event. If on the other hand the demand for autonomy remains clear and persistent, through evil report and good report, through coercion and concession, through adversity and prosperity, in days of disorder when despair has reigned and in law-abiding times rendered calm by hope, there is the proof that nationality is a vital principle, and a permanent force with which liberty must make its account.

How is it then that by the gift of autonomy, time has succeeded in fusing French and British peoples into the nation of Canada, and why do we see a similar fusion proceeding between British and Dutch in South Africa? The question arises partly out of the common confusion between race and nationality. Race is a matter of physical kinship, and kinship is one of the bonds that tend to unite people and at the same time in a measure to separate them from others. But it is only one bond among many. Most modern nations, our own conspicuously, are blends of many races, and are united not so much by common ancestry as by the possession of a common country, common interests, common traditions, a common mode of life and sentiment. Further, where two or more races are intermixed, there is no means of endowing them with independent Governments. The same writ must run over the whole territory. Hence there are three possibilities. One is that one race should hold the reins of power, as generally happens when white and black live together. Another is that the country should be governed from without, and this will generally mean that the administration leans on one of the races within, and makes of it an 'Ascendancy' caste. The third is that the two races should seek to live together and govern themselves with mutual toleration. This is the experiment which has succeeded in Canada, and is succeeding so far as the white races are concerned in South Africa, and which is to be tried in Ireland. In proportion as it succeeds the two races blend, and a new nationality is formed.

But still it may be asked, why should not Ulster claim to be a nation? True, she is but a fragment of Ireland, but then Ireland is but a fragment of the United Kingdom, and St George's Channel[1] is not so very formidable a dividing line as to make all the difference. Our whole argument, it may be said, has rested on the rights of minorities, and Ulster is a minority. Why should not Ulster also be a nation? This at once suggests the counter-question, does Ulster claim to be a nation? Let us bear in mind that the term Ulster is a mode of speech, and that what is meant by it for these purposes is half Ulster, or the city of Belfast with some adjacent counties. Does Belfast, we should more rightly ask, profess and call itself a nation? Not if its desire is, what we have always understood it to be, to remain directly subject to the British Parliament. It is in fact, the focus of an old, but decayed Ascendancy caste, and its desire is to retain what it can save from the wreck of the Ascendancy system. With this demand Liberalism can have no sort of sympathy. If Belfast would condescend to put her case with a little more moderation, and a little allowance for the two sides of the question, it would be easier to meet her views. As long as she declines to make her account with the fact that the great majority of Ireland is Nationalist, and that British Liberalism is resolved to do justice at last to nationalism, she

[1] St George's Channel: the strait which separates Ireland from Wales.

rules herself out of the discussion, and leaves it to British statesmen to act for her rather than with her. Belfast is a Protestant and industrial centre in a land which is predominantly Catholic and agricultural. On both counts she may fear some inequality of treatment, and on both may legitimately receive guarantees. On the major question, that of religion, every Home Rule scheme has proposed ample guarantees and the present Bill does not fall short under this head. The problem of financial and commercial interests is more complex, but it is difficult to see how an Irish Parliament, responsible for the financial soundness of the country, could do anything to cripple the industries of Belfast without being fully aware that in so doing it would be killing the goose that lays the golden eggs. The discussion of this question, however, I must leave to those who are dealing with the financial provisions of the Bill. On the main point we may ask whether, if the Bill is to pass, Belfast will deliberately and persistently demand to be left out of its scope, and separated from Ireland in the sense and degree in which Ireland will be separated from the direct control of Great Britain. If such a demand is put forward not merely in order to wreck Home Rule, but as a substantive proposal seriously intended, it will constitute a new fact. Belfast will then be, indeed, claiming recognition as a miniature nationality, and the claim will be fairly weighed. At present it can only be regarded as highly improbable that such a claim should be maintained or even put forward except in a fighting mood. That Belfast should sustain her opposition to the whole Bill is perfectly natural, but given that there is to be Home Rule as one of the fixed conditions of a settlement, her natural position is that of a centre and rallying point for the dispersed forces of Irish Protestantism. That this is her true function in the Irish Parliament, Belfast must be as well aware as she is that her influence in that Parliament will be more than proportionate to her numerical strength.

We have spoken of nationality as a centrifugal force, as one of the influences tending to division. But there is another side to the question. When a nation obtains self-government it undertakes a new responsibility. It must keep its own peace, balance its own finances, have regard to its own common economic interests. This common responsibility does not make for division. It makes for unity. It enforces a sober regard for the claims of each part. It dictates a measure of mutual consideration which is not developed as long as one party within the country is taught to lean upon an outside power. In the past history of Ireland each party has alike been taught constantly to look to Westminster for its wants, to Westminster for redress of grievances, to Westminster perhaps for vengeance on its foes or at lowest for the means of keeping them in order. This is not the atmosphere in which mutual toleration grows. When Irishmen understand that they must go of themselves unaided and uncontrolled from without they will learn like other men that they must pull together if they are to keep off the rocks. The national element will have the majority in the Irish Parliament, and the first object of this element will be to make Home Rule a success. That they can do only by securing the co-operation, even if it be the grudging and unadmitted co-operation, of the opposition. But Belfast is not bound to content herself with these general probabilities. She has only to formulate intelligible demands consistent with the establishment of a Dublin Parliament to be assured of a respectful and considerate hearing. If she would be content to rest her case on the same basis as that of Irish nationalism itself, recognizing that nationalism must have its rights and submitting only that she in turn is a lesser nation within a nation, it would be possible to deal with her. As long as she stands on her own claims she rules herself out of the discussion.

There are many who regard the recognition of nationality as at best a regrettable necessity. They lay stress on those centrifugal tendencies that we have admitted and they feel that the greater need of mankind is for unity. But the unity which they desire can only come through the development of life in many different centres and with luxuriant divergencies of character. The doctrine of Mazzini that every nation had its own peculiar function to fulfil in the life of humanity was not pure fancy. It is easy to recognize that the leading modern nations have each, in fact, contributed something distinctive, something that would have been blurred and dulled if all had been of one speech and under one rule. Division has meant unrest, friction, war, and suffering. But it has been a necessary condition of collective vitality. Self-respect and self-confidence are necessary to a people that are to do great things, and these they cannot enjoy to the full so long as they are conscious of a mastery that galls their pride. Ireland has contributed to our literature her peculiar strain of humour and of romance, tinged with the melancholy of her historic ill-fortune. The graver tone and gentler view she will never lose, for they belong to a people who will always have behind them the memory of the centuries of that undeserved suffering which opens the eyes of men to the nature of the human tragedy. But the distinctive Irish quality may henceforward be shot with a brighter thread catching the light from her assured future as a nation. As a nation she has her part to play in the English-speaking Commonwealth, questioning the successful practicality of a dominant people with the irony, and tempering its prose with the romance born in the centuries of her probation in the valley of the shadow.

The Historical Evolution of Property, in Fact and in Idea

Summary

1. The general notion of property. It is a right of control over things which society recognizes. It may be absolute or partial, held by one person or many, or by a community, but it must be exclusive as against others, and it must have some permanence.
2. The connection of property with rational purpose, and with freedom.
3. The opposition, in this regard, between property held for use by its owner, and property as a means of controlling the labour of others.
4. Property is a recognized institution in all known societies; but in the simpler societies it is rarely, if ever, a source of 'power'. This side develops with the advance of material civilization, and culminates in the modern inequalities of wealth.
5. Of theories of property we may distinguish (*a*) the Communistic, which really attacks the whole principle of property; (*b*) the Labour theory; (*c*) the Individualistic theory, which finds it essential to character; and (*d*) the Socialistic theory. Need of discrimination between property for 'use' and for 'power', and of the extension of certain forms of State ownership in the interest of personal rights.

The Historical Evolution of Property, in Fact and in Idea[a]

A satisfactory account of the development of property in general has not yet been written, and perhaps in the present state of our knowledge cannot be written. In no department of the study of comparative institutions are the data more elusive and unsatisfactory. The divergence between legal theory and economic fact, between written law and popular custom, between implied rights and actual enjoyment, enables one and the same institution to be painted and, within limits, quite honestly and faithfully painted in very different colours. The legally minded historian will lay stress on forms or principles which have very little bearing on the actual life of the people. The economic historian, impatient of these subtleties, will ask us to look at the actual working of the institution, only to find that by some turn of events the dormant legal principle is awakened, and becomes a potent and perhaps deadly force in the working of a system. The theorist with a generalization to defend can always, by judicious selection and omission, quote travellers, ethnologists, early codes, or points of contemporary custom on his side; for he is singularly unfortunate if he cannot find something either in the every day working of the institution or in its theoretical implications, which, by ignoring other aspects, may be made to tell on his side. But any one who considers the extraordinary difficulty which our own social historians find in presenting a perfectly just picture of landed property in England in any one century, to say nothing of its development through the centuries, will realize the kind of caution which science will demand in

[a] In this paper the social functions of property are examined by the standard of purely humanitarian ethics.

reconstructing the true character of property among a simple people who have no written documents from the statements of travellers, even if they are skilled observers.

A single illustration may suffice. In a simple community practising extensive agriculture a man tells a traveller that this is 'his' land, and that his neighbour's land. The statement is duly printed, and in the end finds its way into a volume on the development of property as evidence of the individual ownership of land, without so much as a note to show the reader whether there has been any enquiry into the conditions of tenure. Another observer may state with equal truth that the land 'belongs' to the tribe, and this remark figures in a work of different tendency as equally good evidence in favour of primitive communism, though there may be nothing to show in what form the land is actually used by the members of the tribe. In some of the Australian tribes good observers tell us that there is no such thing as private property in land.[*] Among others, other writers assure us that land neither belongs to a tribe nor to a group of families but to a single male.[c] Does the difference really lie between the tribes or between the observers? Some light may be thrown on the question and on the general difficulties of method by a passage in Mr Howitt's classical work.[d] Among the coast tribes of New South Wales it appears that the land wherein a child is born is 'his' to hunt in, and even a father or mother may thus 'acquire' land when a child is born to them outside their own locality. 'The place where a man is born', said an old man, 'is his own locality and he has always the right to hunt over it, and all others born there have also the right to do so'. It may safely be said that this is one of the very last forms of title that would occur to a civilized enquirer. The effect of his examination of any single native would be to persuade him that that native owned the land where he was born. It would only be if he happened to examine several born in the same district that he would discover that many men called the same land their own, and that their property in it could neither be described as communal nor as individual.

[*] [Walter Baldwin] Spencer and [F. J.] Gillen, *The Northern Tribes of Central Australia* [(London, 1904)], p. 27, etc.

[c] *E.g.* Grey and Eyre, cited in [Richard] Hildebrand's *Recht und Sitte auf den verschiedenen [wirtschaftlichen] Kulturstufen* [(Jena, 1896)], p. 4.

[d] [Alfred William Howitt,] *The Native Tribes of South East Australia* [(London, 1904)], p. 83.

Where data are so difficult to ascertain, generalization must be unusually precarious. At best it may be possible here to set out a few salient points which may serve to throw light on the very diverse functions of property in the social system, the variations which the conception of property has undergone, and the manner in which these are connected with the general development of society. With this object we will briefly consider (1) the general notion of property, (2) the psychological conditions on which it rests, (3) certain aspects of its social functions, (4) some of the forms which property has assumed at several stages of social development, and (5) the light thrown by these considerations on certain typical theories of property which will be briefly reviewed.

1. The Notion of Property

For purposes of social theory property is to be conceived in terms of the control of man over things. Man needs food to eat, implements to procure it, land to work upon, and for that matter to stand and move upon. That he may supply his needs at all, he must at least temporarily control the implement that he is using, and the spot on which he is working. But that this temporary control or possession may become property, certain further conditions are essential. His possession must in the first place be recognized by others, *i.e.* it must be of the nature of a right. In the second place, with regard to things of a permanent nature, his right must also have a certain permanence. He must be able to count on the use of the thing. His right over it, though it may be limited in time, must not be confined to the moment when he has it in his hands, but must be respected in his absence. Thirdly, his control must be exclusive. If he shares the control of the thing with others, then it is not his private property. But if he and his partners control it to the exclusion of the rest of the world, then it is their joint or their common property. If on the other hand all the world alike can use it, then it is not property at all. Property may be private, joint, or common, but it must vest in some person or persons, and it must be exclusive of other persons.

Exclusive control, however, it must be borne in mind, does not necessarily mean complete control. A may control a thing for one purpose to the exclusion of all the world, B among the rest; yet B may control that same thing for another purpose to the exclusion of all the world, A among the rest. When I take a room in an inn for the night, it is 'mine' for the night to the exclusion of any one else. But the landlord has permanent rights in the room which are exclusive as against me. It may be objected that we ought to say that the landlord has the property, while he gives me only the right of using it. This may seem to accord better with usage, but in the final analysis of property it seems desirable for several reasons to insist that all forms of control are species of one genus. The control over a thing may be complete or partial, and the partial control may ascend by so many gradations till it becomes complete, that it is difficult to know where to draw a line. The only distinction of principle seems to be that between control of a thing for use and enjoyment, and control for the purpose of disposal, sale, exchange, or bequest. The latter kind of control may indeed be regarded as property in the sense of eminent ownership, but to restrict property to this sense would be to leave the manner of its use and enjoyment out of account. A man may only be life-tenant of a landed estate, its disposal after his death being determined by law or the decision of the community, or a previous owner's will. Yet while he lives the man may have complete control of its management, and from generation to generation the same conditions may recur. To leave the life interest out of account would then be to divorce the conception of property from the main conditions of practical control.

It will be seen then that property is a principle which admits of variation in several distinct directions. It is a control which may be more or less fully recognized and guaranteed by society. It may be more or less permanent, more or less dependent on present use and possession or enjoyment. It may be concentrated in one hand, or common to many. It may extend to more, or to fewer, of the purposes to which a thing may be put. But that the control may be property at all, it must in some sort be recognized, in some sort independent of immediate physical enjoyment, and at some point exclusive of control by other persons. Within these limits there is room for indefinite variation in many directions, and the variations are not necessarily dependent on one another.

2. The Psychology of Property

These elementary considerations help us in determining the psychological basis of property, as to which a mere note must here suffice. Some writers speak of an instinct of property. But this is to simplify overmuch. No doubt the higher animals have a rudimentary property. The bone which your dog has once seized is 'his' bone. He resents the attempt to take it from him with an excitement which he does not show in respect to a bone which he has not yet taken. My tame jackdaw steals my pencil and makes off hurriedly with it with all the flutter of conscious theft, or he will play a game with it, dropping it provocatively and picking it up smartly, or going straight at my fingers – the wretch! – when I attempt to recapture it. What happens in these cases seems to be that the interest which a class of objects excites – either through their use for food or, in the exceptional case of the jackdaw, through their inherent attractiveness as nice, bright, peckable things, easily portable in one's bill – is focussed by the first act of seizure or even of attention on a particular object, and that thereupon all the train of feelings or reactions attendant on, or subsidiary to, its use are called forth in response to that object rather than others. This constitutes the mental appropriation of an object; and not only for man, but for the dog with its buried bone, and the bird with its nest, and the jackdaw with its 'cache', the appropriated object becomes a permanent basis of action, something that it can count upon and go back to at need. For man, at all events, his property is above all something that he can rely upon as a permanent home, permanent means of subsistence or enjoyment. Property is thus an integral element in an ordered life of purposeful activity. It is, at bottom for the same reason, an integral element in a free life. This distinguishes property from mere adequate provision with material goods. A man who has his meals set down before him all nicely prepared and measured out by expert authority may be well nourished; but as he has no property beyond his actual plateful, so he has no freedom but to take it or give it to the cat. The man who has a shilling in his pocket is free to eat or drink what he likes up to the limit of the shilling. He may not get so good or sustaining a meal, but he gets his own choice. The man who has a weekly wage is, other things being equal, more free than a man paid by truck,[1] and a man who works on his own land with his own implements is more free, other things being equal, than the wage-earner. At each point the more a man can count on his own exertions applied to his own property, the more he can direct his own activity on the lines which

---

[1] 'paid by truck': to be paid in goods rather than in money.

suit his taste. Some measure of property appears, in short, to be the essential basis of liberty; and conversely the sense of freedom in enjoyment ranks along with the sense of security and permanence among the complex constituents of the pride and joy of ownership.

3. Social Aspects of Property: Use and Power

Unfortunately what is liberty for one man is often the negation of liberty for another. In a developed society a man's property is not merely something which he controls and enjoys, which he can make the basis of his labour and the scene of his ordered activities, but something whereby he can control another man and make it the basis of that man's labour and the scene of activities ordered by himself. The abstract right of property is apt to ignore these trifling distinctions; and theories of property are founded, for example on the right of the labourer to his produce, which completely ignore the fact that as industry develops, the most conspicuous function of property is to secure a part of one man's labour-product for the benefit of another. Both the history and the philosophy of property turn on these two relations of the institution to social life as a whole. On the one hand property is the material basis of a permanent, ordered, purposeful, and self-directed activity. Such upon the whole is the property which a man directly uses or enjoys by himself or in association with his nearest and dearest. On the other hand property is a form of social organization, whereby the labour of those who have it not is directed by and for the enjoyment of those that have. In this sense the control of the owner is essentially a control of labour. It is that 'alchemy' whereby the 'Seigneur lounging in the Œil de Bœuf' extracts the third nettle from the gatherer in the fields and calls it rent. It does not essentially consist in the handling and use of the material thing. It is consistent with as little knowledge of the thing as the average shareholder of an Argentine railway possesses of the whereabouts of 'his' track, who knows that the dividends come in with fair regularity every six months, though he might have difficulty in locating the terminus of the line within 500 miles.

Now these two functions of property, the control of things, which gives freedom and security, and the control of persons through things, which gives power to the owner, are very different. In some respects they are radically opposed, yet from the nature of the case they are intertwined, and their relationship can be traced through the history of the institution, some phases of which may now be indicated.

4. Phases of the Development of Property

In the general sense here given property is found in every known society. A man's clothing, weapons, and tools, a woman's ornaments, the family hut or cave, or at least a marked portion thereof,' are from the first recognized as belonging to the man, the woman, or the family. The inventory of a Vedda's very simple personal estate is given by Dr and Mrs Seligmann:

> One axe, bow and arrows, three pots, a deer skin, a flint and steel, and supply of tinder, a gourd for carrying water, a betel pouch containing betel covers, and some form of box for holding lime, also a certain amount of cloth besides that on the person.[2]

To these personal belongings a man has a right in the sense in which rights are recognized by simple societies. Theft would at lowest be resented by the individual, and there would be a customary form of reparation which he would exact. As soon as any sort of public court is formed it will deal with this right and the wrongs arising out of it, on the same general principles and by the same methods as with others.' To discuss these questions further would be to examine the social basis of rights in general, which is foreign to our purpose. Property is from the first, to all appearances, a right recognized much in the same fashion as rights of the person or marital rights are recognized, and on this side the development follows the same general lines in all cases. The important point for us to consider is what sort of things are objects of property, and whose property they are;

' *E.g.* In the 'Long House' of the Iroquois and other North American Indians. [Lothar] Dargun, 'Ursprung und [Entwicklungs-] Geschichte des Eigentums' (*Zeitschreifi für Vergleichende Rechtswissenschaft* [eds. Franz Bernhöft, Georg Cohn, and J. Kohler (Stuttgart, 1884)], Band 5, p. 37), insists on this point. The Vedda families, according to Dr Seligmann, have their proper place in the joint caves.

' In nine cases out of ten the 'thievishness' attributed by travellers to simple peoples is seen on careful reading to mean that they disregarded the proprietary rights of the whites. Could these peoples describe the morals of the whites, what might they say of the civilized man's regard for their property? It is true that in some cases belongings are taken without leave and without censure, but these are certainly the exception.

[2] C. G. and Brenda Z. Seligmann, *The Veddas* (Cambridge, 1911), p. 117.

or in more ultimate analysis, What sort of exclusive control is exerted over things, and by whom?

Now among the simplest known tribes, who live by gathering fruits, digging roots, and hunting, the possible objects of property may be divided into two categories. On the one hand there are the trivial personal belongings that have been mentioned. On the other hand there is the land, uncleared and uncultivated, but the one great means of subsistence. Of the first kind there is private ownership; but it will be apparent that the life of the little society will be determined principally by liberty or restriction in the matter of hunting or collecting food, that is to say, by the ownership of the land. How then is land owned in these communities? Is it communal or is it personal? If we could answer this question clearly and unambiguously, we should get as near as the evidence is ever likely to bring us to a solution of the problem of primitive property, and in particular of the vexed questions surrounding the nature of the village community. Unfortunately the evidence is not altogether clear and unambiguous. In some instances the communal tenure of the land is beyond doubt. The case of the Central Australians already quoted may serve as an instance. In the first place, among these people the tribe has its known area, with boundaries recognized by the neighbouring tribes. Within the tribe there are divisions and subdivisions, the ultimate unit being a 'local group' of a few families – in one tribe forty individuals constitute the largest existing group – who roam about an area which, like that of the tribe as a whole, is clearly defined. Within this area there is no individual property. It is free to all members of the group, but no one else may hunt in it without permission, and the boundaries are habitually observed. Moreover, ownership is associated with the centres within the area in which the souls of ancestors who lived in the Alcheringa – the great long ago – are deposited, which souls are reincarnated in living members of the group. Within the terms of our definition it is clear that this area is the common property of the group. Writers who deny communal property altogether among the hunting peoples can only deal with a case like this by calling it not property but sovereignty. It is true that the group is substantially an autonomous unit, but the only deduction that can be drawn from this is that political control – if we may use such an expression here – and the right of property are not at this stage differentiated. Indeed, in the case of land this differentiation is not completely effected till a relatively late stage in social development, and it may be doubted whether a complete differentiation is ever possible without socially disastrous consequences. In any case the effective control of the land is in the hands of the group. No single member has an exclusive right against the group, while the group has an exclusive right against all others, and this right is recognized by the others. We cannot refuse to call this common ownership; and if the same system obtained among all hunting people, the starting-point in the development of property in land would be perfectly clear.

But this is not the case. The necessities of hunting and the collection of food may lead to further subdivision, and we find cases, both in Australia and elsewhere, where land is owned by an individual hunter and his family.[f] We saw above that some ambiguity may attach to the evidence in these cases. Let us take an instance where the report is precise. The Veddas are organized in very small groups of families closely related to one another. Each group has its definite hunting area, but within it each man has his own land. This land passes by regular inheritance, or may be given to a son or a son-in-law. It may also be alienated. But whether it is given to the natural heir or to any one else it can only be with the assent of every adult male of the group.[h] In this instance it is clear that immediate ownership is private, and that the eminent ownership is in the group. The control of the group secures the important point, that access to the land will be maintained for those who are by birth its members. As long as this principle is maintained land may be communal property,

---

[f] In ten Australian tribes or groups common ownership is pretty clearly indicated, and in five family ownership. But several authors, *e.g.* [Gideon Scott] Lang, [George] Grey, [Edward John] Eyre, [Edward Micklethwaite] Curr, assert individual ownership. The evidence, however, is often conflicting and in some cases we can only suppose a kind of dual ownership. Thus J. Browne writing in Dr Petermann's [*Geographische*] *Mitteilungen* [(Gotha)] for 1856, describes four West Australian tribes which he knew well, as having land possessed by families and individuals; but he remarks that it is difficult to say in what private property consists, as the tribe roams the whole area without distinction, while if a stranger trespasses, it is resented and a fight ensues. Perhaps the only prerogative of the owner, he says, is to take the lead in this resistance. As to family property, it must be borne in mind that the Australian local group is often so small as to be little more than an enlarged family, so that family and group ownership pass into one another. It should also be noted that rules for the division of the spoils of the hunt are common in Australia. Of twenty cases of which I have information, the food is divided between the whole camp in ten; between the relations, including the wife's relations, in six; while in four the rules are not specified.

[h] Seligmann, pp. 107, 111.

or it may be personal, or the two principles may be intermixed, but in any case it will be held for use and not for power. Its tenure will be occupational, and I think we may provisionally conclude that this is the general characteristic of primitive property in land, that is to say, of the one essential basis of production in the lowest stages of development.[1]

This suggestion is confirmed when we consider the beginning of agriculture. Land at the outset is cleared for the raising of a crop. Its fertility is soon exhausted, perhaps after a single harvest, and the little community moves on to another spot. But the whole amount brought under cultivation at any one time is a very small fraction of the waste belonging to the community and hunted over by any of its

---

[1] Among fifty-five tribes of 'hunters and gatherers' as to whose property system I have found some account, forty-four appear to hold land either as property of the tribe or of a smaller group – clan, village, or band – within the tribe. Of the remainder five are the Australian tribes in which ownership is attributed to the family, and there are left six cases of individual ownership, to which perhaps a few more Australian cases ought to be added. In two or three instances ownership is attributed to the chief, but this seems to be rather as the representative of the community than as true personal property.

In a few cases special clans monopolized the land or the best part of it. Thus among the Thlinkeets, according to Swanton (*Smithsonian Annual Reports*, [vol.] 26), certain clans had no land of their own, and either used the common land of the tribe or had to wait until the more fortunate clans had done with their land for the season. Among the Chilcotin, Carriers, and Western Shushwaps land was the property of the nobles. In the two former cases, according to Father Morice (*Proceedings of the [Royal] Canadian Institute*, 1893), the heads of non-noble families might hunt on the land with the chief's permission. In the latter, according to Teit (*Report of the Jesup Expedition*), the nobles charged rents on the commons, fined them for trespass, and drove them off to the more distant tribal grounds quite in the style of modern civilization. Among the Tsimshian, according to Boas, a clan retained the right to its land even though it moved away; but I do not know whether it could charge anything for its use by others. All these instances are from the relatively developed hunting and fishing tribes of the west coast of North America, where class distinctions had come into being.

In the Torres Straits land may be held in individual ownership and is not infrequently lent or let for a share in the produce, *e.g.* a garden is lent on the understanding that the first-fruits go to the owner ([A. C.] Haddon, [*Reports of the*] *Cambridge* [*Anthropological*] *Expedition* [*to Torres Straits*], vol. 4 [(Cambridge, 1912), p. 147]). One group of these islands is non-agricultural, and private property also obtains here, but whether the leasing system is also known is not clear to me.

The figures given above are from an enquiry which is not quite finished and needs final revision, but are not likely to require any such modification as would invalidate the general rule that, with a few exceptions such as those mentioned, land in a community of hunters and gatherers is accessible to all members of a social group. This, it may be remarked, would hold even in the Australian cases where ownership is assigned to the individual. There is nowhere any hint of a landless class.

members indiscriminately. No difficulty is made about the right to clear a field, but whatever one man has cleared belongs, at least while he tills it, to himself and his family. At this stage private property can hardly be more than a possessory right, for when the last crop has been taken the clearing is really of less value than the waste. 'Arva per annos mutant et superest ager.' There is uncleared land in abundance. It belongs to the community and is open to any one to break up.' Thus there is temporary private possession and permanent common ownership. But on this point more than one possibility arises. Agriculture may become a collective industry, fields being tilled and the harvest gathered by the common labour, as among the Karaya tribes,' and a special store may be set apart for the necessitous, as among the Creeks. But more often, as tillage develops and becomes more intensive, the temporary occupation becomes permanent. The necessity of letting the land lie fallow may be met by a two-field or three-field system, and the recurrent possession of the same plots hardens into permanent ownership. The holding, however, may still be that of the family or of the kindred rather than that of the individual; and the kindred, living together in a Long House with stores in common, constitute a smaller and stricter communism within the community as a whole.' But whether through the break-up of the kindred or as the direct result of the growth of cultivation,''' land may be recognized as the private property of the man who clears or tills it, and may be alienated, sold, or bequeathed." Immediate

---

' Compare the remarks of [Karl Friedrich Philipp] von Martius, [*Beiträge*] *Zur Ethnographie* [*und Sprachenkunde*] *Amerika's* [*zumal Brasiliens* (Leipzig, 1867)], on Brazilian land tenure, which are sufficiently clear, notwithstanding the criticisms of Dargun ('Entwicklungs-Geschichte', pp. 51–4).

' [E.] Ehrenreich, *Veröffentlichungen aus dem* [*Königl[ichen*] *Museum* [*für Volkerkunde*], Band 1 [(Berlin, 1889].

' The Iroquois lived in joint houses containing from five to twenty families and made common store of the food, which was duly distributed among the component families by the superintending matron. The Creeks lived in clustered houses, practising a similar communism ([Lewis Henry] Morgan, *Houses and House Life* [*of the American Aborigines* (Washington, 1881)], pp. 64–8).

''' The evidence does not justify us in laying down a fixed order leading from the community through the kin to the individual. It is more likely that development followed a different course among different people.

'' Thus among the Kayans of Borneo, according to [Anton Willem] Nie[u]wenhuis (*Quer Durch Borneo* [(Leiden, 1904, 1907)]), unbroken land is accessible to any one, but land once tilled passes into private ownership and may be let or exchanged. Among the Hill Dyaks, according to [Henry] Ling Roth ([*The*] *Natives of Sarawak* [*and British North Borneo* (London, 1896)]), land is abundant within the tribal limits,

ownership of the cultivated plots thus passes to the kindred, the family, or the individual. Still the community may retain certain eminent rights and certain powers of control: for example, alienation to an outsider may be forbidden, or allowed only by common consent of the original group," while the right to acquire new land by clearing requires a more definite assent from the community or chief as it becomes more valuable.

Again, the community may retain a general control of cultivation, and may remain the guardian and ultimate court of appeal on questions of the rights and duties of its members, and on all customs regulating the common life. On this side, the old principle survived into the manorial courts of our mediaeval system. Furthermore, the cultivation of the arable is not self-sufficient. As agriculture develops it requires beasts of burden, and a right of grazing on the common pasture and the use of the waste are essential to the maintenance of the tillage. But the pasture and the waste remain common; and if there is meadow land, its use is duly apportioned by the community in accordance with the needs of each holding. Lastly, if holdings become unequal and unsuited to the needs of families, there may be a conscious effort to maintain the partnership by a system of periodical redistribution, as in the case of the Russian *mir*.

Systems like these, though compatible with a considerable development of individual ownership, are still so far primitive that they associate property, not with power, but with use.' At least until property begins to press on the means of subsistence, every boy on growing to manhood will have the basis of his life-economy secured to him by the social structure. He will succeed to his share in the family land, with the right to pasture, meadow, and waste, which it carries with it; and if, through the growth of the family, the lot has become too narrow, he will readily gain the consent of the community to an additional clearing in the waste. If the pressure of population has

---

but very little is individual property, except the private plots near the houses, which are saleable. The locality of the farms is generally settled by the council of the tribe, so that one road may serve all. Among the Sea Dyaks a man acquires a title to the land by clearing it.

" So in early mediaeval Germany, [Richard Karl] Schröder, *Lehrbuch der deutschen Rechtsgeschichte* [(Leipzig, 1889)], pp. 207–8.

' In more than one hundred descriptions of land tenure among agricultural and pastoral peoples of simple culture, I have only found ten cases in which a system of letting or leasing land is suggested.

begun, it is more likely to lead to trouble with neighbouring peoples than with landlessness and poverty at home. Its effects will be seen in tribal unrest, migrations, and wars of conquest. Here then is one possible root of disorganization. But there are others. Men are by nature unequal, and one family will thrive while another decays. If debt-slavery – particularly for non-payment of the wergild[3] – is recognized, men will fall into the hands of creditors for whose benefit in future they may have to till the land, and prisoners of war may be put to the same use.[4] Whole tribes, indeed, may become tributary to a stronger people.[5] Within the community the growth of military organization involves the elevation of the chief and his trusted followers into a nobility standing above the mass of the free men, and this elevation implies at some point or another a corresponding depression. Some one must serve, if some one else is to have leisure to be a nobleman.

But apart from these tendencies, there is another economic movement on which we have not yet touched. In some regions of the world, particularly on the steppes of Eastern Europe and Asia, the pasture land provides opportunity for a different form of development from the hunting stage. The possession of flocks and herds is far more free from communal restrictions than the tilling of the soil; and even if the herds are family property, the power of the father among these peoples is often so great that he deserves to be called the true owner. But what is more important, property in flocks and herds can wax and wane with ease and celerity; and in pastoral societies accordingly, the distinction of rich and poor readily makes its appearance. Some pastoral tribes indeed are slaveholding. In others the poorer members of the community sufficiently supply the need.[6] The definite appearance of the man who is neither provided for as a slave, nor by his own hereditary share in the common basis of subsistence,

---

[4] For serfs of this type among the Germans, see Tacitus, *Germania*, [chap.] xxv; Schröder, pp. 46, 47.

[5] Even a tribe of hunters like the South American Mbaya hold the neighbouring Guanas in a form of serfdom, compelling them to till land for them.

[6] Or there may be a subject tribe who are hewers of wood and drawers of water. *Cf.* [Herman Jeremias] Nieboer, *Slavery as an Industrial System* [(The Hague, 1900)], who finds ten clear cases of the presence and twelve of the absence of slavery among pastoral folk (p. 262 ff.).

[3] 'wergild': 'In ancient Teutonic and old English law, the price set upon a man according to his rank, paid by way of compensation or fine in cases of homicide and certain other crimes to free the offender from further obligation or punishment'(*OED*).

seems to be especially associated with the pastoral stage, and in agricultural societies to be at least largely influenced by the pastoral element. It was in the end the enclosure of the pasture and the waste which destroyed the remains of the common field system in this country and achieved the ruin of the small holder.'

This slight sketch may serve to show the general character of the economy from which the mediaeval organization of Western Europe was evolved. The whole problem of the antecedents of the manor is still entangled in endless controversy; but a survey of the anthropological data on the whole confirms the view that at the back of the entire process we must place 'a village community of shareholders which cultivated the land on the open field system and treated all other requisites of rural life as appendant to it'." The only question is as to the extent to which within this community private property was developed or eminent control maintained. In any case it is probable that land was originally held for use, and that its value to its separate owner was conditioned by the right which it carried to that part of the area which was undeniably common. But we have seen that from the first this system was compatible with inequality, and we have noted several methods by which the inequality might develop. In our own country in the early Middle Ages the growth of the king's power, and then the grant of judicial privileges and correlative fiscal duties to private people, together with corresponding grants to the Church, were continuously at work to convert the village into the manor." Now in the manor the cultivators had certainly to work for the lord as well as for themselves. The lord's property is held 'for power', or perhaps more strictly it is the economic appanage of the legal power which he holds over the inhabitants – it is power held for property. At the same time one good feature of the older system survives. The ordinary child is still born into a system in which the basis of his work and his livelihood is assured to him. He has his virgate or half virgate.[4] At worst – if not a slave" – he is a cottar[5] with

---

' See [R. H.] Tawney, [*The*] *Agrarian Problem in the Sixteenth Century* [(London, 1912)]; and [J. L. and Barbara] Hammond, *The Village Labourer* [*1760–1832* (London, 1911)].

" [Paul] Vinogradoff, [*The*] *Growth of the Manor* [(London, 1905)], p. 365.

' *Cf.* [Frederic William] Maitland, *Doomsday Book and Beyond* [(Cambridge, 1897)].

" Chattel slavery disappeared in England during the twelfth century.

[4] 'virgate': 'an early English land measure, varying greatly in extent, but in many cases averaging thirty acres' (*OED*).

[5] 'cottar': 'a villein who occupied a cot or cottage with an attached piece of land (usually five acres) held by service (with or without payment in produce or money)' (*OED*).

a few acres and the right by practice, if not by stringent custom, to the pasture and the waste. Unfortunately these rights were insecure, and when the strain came, when it became profitable to lay down pasture, to enclose the demesne, and to encroach on the waste, there was no one but the free-holder who was in a firm position for resistance.' In the break-up of the manorial system the serf gained his freedom, but he lost his land. The outline of the story has now been pretty clearly made out, but is too long and complex even for summary here.' With the upshot we are familiar – on the one hand private ownership denuded of the old public obligations; on the other, a landless proletariate whose chief economic privilege is that its members are free to leave their homes and do better elsewhere; and between them the farmer owning his stock but renting his land.

The appearance of the capitalist farmer is, however, only a minor symptom of a vast change in the nature of property which has developed *pari passu* with the private ownership of land on the large scale. In early society we could virtually treat land as the one necessary basis of subsistence; and the fact that land could not be accumulated in private hands apart from personal occupation was noted as a preservative of the common life. In the pastoral stage, however, we saw accumulation of a different kind, and the growth of flocks and herds, the first form of true capital, at once involved the distinction between the possessing and non-possessing classes. The development of industry and commerce has always engendered the same distinction, and has set a problem to legislators whether in Athens or in Rome or in our own time. But as industry is more productive, so accumulation proceeds on a vastly greater scale in our own civilization; and while the borders of political, religious, national, and one may say social, freedom have widened, the inequalities of wealth have only increased. Yet it is not inequality as such that is the fundamental fact of our system. It is the entire dependence of the masses on land and capital which belong to others. Five out of six, I suppose, of the children now born, are born to no assured place in the industrial system. They have of their own no means of subsistence. They have hands and brains, but they have neither land to till nor stock to till

' On the position of the copyholders and the customary tenants, see Tawney.
' See the works already cited of Mr Tawney and Mr and Mrs Hammond; also *The English Peasantry and the Enclosure [of Common Fields]*, by Gilbert Slater [(London, 1905)].

it with. What is more, only a fraction of our population could be supported by agriculture; and for the cotton spinner, the railway man, or the coal miner, there is no sense in talking of his owning the means of production as an individual. The rise of large-scale industry has abolished the possibility of any form of individualism as a general solution of the economic problem.

Thus, while modern economic conditions have virtually abolished property *for use* – apart from furniture, clothing, etc.; that is, property in the means of production, for the great majority of the people – they have brought about the accumulation of vast masses of property *for power* in the hands of a relatively narrow class. The contrast is accentuated by the increasing divorce between power and use. The large landowner stood in some direct governing relation to his estate. Responsibility went with ownership, and even survived the explicit association between land tenure and political functions. The capitalist employer, who began to be differentiated from the workman in the earlier part of the modern period, and who was the prominent feature of the first two generations of the industrial revolution, was still, as the name implies, the employer as well as the capitalist. He himself, that is to say, was actively engaged in carrying out the function which his property made possible. But with the progress of accumulation there came further differentiations. It became more and more indisputable that the possession of capital was one thing and the conduct of business another; and with the rise of the joint-stock system capital became so split up into shares and stocks that it has come to be for its owners nothing more than a paper certificate, or an entry in the books of the Bank of England, which they have never seen, meaning to them only what it brings in by the quarter or the half year. And yet these investments, this capital, is the governing force in the lives of thousands and millions of men scattered throughout the world. It is the instrument by which they are set in motion, by which their labour is sustained, above all, by which it is directed and controlled. The divorce of functions is complete; and what wonder if the owner of capital presents himself to the imagination of the workman merely as an abstract, distant, unknown suction-pump, that is drawing away such and such a percentage of the fruits of industry without making a motion to help in the work?

Lastly, behind the mass of the investors, is the financier who shuffles all these abstract pieces of capital about, controls their application, takes his commission on the proceeds, and constitutes himself the working centre of industry and commerce. The institution of property has, in its modern form, reached its zenith as a means of giving to the few power over the life of the many, and its nadir as a means of securing to the many the basis of regular industry, purposeful occupation, freedom, and self-support.

5. Some Theories of Property

With these few illustrations of the diversity of forms which the institution of property has assumed in the course of social evolution, we may usefully compare some distinctive theories which have been held by thinkers of its basis and functions. We may consider first those who have attacked the institution of private property altogether, in the interests of communism; secondly, those who have found a general justification for the institution of private property either in its economic or in its ethical value; and thirdly, those who have held that the solution lies in the discrimination of kinds of property and the function which each severally performs.

(*a*) Property has sometimes been attacked on philosophical, sometimes on religious grounds. In the *Republic*, the object of Plato is to set out in clearest possible outline the picture of a completely unified State. The State is to be so compact a unity that, if one of its members suffers, it is to feel that it suffers in that member, just as when the finger aches the man feels the ache in the finger. Looking over the rallying points at which the individual can assert himself against the social unity, Plato finds them conspicuously in family life on the one hand and in property on the other, and he proceeds to the abolition of both; at any rate, the guardians, who are to lead the highest, the most completely social, and the most fully philosophic life, can have no room in their minds either for family or for economic cares. Communism is advocated in the interests, not of enjoyment but of austerity; and in this the Platonic philosophers may be regarded as prototypes of the monastic community. In both cases it is open to criticism to maintain that social unity is pushed to a point at which personality is obliterated, and that the independence of material things is expressed in a form in which it defeats itself. Man cannot live without material things, and in so far as he is dependent for his necessaries on the will of others, his life is also dependent upon these others. Where he cannot move hand or foot without them, he abandons self-direction, and the self-denial, which was to give spiritual freedom, ends by denying autonomy altogether.

But the principle of property was also criticized in antiquity from the point of view of Natural Law. Property, it was clear to the thinkers who introduced this conception into ethics, was a human institution. The gifts of nature, the land and its fruits, must originally be free to all men; appropriation was the act of man, and the institutions by which appropriation is regulated derived from man-made laws. Just as by nature all men are free and equal, so by nature they have a right to use the earth and its fruits for their own purposes, to apply their labour to them freely, and to enjoy the product at their will.

This conception of a natural Communism underlying the institutions of positive law was taken up by the Early Church, where it fused with the conception of a Christian Communism, based, not on the Platonic principle of an abstract unity, but on the ideal of brotherly love and mutual aid as between co-religionists, the sons of one Father, the members of one household. This was an ideal which could only be effective among the members of a small community; and when the Church had seriously to undertake the problem of reconciling State law with Christian ethics, it had to fall back on the Stoic distinction between the law of nature and the positive institutions of government. The fabric of society was accepted, and though Communism is proclaimed as the law of nature at the outset of the Canon law, it is not so interpreted as to direct or to qualify those institutions of State which determine the conditions on which property is held, and by which wealth is distributed, excepting in so far as it secures the levy of a tax on wealth for the service of the Church and of the poor. The theory of Communism, as qualified by respect for established institutions, becomes a doctrine of charity.

In point of fact, as a political doctrine, Communism is an emotion rather than a system. In a small community it has its place. Every family, while the members live together, is in essence a communistic unit; and Communism may be conceived as operating successfully among any small group of enthusiasts as long as the enthusiasm is maintained. In the larger world the communal principle has its place only in respect of the enjoyment of those things in which no correlative performance of duty is requisite. Public spaces, recreation grounds, the advantages of lighting, and, in some respects, of cleaning, sanitation, order and good government, are common property in the strict sense of the term. Everybody can enjoy them without payment, for some of them are things which cannot exist at all unless they are available for every one, and others cost no more when available to all than they would if restricted to a few. But Communism of this kind only touches the outside of life.

(*b*) For the regular working of the economic order it has been clear to most thinkers that there must be some systematic apportionment of the instruments of production, and the fruits of industry. The social organism has many functions, and each function requires its due stimulus and sustenance; hence the most popular theory of property associates it with the right to labour and the product of labour. On this basis Locke finds a justification for property antecedent to positive law. By the law of nature the earth stood open to all men, but also by the law of nature a man had the right of property in his own person, and in that which he wrought with his hands. Accordingly, that in which he 'mixed his labour' became his own, and this would include the portion of soil which he reclaimed by occupation and tillage. But in this conception, as Locke apparently recognizes, property is limited by use: 'As much as any one can make use of to any advantage of life until it spoils, so much he may by his labour fix, and property in whatever is beyond this is more than his share, and belongs to others.' Hence Locke protests that his theory is incompatible with 'engrossing'. Unfortunately he only works it out for 'Americans', as typical instances of people who live under conditions where land is still superabundant. And when he comes to consider property as an established institution of organized society, he can only tell us what is painfully obvious, that 'it is plain that the consent of men have agreed to a disproportionate and unequal possession of the earth – I mean out of the bounds of society and compact, for in governments the laws regulate it, they having by consent found out and agreed in a way how a man may rightfully, and without injury, possess more than he himself can make use of, by receiving gold and silver'.

Locke, it is true, states in general terms that laws and government ought to accommodate themselves to the principles of natural law;

= Second Treatise on Civil Government, chap. v. [For a more intelligible variant of this passage see *Two Treaties of Government*, Book II, chap. v., ed. Peter Laslett, 2nd edn (Cambridge, 1967).]

and if we press this principle in the case of property, it seems clear that Locke might be led, if he were living now, to somewhat radical conclusions. Be this as it may, we find in Locke the basis of a view which is at once a justification of property, and a criticism of industrial organization. Man has a right, it would seem, first to the opportunity of labour; secondly, to the fruits of his labour; thirdly, to what he can use of these fruits, and nothing more. Property so conceived is what we have here called property for use. The conception is individualistic, but it may be given a more social turn if we bear in mind, first of all, that society as a collective whole is that which determines the structure and working of economic institutions; and secondly, that in a society where men produce for exchange, labour is a social function, and the price of labour its reward. Locke's doctrine would then amount to this, that the social right of each man is to a place in the economic order, in which he both has opportunity for exercising his faculties in the social service, and can reap thereby a reward proportionate to the value of the service rendered to society.

(*c*) But there exists a much more radical Individualism than Locke's, which also ascends to antiquity. The Aristotelian criticism of Plato proceeds partly from the just conception that unity is only one feature of social life, and that the true community must be a whole of many diverse parts. It rests also upon the conception that property is among the external good things which are necessary to the full expression of personality. In emphasizing this side of the matter it may be allowed that Aristotle lets the communal principle evaporate into a mere pious aspiration. Private possession and common use is a pleasant phrase, but, we may safely maintain, remains a mere phrase. It is no organic law for society to lay down, that men should use their possessions in the spirit of the proverb that 'the things of friends are common'.

The centre of this line of thought is the conception that property is an instrument of personality, and in that form it has been revived and has played an important part in modern thought. In general terms, what has been said at the outset will have justified this principle by anticipation. Material things that a man can count upon as his own, that he can leave and return to, that he can use at his will, are, we have admitted, the basis of a purposeful life, and therefore of a rational and harmonious development of personality. But as a basis of the institution of property, this principle carries with it consequences which seem too often to be overlooked. On the one hand it carries the condemnation of a social system in which property of the kind and amount required for such development of personality is not generally accessible to all citizens, who do not forfeit their right by misfeasance. A society which should accept this principle, could not tolerate anything like the existing distribution of wealth, could not permit those methods of accumulation which concentrate wealth in the hands of the few, and leave the many – so far as the practical object of earning their living is concerned – as naked as they were born. Cherished as a Conservative principle, it has in it the seed of Radical revolution. And secondly, if this principle would require the universal distribution of the means of subsistence, it would also limit the accumulation of property by the measure of that which is healthy for the soul. The possession of property which emancipates from toil, the possession of property which makes, not for the guidance of self, but for the control of others, stands on this principle condemned; and what is a justification of property becomes a reprobation of riches. Ethical individualism in property, carried through, blows up its own citadel.

(*d*) There remains the Socialistic conception of property, the term by which in general we may express any theory which distinguishes between the appropriation of the means of production and the appropriation of the fruits of labour. The difficulty of this theory, considered merely as a theory – for we are not here concerned with practical applications – is, in the first place, to discriminate neatly between the two kinds of property; and in the second place, to determine the conditions of access for the individual to the means of production, and the ethical basis and measure of his reward. But at the outset let us be clear as to the distinction between the Socialistic principle and the Communist. To the Communist all things are equally the objects of enjoyment, without payment made or service rendered. To the Socialist – or indeed to any society so far as the socialistic principle is applied – property is not common to all, but is held in common for all, and its assignment or apportionment is a matter of collective regulation. There is no enjoyment without a correlative performance of function. The problem before the Socialist has always been to consider how this collective regulation can be accommodated to the free initiative and enterprise of the individual; and it may be doubted whether, upon purely socialistic principles, this problem is capable of solution.

The problem is complicated by the psychological difficulties of democratic organization. We talk easily of a common property, of a common industry directed to the common good and organized by the general will; but where is the general will? Is it a figment of the rhetoricians, or is it a working reality in actual life? In practice, does it mean a collective decision, to which the ordinary man contributes, and in which therefore his personality may, in a genuine sense, be said to be expressed? Or does it mean the fiat of statesmen and of experts, sheepishly accepted by the crowd because they see no way of escaping it? On the former alternative, collective property might truly be regarded as having that same organic relation to personality as is possessed by the peasant's plot of ground in relation to the proprietor, who knows the capacity of every square yard of it. In the latter alternative, collective industry becomes a mechanism, in which each man might be reduced to the part of an unthinking cog, grinding his grind with no more freedom than the factory hand under the capitalist employer, and with no more sense of the social value of his work than the machine-minder performing a fragmentary process in the manufacture of an article, which, whether sound or unsound, wholesome or unwholesome, will go to the use or the annoyance or the injury of people whom he has never seen and never will see. Considerations such as these have led some of the more generous minds of our own time to look for the reform of property rather in a revived individualism than in furthering the collectivist tendencies, which, of late years, have influenced legislation. Their ideal would be something like the mediaeval organization, without its restrictions on personal freedom. They sigh for the day of the small landed proprietor and the master-workman.

In relation to the land this conception, no doubt, has a certain limited applicability; but in the main its development seems barred by the hard facts of economic development, making for the large scale of production and the complex interchange of goods throughout the world market. Yet the principle is in so far just that it recognizes an indestructible core of value in the idea of property. Only it has to be maintained that, if private property is of value, for reasons and within limits that have been indicated, to the fulfilment of personality,

197

common property is equally of value for the expression and the development of social life. The problem of modern economic reorganization would seem to be to find a method, compatible with the industrial conditions of the new age, of securing to each man, as a part of his civic birthright, a place in the industrial system and a lien upon the common product that he may call his own, without dependence either upon private charity or the arbitrary decision of an official.

The other side of this problem is that of securing for the State the ultimate ownership of the natural sources of wealth and of the accumulation of past generations, together with the supreme control of the direction of industrial activity and of labour contracts. We cannot reconstitute the early commune. We cannot secure for each man his inheritance, his virgate, and his plough team. What we have to aim at would seem to be an analogous relation between the individual and the community, adapted to the complexity of modern conditions, combining the security of the old regime with the flexibility and freedom of the new, partly by education and training, partly by the supervision of industrial organization. We have to restore the contact between the individual and the instruments of labour. We have to assure him of continuity in employment, and – given reasonable industry and thrift – of provision against the accidents of life and the periods of helplessness. And for these purposes we have to restore to society a direct ownership of some things, but an eminent ownership of all things material to the production of wealth, securing 'property for use' to the individual, and retaining 'property for power' for the democratic state.

Index

Cambridge Texts in the History of Political Thought

Ferguson *An Essay on the History of Civil Society* (edited by Fania Oz-Salzberger)
0 521 44736 4 paperback
Filmer *Patriarcha and Other Writings* (edited by Johann P. Sommerville)
0 521 39903 3 paperback
Fletcher *Political Works* (edited by John Robertson)
0 521 43994 9 paperback
Sir John Fortescue *On the Laws and Governance of England* (edited by Shelley Lockwood)
0 521 58996 7 paperback
Fourier *The Theory of the Four Movements* (edited by Gareth Stedman Jones and Ian Patterson)
0 521 35693 8 paperback
Gramsci *Pre-Prison Writings* (edited by Richard Bellamy)
0 521 42307 4 paperback
Guicciardini *Dialogue on the Government of Florence* (edited by Alison Brown)
0 521 45623 1 paperback
Harrington *The Commonwealth of Oceana* and *A System of Politics* (edited by J. G. A. Pocock)
0 521 42329 5 paperback
Hegel *Elements of the Philosophy of Right* (edited by Allen W. Wood and H. B. Nisbet)
0 521 34888 9 paperback
Hegel *Political Writings* (edited by Laurence Dickey and H. B. Nisbet)
0 521 45979 3 paperback
Hobbes *On the Citizen* (edited by Michael Silverthorne and Richard Tuck)
0 521 43780 6 paperback
Hobbes *Leviathan* (edited by Richard Tuck)
0 521 56797 1 paperback
Hobhouse *Liberalism and Other Writings* (edited by James Meadowcroft)
0 521 43726 1 paperback
Hooker *Of the Laws of Ecclesiastical Polity* (edited by A. S. McGrade)
0 521 37908 3 paperback
Hume *Political Essays* (edited by Knud Haakonssen)
0 521 46639 3 paperback
King James VI and I *Political Writings* (edited by Johann P. Sommerville)
0 521 44729 1 paperback
Jefferson *Political Writings* (edited by Joyce Appleby and Terence Ball)
0 521 64841 6 paperback
John of Salisbury *Policraticus* (edited by Cary Nederman)
0 521 36701 8 paperback
Kant *Political Writings* (edited by H. S. Reiss and H. B. Nisbet)
0 521 39837 1 paperback
Knox *On Rebellion* (edited by Roger A. Mason)
0 521 39988 2 paperback
Kropotkin *The Conquest of Bread and other writings* (edited by Marshall Shatz)
0 521 45990 7 paperback
Lawson *Politica sacra et civilis* (edited by Conal Condren)
0 521 39248 9 paperback
Leibniz *Political Writings* (edited by Patrick Riley)
0 521 35899 x paperback
The Levellers (edited by Andrew Sharp)
0 521 62511 4 paperback
Locke *Political Essays* (edited by Mark Goldie)
0 521 47861 8 paperback
Locke *Two Treatises of Government* (edited by Peter Laslett)
0 521 35730 6 paperback
Loyseau *A Treatise of Orders and Plain Dignities* (edited by Howell A. Lloyd)
0 521 45624 x paperback
Luther and Calvin on Secular Authority (edited by Harro Höpfl)
0 521 34986 9 paperback
Machiavelli *The Prince* (edited by Quentin Skinner and Russell Price)
0 521 34993 1 paperback
de Maistre *Considerations on France* (edited by Isaiah Berlin and Richard Lebrun)
0 521 46628 8 paperback
Malthus *An Essay on the Principle of Population* (edited by Donald Winch)
0 521 42972 2 paperback
Marsiglio of Padua *Defensor minor* and *De translatione Imperii* (edited by Cary Nederman)
0 521 40846 6 paperback
Marx *Early Political Writings* (edited by Joseph O'Malley)
0 521 34994 x paperback
Marx *Later Political Writings* (edited by Terrell Carver)
0 521 36739 5 paperback

James Mill *Political Writings* (edited by Terence Ball)
  0 521 38748 5 paperback
J. S. Mill *On Liberty*, with *The Subjection of Women* and *Chapters on Socialism* (edited by Stefan Collini)
  0 521 37917 2 paperback
Milton *Political Writings* (edited by Martin Dzelzainis)
  0 521 34866 8 paperback
Montesquieu *The Spirit of the Laws* (edited by Anne M. Cohler, Basia Carolyn Miller and Harold Samuel Stone)
  0 521 36974 6 paperback
More *Utopia* (edited by George M. Logan and Robert M. Adams)
  0 521 40318 9 paperback
Morris *News from Nowhere* (edited by Krishan Kumar)
  0 521 42233 7 paperback
Nicholas of Cusa *The Catholic Concordance* (edited by Paul E. Sigmund)
  0 521 56773 4 paperback
Nietzsche *On the Genealogy of Morality* (edited by Keith Ansell-Pearson)
  0 521 40610 2 paperback
Paine *Political Writings* (edited by Bruce Kuklick)
  0 521 66799 2 paperback
Plato *The Republic* (edited by G. R. F. Ferrari and Tom Griffith)
  0 521 48443 X paperback
Plato *Statesman* (edited by Julia Annas and Robin Waterfield)
  0 521 44778 X paperback
Price *Political Writings* (edited by D. O. Thomas)
  0 521 40969 1 paperback
Priestley *Political Writings* (edited by Peter Miller)
  0 521 42561 1 paperback
Proudhon *What is Property?* (edited by Donald R. Kelley and Bonnie G. Smith)
  0 521 40556 4 paperback
Pufendorf *On the Duty of Man and Citizen according to Natural Law* (edited by James Tully)
  0 521 35980 5 paperback
The Radical Reformation (edited by Michael G. Baylor)
  0 521 37948 2 paperback
Rousseau *The Discourses and other early political writings* (edited by Victor Gourevitch)
  0 521 42445 3 paperback
Rousseau *The Social Contract and other later political writings* (edited by Victor Gourevitch)
  0 521 42446 1 paperback
Seneca *Moral and Political Essays* (edited by John Cooper and John Procope)
  0 521 34818 8 paperback
Sidney *Court Maxims* (edited by Hans W. Blom, Eco Haitsma Mulier and Ronald Janse)
  0 521 46736 5 paperback
Sorel *Reflections on Violence* (edited by Jeremy Jennings)
  0 521 55910 3 paperback
Spencer *The Man versus the State* and *The Proper Sphere of Government* (edited by John Offer)
  0 521 43740 7 paperback
Stirner *The Ego and Its Own* (edited by David Leopold)
  0 521 45647 9 paperback
Thoreau *Political Writings* (edited by Nancy Rosenblum)
  0 521 47675 5 paperback
Utopias of the British Enlightenment (edited by Gregory Claeys)
  0 521 45590 1 paperback
Vitoria *Political Writings* (edited by Anthony Pagden and Jeremy Lawrance)
  0 521 36714 X paperback
Voltaire *Political Writings* (edited by David Williams)
  0 521 43727 X paperback
Weber *Political Writings* (edited by Peter Lassman and Ronald Speirs)
  0 521 39719 7 paperback
William of Ockham *A Short Discourse on Tyrannical Government* (edited by A. S. McGrade and John Kilcullen)
  0 521 35803 5 paperback
William of Ockham *A Letter to the Friars Minor and other writings* (edited by A. S. McGrade and John Kilcullen)
  0 521 35804 3 paperback
Wollstonecraft *A Vindication of the Rights of Men* and *A Vindication of the Rights of Woman* (edited by Sylvana Tomaselli)
  0 521 43633 8 paperback